Administrative Information Systems

Note to the Student

Dear Student,

If you winced when you learned the price of this textbook, you are experiencing what is known as "sticker shock" in today's economy. Yes, textbooks are expensive, and we don't like it anymore than you do. Many of us here at Kent have sons and daughters of our own attending college, or we are attending school part time ourselves. However, the prices of our books are dictated by the cost factors involved in producing them. The costs of paper, designing the book, setting it in type, printing it, and binding it have risen significantly each year along with everything else in our economy. You might find the following table to be of some interest.

Item	1967 Price	1986 Price	The Price Increase
Monthly Housing Expense	$114.31	$686.46	6.0 times
Monthly Automobile Expense	82.69	339.42	4.1 times
Loaf of Bread	.22	1.00	4.6 times
Pound of Hamburger	.39	1.48	3.8 times
Pound of Coffee	.59	2.45	4.2 times
Candy Bar	.10	.40	4.0 times
Men's Dress Shirt	5.00	25.00	5.0 times
Postage	.05	.22	4.4 times
Resident College Tuition	294.00	1,581.00	5.4 times

Today's prices of college textbooks have increased only about 2.8 times 1967 prices. Compare your texts sometime to a general trade book, i.e., a novel or nonfiction book, and you will easily see significant differences in the internal design, quality of paper, and binding. These features of college textbooks cost money.

Textbooks should not be looked on only as an expense. Other than your professors, your textbooks are your most important source for what you hope to learn in college. What's more, the textbooks you keep can be valuable resources in your future career and life. They are the foundation of your professional library. Like your education, your textbooks are one of your most important investments.

We are concerned, and we care. Please write to us at the address below with your comments. We want to be responsive to your suggestions, to give you quality textbooks, and to do everything in our power to keep their prices under control.

Wayne Barcomb

Wayne A. Barcomb
President

Kent Publishing Company
20 Park Plaza
Boston, MA 02116

Administrative Information Systems

People and Technology

Thomas Keller, Ed.D.
Arizona State University

Ernest N. Savage, Ed.D.
Bowling Green State University

KENT PUBLISHING COMPANY
A Division of Wadsworth, Inc.
Boston, Massachusetts

Editor: Read Wickham
Production Editor: Leslie Baker
Interior Designer: Linda Ziedrich
Cover Designer: Steve Snider
Manufacturing Manager: Linda Siegrist

Kent Publishing Company
A Division of Wadsworth, Inc.

Printed in the United States of America
1 2 3 4 5 6 7 8 9 — 91 90 89 88 87

Library of Congress Cataloging-in-Publication Data

Keller, Thomas, 1950–
Administrative information systems.

Includes index.
1. Office management. 2. Office practice—Automation—Management. 3. Management information systems. I. Savage, Ernest N., 1946– II. Title.
HF5547.K44 1986 651.7 86-7481
ISBN 0-534-06240-7

This text is dedicated to

Jacque, Andy, and Kristen
Louise and Marc

for steadfast love and support

Preface

In recent years, methods of operation in business organizations have changed dramatically to meet the challenges of today's world economy. Greater emphasis is placed on the administrative office today than ever before. Issues such as productivity, human resources management, and technology, which once were topics of discussion in warehouse and factory settings, are now focused directly on the administrative office environment. It is imperative that today's administrative office managers use every human and technological resource available to transform the office into an effective administrative information system.

This text is designed and written to aid students, business managers, government officials, and educators in transforming the isolated manual offices of yesterday to tomorrow's automated offices. Most texts currently on the market do an excellent job of describing office practices as they have been performed for decades. However, for the most part these texts have merely added chapters to previously written editions, giving little thought to the changing role of the administrative office. The results have been large, encyclopedia-like office manuals that are filled with outdated material and sketchy glimpses of the future. This process has forced instructors to teach office management from a strictly theoretical basis.

Administrative Information Systems: People and Technology was written as a practical guide to administrative office management. It is intended to be a bridge between the theoretical and the applied instructional approaches. This text provides only the essential material from traditional office management references while giving specific examples and the managerial strategies necessary for developing effective administrative information systems.

TEXT STRUCTURE

The text is divided into four parts. Part 1, "Administrative Organization," describes both the office managerial process and the administrative office organizational structure. Part 2, "Administrative Functions," provides the reader with a detailed description of the major administrative office functions as they exist in today's offices. These functions include word processing, records management, micrographics, reprographics, forms control, telecommunications, and budget analysis. Part 3, "Administrative Information Systems," consists of seven chapters that describe the various integrated systems that make up today's administrative information system. The main theme of this portion of the text is the "systems approach." Although there is a substantial amount of technology described in Part 3, it is presented from the manager's perspective in a clear and concise manner. Chapters 8 through 13 provide the reader with many step-by-step procedures for developing effective administrative information systems. Part 4, "Human Resources Management," includes very important information on the most important of all resources—the human resource. Part 4 is written as a manager's guide to acquiring, training, motivating, measuring, compensating, and retaining administrative office personnel.

Individual instructors may desire to cover these topics in an order other than the one presented here. Instructors are encouraged to utilize this text in the manner most conducive to their students' understanding.

TEXT FEATURES

Numerous important features are incorporated in *Administrative Information Systems: People and Technology.*

- The concept of systems theory is included in the discussion of the evolution of management theory.
- The detailed descriptions of strategies for automating many of the traditional office functions provide the reader with greater insight into the uses of computer technology in the administrative office.
- The reader is provided with a practical guide for using systems analysis techniques as part of his or her managerial skill set. These techniques are utilized throughout the text.
- Chapter 9, "Ergonomic Designs and Productivity," is a very timely discussion for today's managers. This chapter emphasizes the delicate relationship between people and technology.
- A major strength of this text is its managerial approach to evaluating, acquiring, and utilizing computer technology. The strategies presented here have been developed and utilized by the authors in actual business contexts.

□ The human resources management issues are presented from the workers' perspective as well as from the management viewpoint. Both points of view are discussed in the framework of the rapidly changing job market.

In addition to these important features, chapter summaries and student activities are provided as instructional aids at the end of each chapter.

INSTRUCTOR'S MANUAL

The instructor's manual that accompanies *Administrative Information Systems: People and Technology* provides guidelines for the instructor to follow with respect to curriculum timelines, sex-equity and special needs issues, and the availability of resource materials. It also presents a strategy for modifying curriculum in order to create and maintain a contemporary focus.

Each chapter is analyzed in an objective and subjective manner. Objective testing takes the form of "Test Your Knowledge" review questions. By answering these questions, students will be able to review and evaluate their understanding of each chapter's content. Answers to these questions can be found at the back of the instructor's manual. Subjective testing requires students to respond to simulation and case study scenarios. This type of activity requires students to address the main issues of the chapter and also synthesize information from previous chapters and outside sources. Sample responses are at the back of the instructor's manual.

ACKNOWLEDGMENTS

Our thanks go to the reviewers of this manuscript for their help and suggestions:

James C. Bennett
University of Texas at Austin

Roger Bloomquist
University of North Dakota

Catherine Boudreau
Massasoit Community College

Chet Bulgia
Broome Community College

Lillian Chaney
Memphis State University

Barbara Christoff
Monroe Community College

Carolyn Dolecheck
Northeast Louisiana University

Mary Evelyn Galbraith
Sam Houston State University

Beverly House
University of New Orleans

Velma Jesser
Lane Community College

Dora Johnson
Central Piedmont Community College

Gloria Mitchamore
North Harris County College

Karen Munson
Tacoma Community College

Linda Sarlo
Rock Valley College

Elaine Schmittke
Nassau Community College

John B. Smith
Bucks County Community College

Contents

Administrative Information Systems

PART 1 ADMINISTRATIVE ORGANIZATION

Part 1 of *Administrative Information Systems: People and Technology* describes the managerial process and the administrative office structure. Special emphasis is given to the changing nature of administration in the Information Age.

1 The Office Managerial Process

OBJECTIVES At the conclusion of this chapter, you should be able to:

1. Discuss the significant aspects of management theory associated with the Scientific Management Era, the Human Relations Era, the Behavioral Science Era, and the Systems Era.
2. Identify and describe the various functions of management.
3. Explain the management responsibilities of the administrative office manager.
4. Discuss the various aspects of administrative information systems with regard to the administrative office.

INTRODUCTION

Management can be defined as the process of organizing the activities of people to achieve goals. Humans have attempted to organize their activities for thousands of years. Recorded history is replete with examples of how effective management strategies have served tribes, armies, governments, and business organizations. There is also substantial evidence documenting ineffective management strategies that have been utilized by humankind throughout the ages.

The managerial process has slowly evolved over the years. On many occasions, it has taken different directions and pursued different emphases. Modern management theory has been well documented during this century, to the extent that today's managers have a wealth of tested management strategies available to them.

THE EVOLUTION OF MANAGEMENT THEORY

Management theory experts indicate that the evolution of management theory has moved through at least three distinct periods. These periods are described as the Scientific Management Era, the Human Relations Era, and the Behavioral Science Era. It appears that management theory has once again taken on a new emphasis, which incorporates computer systems technology, and therefore may be called the Systems Era.

The Scientific Management Era

The Scientific Management Era came into being as the result of the industrial revolution in the United States. For the first time in United States history, new mechanical methods of producing goods were being developed. In general, American workers were unprepared for this type of employment. It was expected that they, like the new machines, would become more productive. In order for this increase in total worker/machine productivity to come about, the efficiency of management also had to increase.

The efforts of Charles Babbage and Frederick Taylor provided a framework for controlling the factors of production within organizations. Babbage was responsible for developing such concepts as mechanization, work measurement, specific job costs, and salary incentives in the 1830s. Frederick Taylor designed his "Principles of Scientific Management" during the late 1800s and early 1900s. His principles are based on the concept that all persons will not perform all jobs equally well. The efforts of Babbage and later of Taylor identified differences in people's ability to perform certain tasks. By measuring performance, Babbage and Taylor could determine better work methods and tools (mechanization) to reduce the time and cost of specific job tasks.

> There is no question that the tendency of the average man is toward working at a slow easy gait, and it is only after a good deal of thought and observation on his part or as a result of example, conscience, or external pressure that he takes a more rapid pace.
>
> Frederick Taylor, 1919

In those times of rapid industrial expansion, efficiency was of the greatest importance. Taylor and French mining engineer/geologist Henri Fayol are credited with the early development of job engineering. The efforts of both men, especially Taylor, were obviously directed at improving corporate efficiency, or "productivity" as we call it today. Taylor firmly believed that there was one "best way" of performing a specific job task, and that through job analysis, organizational efficiency could be greatly improved.

The husband and wife team of Frank and Lilian Gilbreth also supported the scientific management movement. The Gilbreths used stopwatches and motion pictures in their development of time and motion theory. These studies, as well as their research into worker fatigue as it related to health and productivity, significantly contributed to the success of this era.

During the early 1900s, William H. Leffingwell was developing his "Five Principles of Work." His efforts were directed specifically at administrative office activities. Leffingwell's "Five Principles of Work" encouraged managers of the day to:

1. plan the work;
2. schedule the work;
3. execute the work;
4. measure the work; and
5. reward the worker.

Leffingwell's early efforts at office work management earned him the title of "Father of Office Management."

The Scientific Management Era extended into the 1930s. Luther Gulick and Lyndall Urwick elaborated on the earlier efforts of Babbage, Taylor, and Fayol, and edited a book in 1937 entitled *Papers on the Science of Administration.* Gulick developed the acronym POSDCORB (Planning, Organizing, Staffing, Directing, Coordinating, Recording, Budgeting) to describe administrative activities as the result of his research of the United States presidency. Urwick's main contributions were the concepts of "span of control" and "delegation of authority." *Span of control* refers to the number of people directly supervised or managed. *Delegation of authority* is a management strategy which passes on (delegates) the power (authority) to perform certain tasks to individuals who ordinarily do not possess the authority to perform these tasks.

The underlying philosophy of this era could be described as strictly task-oriented. Emphasis was given to the needs of the organization, to the exclusion of the needs of the people within the organization.

The Human Relations Era

Even as Gulick and Urwick were presenting their efforts, the development of administrative management was taking a dramatic turn. A group from Harvard Business School, headed by Elton Mayo, was called into the Hawthorne Works of the Western Electric Company by the company's employee manager to assess the effects of illumination on worker efficiency. These research efforts, which become known as the "Hawthorne Studies," helped to change the philosophy of administrative management from an organization-oriented mode of operation to an emphasis on the needs of the individual within the organization. The study found that worker productivity increased, not as a result of the level of illumination, but rather as a result of the amount of attention given to the workers and the involvement of the workers in the decision-making process.

> However unexpected it may have been, one major finding of these studies was the realization that "human" variability is an important determinant of productivity.
>
> Fritz Roethlisberger, 1939

The Human Relations Era, which spanned the 1940s and much of the 1950s, gave administrators a new set of management principles and techniques. As a result of the Hawthorne studies, the theories of group dynamics, communication, democratic leadership, and participative supervision became popular concepts.

- ☐ *Group dynamics:* the utilization of input from various members of the work group in order to solve problems.
- ☐ *Communication:* the establishment of communication policies and procedures to facilitate the flow of information throughout an organization.
- ☐ *Democratic leadership:* a leadership style which encourages input from subordinates for problem solving, policy making, and so on.
- ☐ *Participative supervision:* a supervision strategy which allows subordinates to participate in the supervision of a given work group or area.

The Behavioral Science Era

Economic expansion continued into the 1960s. In the corporate world, administrators searched for new management techniques. Management by objectives (MBO), early systems studies, and other techniques were developed to deal with the tremendous industrial expansion and competition within the private sector. MBO is a method of appraising the performance of an organization's managers. It emphasizes the evaluation of the measurable results of an organization's objectives.

It would be an oversimplification to suggest that the Behavioral Science Era integrates the positive aspects of the two previous eras. However, this period does reflect an understanding and acceptance of the need for sound, efficient management techniques, as well as the importance of addressing the needs of the individual within the organization. This recognition of the positive aspects of the Scientific Management and Human Relations Eras is depicted quite clearly in the Getzels/Guba model shown in Figure 1.1. This model looks at an organization in a dynamic manner, as a living and breathing entity that must reflect both human and organizational considerations. Jacob Getzels and Egon Guba were instrumental in developing an administrative theory which identifies the workplace as a complete social system.

In any social system such as a business, there are role expectations of individuals that are related to the goals and objectives of the institution. This dimension of the system is known as the *nomothetic* dimension, and represents the main focus of the Scientific Management Era. The social system is also made up of people who bring to the organization their own distinct personalities and needs. This dimension is known as the *idiographic* dimension, and represents the main focus of the Human Relations Era.

During the Behavioral Science Era, administrators attempted to devise strategies which addressed workers' needs and concerns in an effort to increase organizational efficiency and productivity. In es-

FIGURE 1.1
The Getzels/Guba model

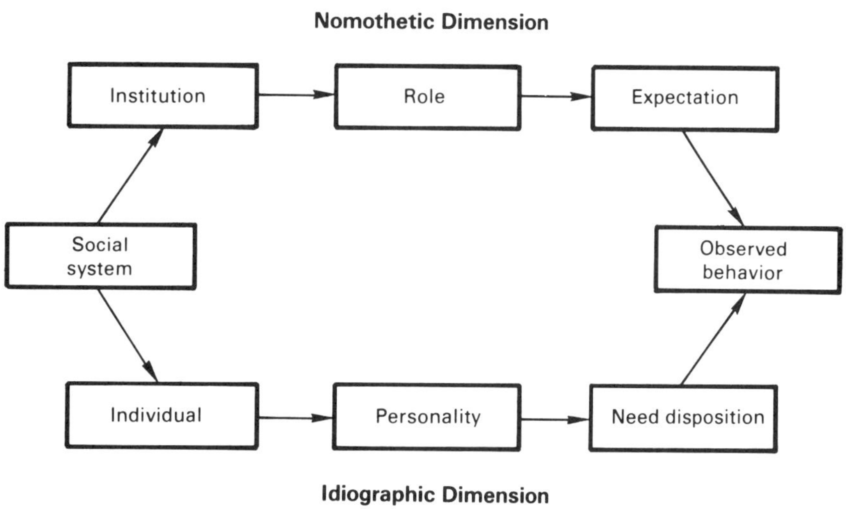

sence, this era attempted to deal with the interaction between the two dimensions of the Getzels/Guba model.

The Systems Era

Management strategies for the 1980s have incorporated the use of the most powerful tool of this century—the electronic computer. Tremendous advances in microcomputer technology and management software have paved the way for the widespread use of computer systems technology.

The pervasive nature of computer systems applications within the organizational structure requires that administrators have a substantial understanding of systems analysis and design techniques. Administrators are rapidly discovering that although computer systems are versatile and powerful business tools, they can be troublesome additions to the organization if they are poorly designed, implemented, or understood.

Systems theory incorporates an understanding of information flow and the technology available to process and disseminate the information generated by an organization. Although there are various systems formats, the primary aspects of systems analysis and design include systems investigation, systems analysis, systems design, systems implementation, and systems evaluation.

- ☐ *Systems investigation:* a study conducted to determine the managerial and operational objectives of an organization.
- ☐ *Systems analysis:* a study conducted to determine the existing method(s) of operation, problem areas, and so on.
- ☐ *Systems design:* the process of designing a new method of operation or modifying an existing process.
- ☐ *Systems implementation:* the process of installing the new or modified system.
- ☐ *Systems evaluation:* the process of establishing a measurement program to determine the success/failure of the new system.

Administrators must understand that although the work effort may be departmentalized, the departments' functions are not isolated. Previous management structures required managers to disseminate the information throughout the organization. Today's computer systems, combined with communication systems, have been designed to provide this dissemination service. However, administrators must be able to coordinate the objectives of the organization with the expanding technology base, and thus they need to understand the primary aspects of systems analysis and design.

Although the Systems Era has not been completely defined, the philosophy of this period embraces the idea that computer systems technology provides a new dimension to management technique which addresses organizational objectives as well as the needs of the individual within the organization. Thus, administrative systems technology is an essential tool for the office manager.

MANAGEMENT FUNCTIONS

Managers perform a variety of activities. Most of these activities fall into the categories of planning, organizing, staffing, directing, and controlling.

Planning The planning function of most organizations is of critical importance. The ability to effectively plan for the future is a valuable commodity in a highly competitive environment and in difficult economic times. Today, numerous planning strategies are available to managers to aid them in both short- and long-term planning. Computer software packages are available to aid managers in planning budgets, personnel requirements, equipment depreciation, and plant expansion, in addition to other highly sophisticated managerial functions.

Organizing The organizing function is primarily concerned with coordinating the people, equipment, and procedures of the organization. As one might expect, the organizing function is the direct result of the planning function. Managers charged with organizing activities must work with the management efforts of those involved in the planning function. It is imperative that managers be aware of the organization's objectives so that they can effectively organize employees, equipment, and procedures.

Staffing The primary activities that are associated with the staffing function include employee selection, orientation, training, and development, as well as the determination of job requirements, tasks, and responsibilities. A shortage of qualified business office personnel is predicted for this decade. Thus, the staffing function will continue to play a key role in the management process.

Directing Managers spend different amounts of time supervising and directing employees. Some managers spend large amounts of time in direct contact with subordinates, while other managers are rarely involved in supervising employees. An understanding of the formal and the informal lines of authority and communication is essential to the effective supervision of employees. Managers and employees who understand the formal and informal organizational structures can utilize the information obtained to meet the organization's objectives. They can also address many of the needs and concerns of the employees (i.e., safety, overtime, break schedules, etc.).

Controlling The controlling function monitors and makes adjustments to the actual operation of the various functional units of the business enterprise. The functional areas such as production, marketing, accounting, and finance perform specific duties for the organization. These tasks should be monitored and adjusted to ensure that the departmental efforts coincide with the objectives of the organization.

ADMINISTRATIVE OFFICE MANAGEMENT

The administrative office usually provides clerical and records management activities for the organization. These activities include word processing, telecommunications, information management, reprographics, and micrographics. In the past, each department was responsible for the specific function of its own office, and the administrative office handled general correspondence and filing. Today's office computer systems can be organized in a network configuration to service all of the functional areas of the organization.

This type of administrative office organization has critical implications for the office administrator. It is imperative that office administrators develop the systems skills that are necessary to coordinate the functions of the administrative office with the technology in a manner which services each of the functional units or departments of the organization. Administrative office managers in today's offices are responsible for computer systems evaluation and acquisition procedures, software evaluation, systems analysis and design, job descriptions, performance evaluations, and employee supervision, as well as the clerical and records management functions.

ADMINISTRATIVE INFORMATION SYSTEMS

The development of office computer systems has given office administrators the technical capability to gather, process, file, and retrieve information in a very efficient manner. Getting the right information to the right people at the right time so that informed decisions can be made is the primary goal of any well-designed administrative information system.

The computer system alone does not constitute an administrative information system. It is merely the tool used to facilitate the flow of information. Data base administrators are responsible for creating the structure which coordinates the functions of the organization with computer technology in a manner which accurately processes the data and then disseminates that information to the individuals who make decisions.

Properly constructed administrative information systems can provide several advantages to the organization. Administrative information systems provide a data base of information to be shared by the functional units of the organization. If properly developed, the data base offers greater control over the functions of the organization and reduces operating costs by more efficiently processing the data.

SUMMARY

1. Management can be defined as the process of organizing the activities of people to achieve goals.
2. Management theory has been documented through four distinct periods. They are the Scientific Management Era, the Human Relations Era, the Behavioral Science Era, and the Systems Era.
3. Tremendous advances in microcomputer technology and management software have paved the way for the widespread use of computer systems technology by administrators and managers.
4. The primary features of systems analysis and design are systems investigation, systems analysis, systems design, systems implementation, and systems evaluation.
5. The functions of management are planning, organizing, staffing, directing, and controlling.
6. Administrative office managers in today's organizations are responsible for computer systems evaluation and acquisition procedures, software evaluation, systems analysis and design, job descriptions, performance evaluations, and employee supervision, as well as clerical and records management functions.
7. The intent of administrative information systems is to get the right information to the right people at the right time so that informed decisions can be made.
8. Properly designed administrative information systems offer control over the functions of the organization and reduce operating costs.

STUDENT ACTIVITIES

Active Orientation

1. Visit a small- to medium-size company and interview a manager who has primary responsibility for at least one office management

function. Identify at least five duties that this person performs. Present your findings to the class for clarification and discussion.

2. Review the works of Mary Parker Follett or some of the writings of Fritz Roethlisberger, Herbert Simon, Max Weber, or William Leffingwell. Identify their management theories and any significant contributions that they may have made.

Independent Problems

1. Many people feel that selecting the best components from each of the management theory periods will build a model for management success. Do you agree? Justify your answer.

2. Management information systems can work at any organizational level and even at the personal organizational level. We all have several functional areas from which to receive input: school, work, family, and other social institutions. Using the characteristics of management information systems:

- ☐ develop your own personal system;
- ☐ state your objectives; and
- ☐ list the advantages of using a system of this type.

REFERENCES

Roethlisberger, F. J., and Dickson, W. J. *Management and the Worker.* Cambridge, MA: Harvard University Press, 1939.

Taylor, Frederick W. *Principles of Scientific Management.* New York and London: Harper and Brothers Publishing Company, 1919.

2 The Administrative Office

OBJECTIVES At the conclusion of this chapter, you should be able to:

1. Define the term *administrative office.*
2. Identify the various functional areas of an organization.
3. Describe the primary role of administrative office personnel.
4. Distinguish between line and line-and-staff organizational structures.
5. Describe the authority-responsibility relationship with respect to managerial personnel.
6. Contrast a centralized with a decentralized form of organizational structure.
7. Describe the role of the informal organization.

INTRODUCTION

There have been tremendous increases in administrative office activities in recent years. Today, more than fifty percent of the workforce in the United States consists of office workers. In 1985, more than $786 billion was paid to office workers for wages, salaries, and benefits. The demands placed upon business offices are extremely challenging. It is estimated that by 1990, seventy percent of all workers will be employed in information-related jobs. Other estimates indicate that nearly 300,000 new office jobs will be available each year through 1990.

This dramatic shift in available jobs from the industrial setting to the office setting has created some serious cost/performance problems for organizations. Although it has been a standard practice for many decades to measure productivity on the assembly line, managerial productivity has not been considered in most organizations. Recent productivity studies have indicated that factory productivity has increased by eighty-four percent in the past decade, while managerial productivity has increased at a rate of only four percent over the same time period. In addition, office costs are rising at an annual rate of fifteen percent and managers and professionals account for seventy-five to eighty percent of all office costs. These data indicate a clear need to establish new and effective office systems structures in business and government offices in the United States.

If office administrators are to effectively address these challenges, they must embrace the available office systems technology. In order to utilize office automation concepts, office managers must fully understand administrative office objectives, organizational structure, and office information systems. Therefore, now more than ever, it is essential that office administrators develop and apply sound organizational principles to the administrative office work effort.

Administrative offices are centralized facilities that have, as their primary function, the control of office activities and services. Typical functions of administrative offices include the overall responsibility for human resources, training and development, word processing, records management, reprographics and micrographics, and their related activities. The extent of responsibility that administrators in these offices have is dependent upon the types and sizes of the organizations that they serve.

The chief administrative officer of an administrative office is called the administrative office manager. This middle-management individual has direct responsibility for the entire administrative office.

ADMINISTRATIVE OFFICE OBJECTIVES

Organizations do not consist of isolated, independent departments. The various functional areas of an organization, such as marketing, manufacturing, accounting, finance, and human resources, must interrelate. These major functional areas, which are illustrated in Figure 2.1, must perform in harmony with each other if organizational objectives are to be attained. These objectives relate to the criteria to be met, the conditions under which they will be met, and the acceptable performance that is expected. Simply stated, organizational objectives relate to where the organization is going, how it expects to get there, and what vehicles will be used to reach the destination.

The administrative office and its human resources play a major role in coordinating the activities of the major functional units. It is critical, therefore, that office administrators understand the objectives of the organization so that the administrative objectives are consistent with those of the entire organization. It is always easier for a team to do something if everyone pulls in the same direction.

ORGANIZATIONAL STRUCTURE

Organizational structure is a management concept which, when illustrated, depicts the relationships among people, their duties, and their responsibilities. Organizational charts such as the one shown in Figure 2.2 graphically represent these relationships. The chart illustrates the flow of information, as well as the lines of authority. Although the organizational chart is only a paper document, it provides an excellent reference for managers and analysts who are interested in monitoring the functions of the organization.

OFFICE ORGANIZATIONAL STRUCTURE

The organizational structure of the administrative office determines the authority and responsibility relationships among employees. It

FIGURE 2.1
Functional areas of the organization

- ☐ Marketing Department
- ☐ Accounting Department
- ☐ Manufacturing Department
- ☐ Management Information Systems Department
- ☐ Finance Department
- ☐ Administrative Services

FIGURE 2.2
Corporate organizational chart

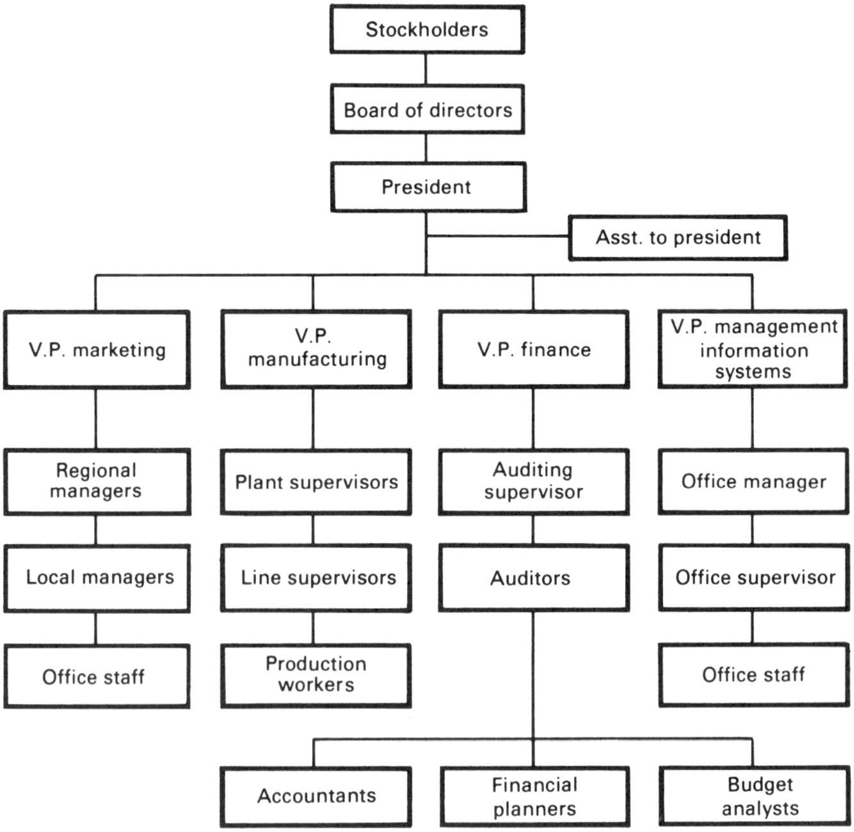

should be designed so that office activities such as records management and word processing effectively address the objectives of the organization. As one might imagine, drawing an organizational chart which reflects all of the interrelationships between the administrative office and the functional departments results in a rather confusing diagram. However, the office organizational structure should be documented in a chart form like Figure 2.3 to indicate each function that is performed. It should be made clear that these operations are performed for each of the major functional units. Without this kind of documentation, it would be impossible to determine authority, responsibility, and information processing channels in medium to large organizations. There are two basic forms of organizational charts that are used to illustrate these relationships: line and line-and-staff organizational structures.

Line Organization

Line organization is the basic form of organizational structure that flows in an unbroken line from the president of the company to the

FIGURE 2.3
Office organizational chart

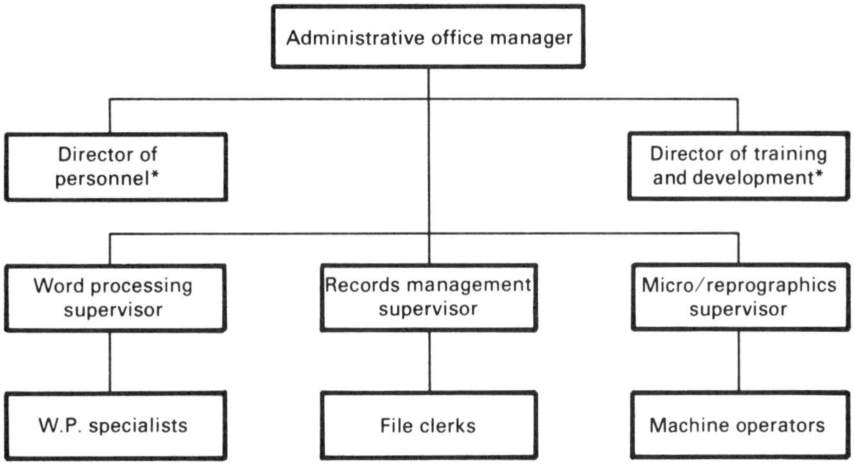

*Sometimes these positions are not under the control of the Administrative Office Manager.

individual office worker. Direct authority in line organizations flows vertically from top to bottom. This form of organizational structure is popular in new or very small businesses where levels of supervision and management are not possible. However, pure line organization structure is virtually nonexistent in large organizations.

Advantages of line organization. Line organization provides numerous advantages to its users. The simplistic design makes it easy for employees to understand; the lines of authority, responsibility, and accountability are clearly defined by the top-to-bottom design. Most important, however, is the fact that the process of decision making is clear and concise in line structure organizations because of the direct lines of authority which are inherent in its form.

Disadvantages of line organization. The simplistic design of line organization breaks down as the organization expands. Once growth begins, the duties and responsibilities of the individuals within the organization increase, creating the need for staff support such as clerical help, records management, and report preparation. Line organization does not provide for staff assistance.

Once staff functions are provided, pure line organization is destroyed. It is similar to adding three more coaches to a sports team; there is a possibility for confusion regarding function and responsibility. However, once responsibilities are determined and communicated, the extra expertise provided should lessen the need for regimentation on the part of the individuals at the top of the organization. Those individuals will then have more flexibility and opportunity to observe

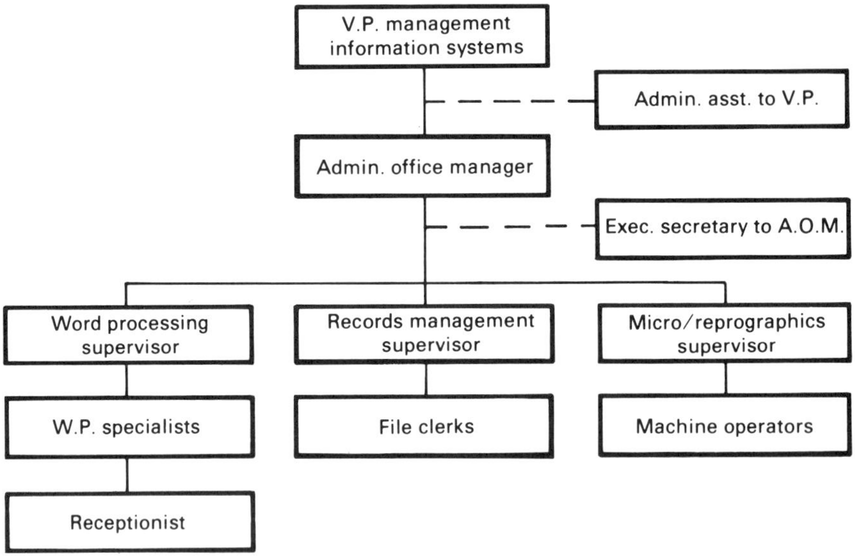

FIGURE 2.4 *Line-and-staff organization*

the functions of the entire organization. A strict line organization places organizational control and survival in the hands of a few significant management people. This limitation forces line organizations to seek replacement personnel from outside the organization instead of promoting from within.

Line-and-Staff Organization

The line-and-staff organizational structure that is shown in Figure 2.4 is the most popular form of organizational design. Line-and-staff organization provides for the same type of top-to-bottom authority system that pure line organization has, but it also recognizes the need for support staff positions in most organizations. The major distinction between line positions and staff positions is that line positions exist to achieve the primary objectives of the organization, while staff positions are designed to provide support to the line positions. Examples of typical staff functions are personnel and administrative services.

Advantages of line-and-staff organization. The major advantage of line-and-staff organization is that the staff support allows line management personnel the opportunity to spend more time with management applications such as planning, organizing, directing, and controlling, and thus focus more closely on their particular area of expertise. Staff personnel benefit from line-and-staff organization by being able to work closely with line personnel for possible advancement.

Disadvantages of line-and-staff organization. Many of the disadvantages of line-and-staff organization can be attributed to poor interpersonal relationships; conflicts can develop between line and staff personnel. These conflicts can occur when line personnel fail to acknowledge the efforts and expertise of staff workers or when staff personnel exceed their authority within the organization. The concept of staff as being a support function should not be confused with a lack of authority. Staff functions are, in many cases, very powerful and hold high authority. The administrative assistant and executive secretary are two examples of staff employees possessing power and authority.

In addition to staff support designations, further organizational definition is usually needed. This definition is usually developed along product or function lines. This departmentalization provides the organization with an opportunity to manage its resources according to similar work groupings.

Departmentalization

Departmentalization is the process of arranging the basic organizational units to facilitate the performance of similar specialized functions or tasks. The activities of these units are grouped to facilitate the various tasks of the organization. Organizations can coordinate the people and equipment needed to perform similar tasks by dividing the work effort into departments.

Typical departmental distinctions are made by the nature of the work to be performed, the product line, the customer or services to be provided, and special projects. Marketing, research and development, and production are some examples of departments that are often found in business organizations. Within each departmental grouping, lines of authority and responsibility must be developed so that work assignments can be efficiently assigned and monitored.

AUTHORITY-RESPONSIBILITY RELATIONSHIP

Authority is the right and the corresponding power to make decisions. Responsibility relates to the necessity to properly complete the tasks that are assigned. Authority and responsibility are often controversial topics. Controversy tends to arise when an individual or organization fails to take responsibility for a particular action or exceeds its authority on a given matter.

Few people would disagree with the idea that individuals should be given an appropriate level of authority to carry out the responsibilities of their positions. However, a proper balance is critical for healthy interpersonal relationships as well as a productive environment. Taking responsibility for specific organizational functions is critical to efficient, productive work. In many situations, individuals cannot possibly perform all the tasks for which they are responsible. Under these conditions, they should exert the sound management ap-

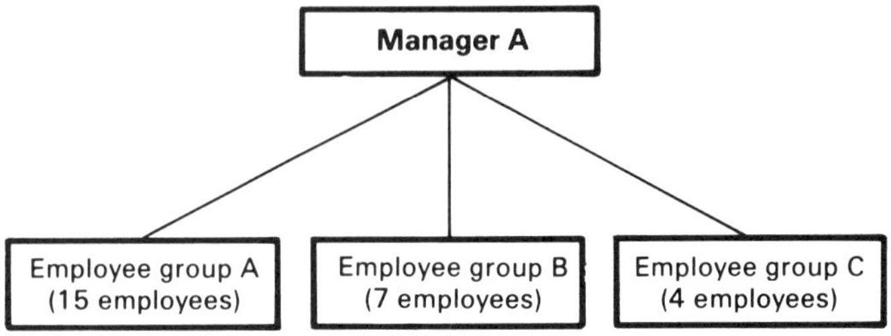

FIGURE 2.5
Span of control

proach of delegating the authority to someone else, thus developing a "span of control." Span of control, which is illustrated in Figure 2.5, refers to the number of subordinates that an individual can effectively manage.

There is no magic number for optimum efficiency in a span of control. Rather, the following factors should be considered: the manager's responsibilities, the type of work to be performed by the subordinates, the hierarchical level in the organization, and the experience level of both the manager and the subordinates. The delegation of authority to perform tasks is a practical procedure. However, even though the authority for the performance of a task is given to a subordinate, the responsibility for the task will always remain with the person who is originally charged with the responsibility. In order to control these authority and responsibility relationships, organizations usually establish centralized or decentralized control procedures.

Centralization and Decentralization

There are two basic methods of control over the functions of an organization: centralization and decentralization. Centralization refers to the unique location of organizational jurisdiction for similar activities; one individual or department performs a particular function for the entire company. A records management center is an example of a centralized function. In a decentralized organizational structure, several individuals or departments may have responsibility for similar activities. For example, order processing (purchase orders, shipping, and invoicing) can be handled on a regional (decentralized) basis to provide more rapid responses to customer needs.

Some organizations prefer centralized control of activities while others could not function under centralized control. Centralization tends to work best for those organizations with large amounts of paper work, relatively few product lines, and localized operations. Decentralization, on the other hand, seems to work best in organizations that are extremely large and diversified and have production facilities in various locations.

Advantages of centralization. Some of the advantages of centralization are:

1. less duplication of effort and equipment;
2. fewer training requirements and better utilization of employees;
3. greater standardization of work processes; and
4. more efficient handling of peak workloads.

Disadvantages of centralization. Some of the disadvantages of centralization are:

1. technical expertise may not be evenly distributed throughout the organization;
2. confidentiality of documents inhibits processing;
3. work flow bottlenecks can develop because of absenteeism or differing job priorities; and
4. the decision-making process may be too slow because of the inaccessibility of certain individuals.

Advantages of decentralization. Some of the advantages of decentralization are:

1. the decision-making process is usually streamlined;
2. there is more flexibility of work flow design; and
3. there is even distribution of expertise.

Disadvantages of decentralization. Some of the disadvantages of decentralization are:

1. the possible duplication of work;
2. the potential of staffing duplication; and
3. the fact that peak workload assignment shifts are difficult.

INFORMAL ORGANIZATIONAL STRUCTURE

The formal organizational structure is represented by an organizational chart and written operations manuals. However, most organizations, like most social structures, contain a subculture that is essential to its existence, efficiency, and effectiveness. This phenomenon is known as the "informal organizational structure."

The informal organizational structure is the actual method of operation in an organization. Many times the formal and the informal organizational structures vary significantly. It is imperative that administrators understand the informal organizational concept because it can be a very effective device for communication within an organization. Informal structure allows employees the opportunity to share information, opinions, and grievances. This communication flow, which has been termed “the grapevine,” is healthy and can be of great benefit to the administrative organization.

PROFESSIONALISM

A great deal of professional growth and development can occur outside of a person’s workplace. A manager’s ideas could develop into useful policies as a result of his or her interactions and involvement in organizations that reflect and support the profession of administrative office management. The most significant organization that can serve the professional needs of the office manager is the Administrative Management Society (AMS). Through this organization, an administrative office manager can become a Certified Administrative Manager (CAM), which may facilitate advancement and increase professional growth and development.

Other associations which could be of benefit to the administrative office manager are the Association of Records Managers and Administrators (ARMA), the Association for Systems Management (ASM), the Association for Information Systems Professionals (AISP), the Business Forms Management Association (BFMA), the Office Systems Research Association (OSRA), and the Data Processing Management Association (DPMA). Most professional organizations offer periodicals, newsletters, information on the state of the art, and other related opportunities for professionals.

SUMMARY

1. Administrative offices are centralized facilities that have, as their primary function, the control of office activities and services.
2. Today more than fifty percent of the United States workforce consists of office workers.
3. In order to meet the many challenges facing office administrators, office automation must be utilized.
4. The development of sound organizational objectives is critical for the successful execution of the various office functions.
5. Office administrators should utilize organizational charts to plan for administrative office activities.
6. Line and line-and-staff organizational structures provide administrators with descriptions of the flow of authority and communication within the organization.

7. Departmentalization is a method of coordinating the people and equipment needed to perform similar tasks.
8. Administrators can delegate the authority for various tasks to subordinates; however, the responsibility always remains with the administrator.
9. Centralization and decentralization are the two basic methods of controlling the functions of an organization.
10. The informal organizational structure identifies the actual methods of operation and communication within an organization.
11. Membership in professional organizations can improve professional growth and development.

STUDENT ACTIVITIES

Active Orientation

1. Visit a company that employs less than twenty-five full-time employees. Develop an organizational chart for the company and identify the line-and-staff organizational functions. (If it is more practical, invite a management official to visit your classroom to discuss this material.)

2. Independently interview a management employee and a production employee from the same company. Describe their formal organizational function, and interpret from the following questions the informal organizational structure.

- ☐ How does management get input from the workers on new policy and procedure changes?
- ☐ How do labor grievances get to the attention of management before any formal procedures begin?
- ☐ Is there a "grapevine" in the company? If so, how does it work?
- ☐ Are the "real powers" in the company those individuals who are listed in responsible positions on the company's organizational chart?

3. As a class, investigate the student membership and student club membership costs of the various organizations identified in the professionalism section of the chapter; then determine the advantages and disadvantages of belonging to each organization.

Independent Problems

1. Develop an organizational chart for XYZ Industries, a manufacturer of cardboard boxes which has production facilities in Los Angeles, Detroit, and New York. Use a decentralized control structure and use only typical departmental units.

2. Describe how the administrative office manager could use the "grapevine" to better meet organizational objectives. Discuss your ideas with the class.

PART 2 ADMINISTRATIVE FUNCTIONS

Part 2 of *Administrative Information Systems: People and Technology* describes the most common administrative functions in today's office. Word processing, records management, micrographics, reprographics, forms control, telecommunications, and budget analysis functions are discussed.

3 Word Processing

OBJECTIVES At the conclusion of this chapter, you should be able to:

1. Define the term *word processing.*
2. Determine those office activities that contribute to the cost of written business communications.
3. Identify the phases of an effective word processing system.
4. Distinguish between a stand-alone word processor and a shared-logic word processor.
5. List the objectives of a word processing system.
6. Identify the various types of word processing technology.
7. List the common software features of word processing packages.

INTRODUCTION

Word processing is the most current term used to describe the clerical activities, which include the preparation of business letters, memos, and reports, in today's business office. The word processing system can be defined as the utilization of people, procedures, and equipment to produce written business documents. Word processing systems are designed to provide an organized means for not only producing business documents but also for controlling their cost.

WORD PROCESSING COSTS

Clerical activities have become an increasingly expensive business office function. Of the 1.5 trillion dollars paid out to United States workers for wages, salaries, and benefits in 1985, fifty-one percent went to office workers. When one considers this fact, it is apparent that the clerical activities represent a major expense item for business organizations.

Wages, salaries, and other benefits are major factors associated with the cost of each clerical activity in a business organization. One such activity is the typing of a business letter. These costs are itemized in Figure 3.1. The Dartnell Institute of Research has charted average business letter costs since 1930. These costs are shown in Figure 3.2. Dartnell also reports that in 1940, the average length of a business letter was 240 words, compared to an average length of 175 words in 1980. These statistics highlight the need for efficiency in letter production. Using these data in another way demonstrates that, since 1940, the office industry has experienced a greater than tenfold increase in

FIGURE 3.1
Cost of producing one business letter

Dartnell Institute of Research
Letter Cost—1983

Cost Factor	Average Cost
Dictator's time	$2.00
Secretary's time	2.18
Non-productive time	.63
Fixed charges	2.17
Materials cost	.24
Mailing cost	.38
Total cost	$7.60

FIGURE 3.2
Average letter costs 1930–1983

Year	Cost	Year	Cost
1930	$ .30	1975	$3.79
1935	$ .52	1976	$4.17
1940	$ .72	1977	$4.47
1953	$1.17	1978	$4.77
1960	$1.83	1979	$5.59
1964	$2.32	1980	$6.07
1968	$2.54	1981	$6.63
1973	$3.31	1982	$7.11
1974	$3.41	1983	$7.60

letter costs, while the number of words per letter has been reduced by more than twenty-five percent.

Today's modern business offices are attempting to break the expensive dictation–transcription–typing cycle through the utilization of office computer systems technology. These efforts have already resulted in the creation of word processing centers that replace the typing pool concept in many business organizations.

WORD PROCESSING AND ORGANIZATIONAL STRUCTURE

The creation of word processing systems within organizations has had its effect on the organizational structure. The typical office organizational chart may now appear in different formats, as is shown in Figures 3.3 and 3.4. Typically, the format will change the titles of Typing Supervisor and Clerk Typist to Word Processing Supervisor and Word Processing Specialist respectively.

FIGURE 3.3
Traditional office structure

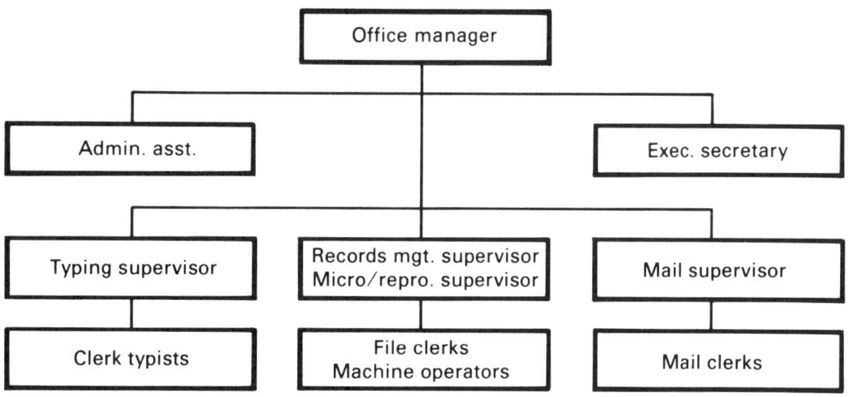

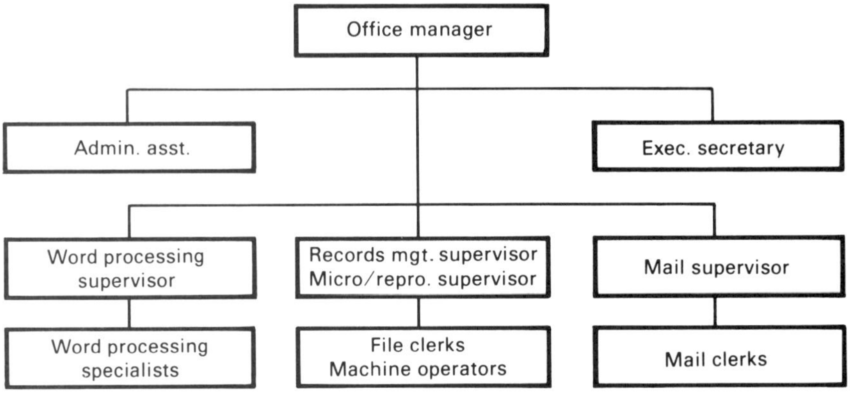

FIGURE 3.4 *Automated office structure*

OBJECTIVES OF A WORD PROCESSING SYSTEM

Once the administrative office manager understands the organizational structure and he or she becomes aware of the organization's long-range goals, the objectives for the new word processing system can be developed. These objectives should take the form of the expected benefits in the development of the new system. The following are examples of objectives relating to the implementation of a word processing system:

1. to reduce cases of redundant work activities in the office;
2. to provide more control over job assignments;
3. to provide more control of job supervision;
4. to increase office production;
5. to increase accuracy;
6. to provide a greater opportunity to measure output; and
7. to provide the opportunity to assign more management duties to nonmanagement personnel.

Setting objectives in the form of expected benefits will provide the administrative office manager with a blueprint for designing a word processing system which is responsive to organizational objectives.

Phases of a Word Processing System

Word processing systems consist of a series of steps that are designed to achieve the objectives of the office. These steps are illustrated in Figure 3.5.

Step 1: Input. Information is supplied to word processing specialists in rough draft form from handwritten copy, dictation, telephone messages, or computer terminals.

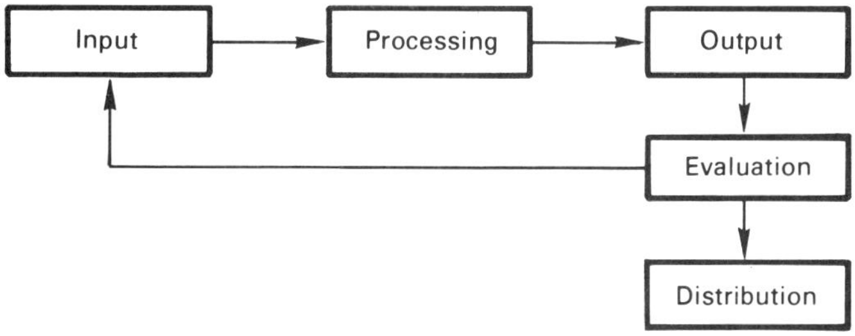

FIGURE 3.5 *Phases of a word processing system*

Step 2: Processing. The word processing specialist edits the input document using a typewriter, electronic typewriter, or word processor. The edited document is prepared according to established departmental formats for letters, interoffice memos, reports, business forms, or manuscripts.

Step 3: Output. During the output phase, the edited document is sent to the originator for review. The edited document can be delivered in hard-copy form (on paper) or through a computer terminal hook-up.

Step 4: Evaluation. The person who originated the document evaluates the edited document. If the document is acceptable, it is signed or initialed and forwarded for distribution. If the document is not acceptable, it is returned to the word processing specialist (step 2) for additional editing.

Step 5: Distribution. Once an edited document is approved, it may be distributed in many forms—U.S. Post Office mailing, private carrier, interoffice mail, facsimile, or computer terminal distribution (electronic mail).

WORD PROCESSING TECHNOLOGY

Office systems technology in the area of word processing is rapidly advancing. Typical word processing equipment that is used in today's business offices includes dictation equipment, electronic typewriters, and word processors.

Dictation Equipment

Dictation machines provide a means for individuals to "voice" input to the word processing system. The originator does not have to write down the information; he or she merely has to vocally record what must be processed. There are many types of dictation machines, as shown in Figure 3.6. These range from desk top recorders and tran-

FIGURE 3.6
Desk top and portable recorders

Courtesy of Lanier, Inc.

scribers to portable units. Common features of these dictation machines include an indexing capability for comments and directions to transcribers, fast forward and fast reverse, and dictation review.

Electronic Typewriters

Electronic typewriters, as shown in Figure 3.7, are devices which utilize microprocessors to perform limited text editing of typed documents. Most electronic typewriters have small visual display windows that allow the user to see a line or two of the typed document. These units also contain limited memory to store documents for later use. The development of electronic typewriters was stunted by the rapid growth of low-cost word processors. These word processors provided many additional features for only a few more dollars. In today's market, electronic typewriters are considered a poor purchase when price or performance is truly desired.

Word Processors

There is a multitude of word processing equipment to choose from today. Word processors differ from electronic typewriters in that word processors possess much larger memory capacity, removable memory media such as magnetic disks and diskettes, large visual displays of text, and multiple print style possibilities. The two types of word processors are stand-alone units and shared-logic systems.

Stand-alone word processors. Stand-alone word processors, like the one shown in Figure 3.8, are designed to operate independently from other machines. The stand-alone units utilize keyboard data entry, microprocessors for computing power, visual display terminals (VDT) for viewing full pages of text, removable disk storage, and a wide variety of print capabilities.

FIGURE 3.7
Electronic typewriters

Electronic 75 (1979)

Correcting Selectric III (1980)

Electronic 65 (1982)

Electronic 85 (1982)

Wheelwriter 3 (1984)

Wheelwriter 5 (1984)

Quietwriter 7 (1984)

Courtesy of International Business Machines Corporation

FIGURE 3.8
Stand-alone word processor

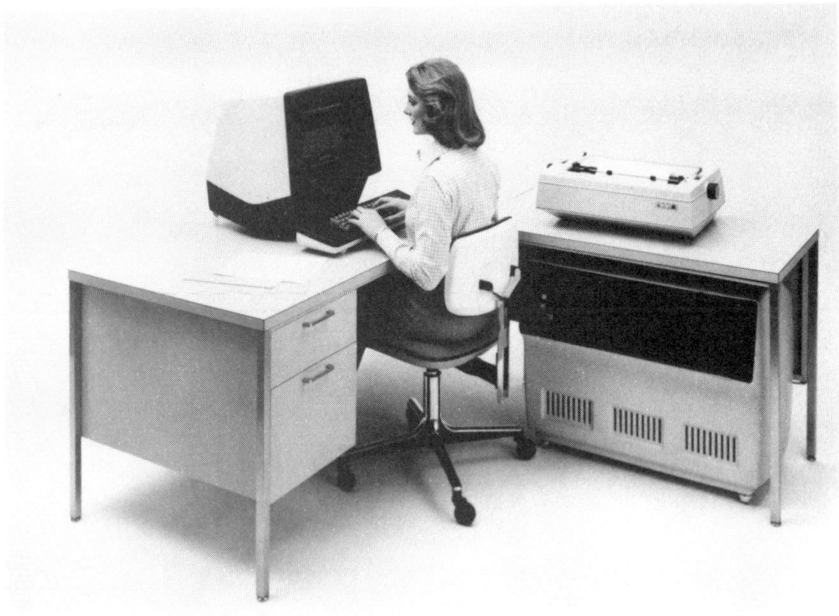

Courtesy of Lanier, Inc.

Shared-logic word processors. Shared-logic word processing systems, such as the one shown in Figure 3.9, are designed to allow many people to use one word processing software package that is stored in the central computer memory. For example, marketing and production departments might have computer terminals that are linked to the same computer memory. Shared-logic systems usually contain more memory for document storage and a more sophisticated word processing package than stand-alone units.

COMMON FEATURES OF WORD PROCESSING PACKAGES

The functions of word processing packages vary according to the manufacturer. However, typical systems contain text origination, text editing, and block move features.

Text Origination

All word processing software allows the operator to enter original text material (see Figure 3.10). As the originator types the document, he or she has the option to select automatic indentation, justification of right margins, centering, page numbering, decimal alignment, and other features.

FIGURE 3.9 *Shared-logic word processor*

Courtesy of Lanier, Inc.

Text Editing Once the document has been entered, the word processing specialist has the option to search the document for specific items for editing such as deletion or replacement. This technique is called "global search and replace." As an example, the word processing specialist can search for the first occurrence of the word "table" and replace it with the word "desk." The word processor can then replace the word "table" with the word "desk" each time it occurs throughout the document.

The word processing specialist can also run the document against a program that checks spelling. This program may contain 50,000 or more words, plus a user-defined list of additional words. The system checks each word from the document against the words on its lists. The unmatched words and misspelled words are highlighted or listed on the visual display for action by the word processing specialist.

Block Move Another common feature of word processors is the block move. This technique allows the operator to designate a block of text within the

FIGURE 3.10
Text origination

document and move that block of text to a new location within the document, as is shown in Figure 3.11.

WORD PROCESSING CENTERS

The development of word processing centers within organizations has touched off debate as to whether word processing workstations should be centralized in one location or decentralized, and distributed throughout the organization as needed.

The Centralized Approach

The centralized approach to word processing, as illustrated in Figure 3.12, services various departments in the organization under the control of the word processing supervisor. Some organizations have abandoned a centralized word processing center because bottlenecks developed in work flow because of poor job assignment practices. It is important that a complete systems analysis be conducted to determine the best word processing approach for an organization. This approach will provide the data to determine whether or not a centralized word processing center is workable.

The Decentralized Approach

Providing word processing equipment and support where it is needed within the organization is known as the decentralized approach. As is

FIGURE 3.11
Text editing and block move

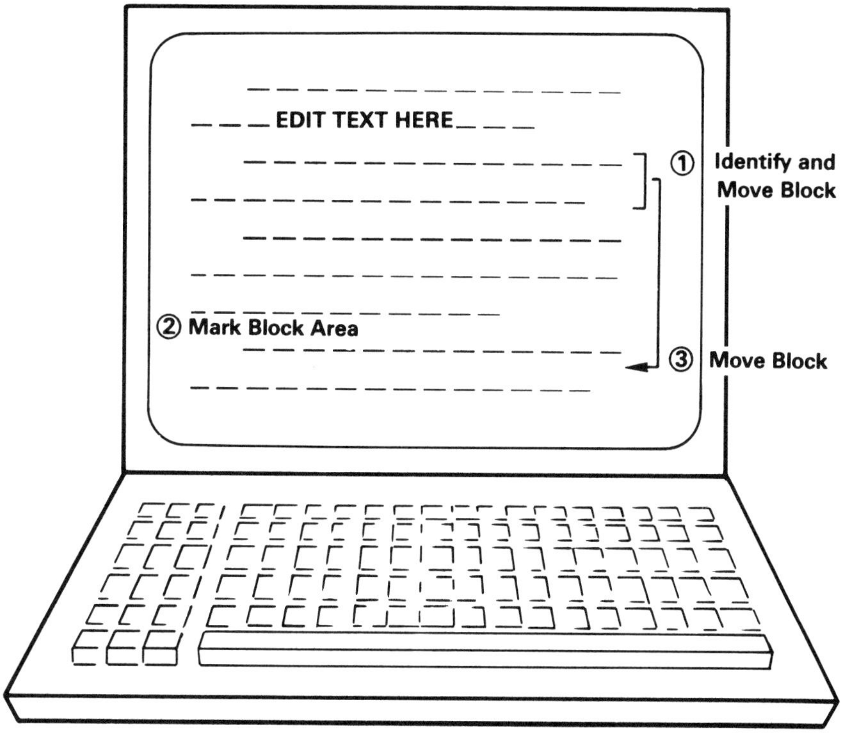

FIGURE 3.12
Centralized word processing environment

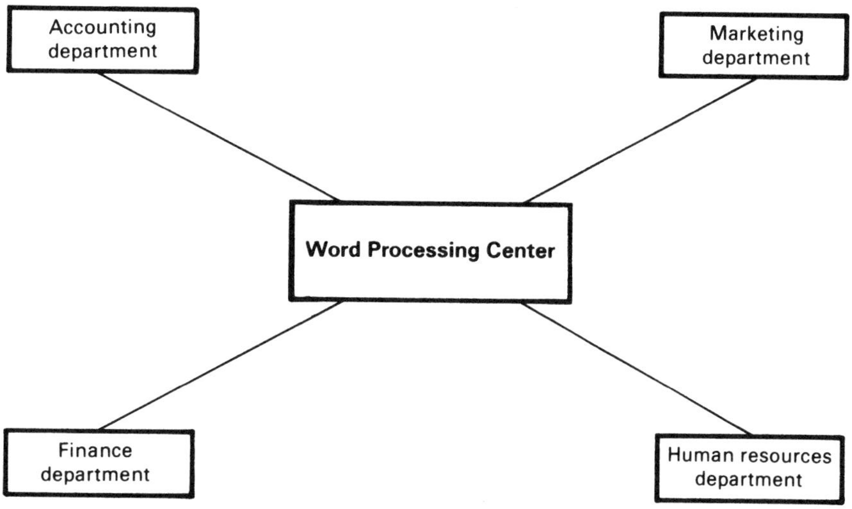

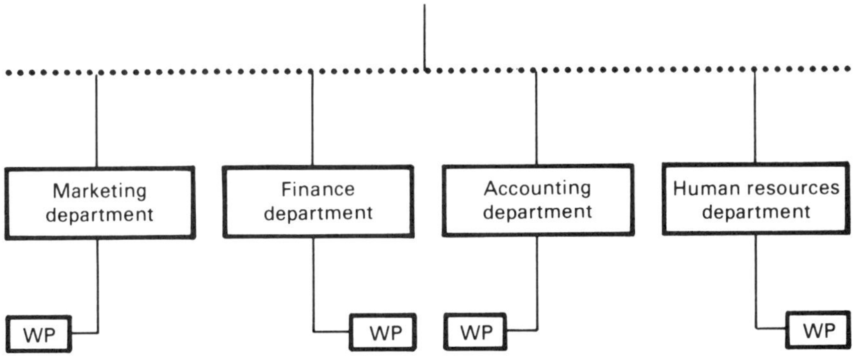

FIGURE 3.13 *Decentralized word processing environment*

shown in Figure 3.13, each area is responsible for its own word processing activities. The inherent danger with the decentralized approach is that in some cases no overall control of word processing growth is exercised. This tends to result in a lack of evaluation of word processing effectiveness, the proliferation of incompatible equipment, and the underutilization of equipment. Recent price reductions, coupled with the development of sophisticated business software, have made it easier for organizations to consider the decentralized approach. However, strategies for effective control are essential.

SUMMARY

1. Word processing utilizes people, procedures, and equipment to produce written business documents.
2. Word processing has changed the job titles and responsibilities of some office personnel. For example, clerk typists are now referred to as word processing specialists.
3. Implementing a word processing system can lead to greater office productivity.
4. The phases of a word processing system are input, processing, output, evaluation, and distribution.
5. Word processing software features include text originating and text editing.

STUDENT ACTIVITIES

Active Orientation

1. In groups of four, develop the best possible solution to the following situation.

As budding entrepreneurs, you have decided to begin your own word processing center. Assuming that you have enough money for the best possible equipment, develop a plan for your company according to the:

- ☐ services you plan to provide.
- ☐ equipment that you will need to provide those services. (Do some investigating here. List the brand, model, associated software, quantity, and approximate cost for this equipment.)
- ☐ phase organization of your system. (A flowchart will be effective here.)

Independent Problems

1. Compare and contrast two of several word processing packages according to their common features.

2. Attempt to justify the average cost of a letter according to the various cost factors. For example, why is the dictator's time more expensive than the secretary's time, and what is meant by "fixed charges"?

3. Cite two examples where it would be best to purchase a shared-logic word processor.

4. How would you justify the incorporation of a word processing system to your boss in a company that solicits money for a charity?

4 Records Management

OBJECTIVES At the conclusion of this chapter, you should be able to:

1. Describe the records management cycle.
2. List the objectives of a records management program.
3. Describe strategies for operating a records management program.
4. Identify the various records management personnel.
5. Discuss the different types of filing procedures and file organization.
6. Outline an effective records retention schedule.
7. Discuss the role of the computer in records management.

INTRODUCTION

The management of records costs businesses, government agencies, and educational institutions billions of dollars annually. Every organization responds or reacts to its environment according to the information it collects, maintains, and stores. The quality and availability of this accumulation of information directly determines the effectiveness of the organization's decision-making process. If the members of an organization are to have the right information at the right time in order to decide a business matter, then the records management system must be current, flexible, and responsive.

THE RECORDS MANAGEMENT FUNCTION

Records management can be described as those functions which create, maintain, store, retrieve, and dispose of the documents of the business organization. These activities represent the very fiber of the business. The records of a business contain the facts and figures indicating revenues, expenses, liabilities, payroll, inventory, sales figures, and legal contracts.

The importance of an effective records management program cannot be overstated. Thousands of new businesses are formed every week in the United States. Most of these new businesses fail within the first year, not because they have an undesirable product or service to sell, but because they cannot effectively manage their own records systems.

Objectives of a Records Management Program

The primary objectives of a business organization's records management program are:

1. to furnish accurate and complete information;
2. to process recorded information efficiently; and
3. to provide information at the lowest cost possible.

The design of the records management program of a business depends primarily on the size of the organization and the type of business activity conducted by the organization. The organizational chart depicted in Figure 4.1 indicates the position of the records management structure within the administrative office.

THE RECORDS MANAGEMENT PROCESS

The employees of a records management center are responsible for the creation, maintenance, storage, and disposition of business records.

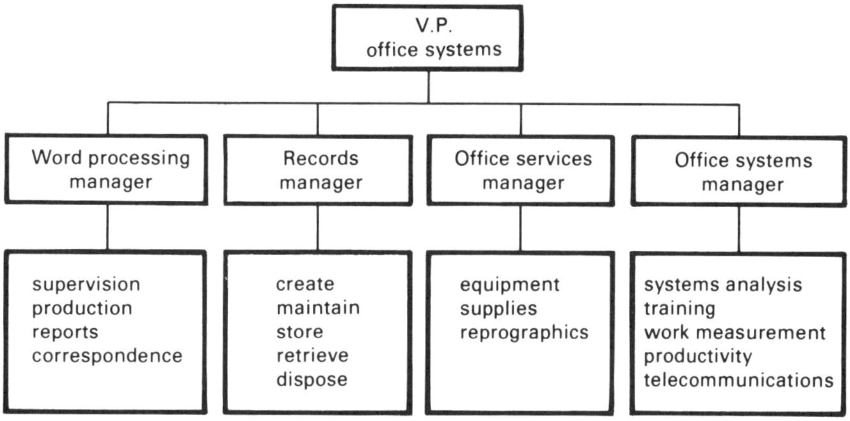

FIGURE 4.1
Records management area—administrative office

Records Creation

The proliferation of files within a business are a major problem. Recent government studies indicate that for every twenty pieces of paper filed in a typical business, only *one* is ever requested after the first filing. This inefficiency is usually the result of a poorly designed or nonexistent policy on records creation.

A policy should be established in each organization that states the procedures for creating new files. Files are the official documents of an organization. Business files typically include daily correspondence, legal documents, historical papers, and operations and procedural manuals. The records manager should be given the exclusive power to create files within the organization. A file requisition procedure, such as the one in Figure 4.2, should be established so that each time a departmental unit requests the creation of a file, the records management personnel can work with the requesting department to either create a new file or modify an existing file to suit the requesting department's needs. The file requisition procedure states that the department should submit the request in a format that describes the need for the file, its intended use, specifications for the file, the estimated length of time the file is to be maintained, and any security considera-

FIGURE 4.2
File requisition procedure

- ☐ Department requests creation of a file
- ☐ Records area searches existing files for similar file
- ☐ Records area approves request for new file or modifies existing file
- ☐ Requesting department and records area personnel develop new file

tions which may be needed. The records department personnel then check the request against any similar files which may already exist. If a similar file or files are found, suggestions are made to the requesting department concerning possible file consolidation. If no similar files are found and the file warrants creation, then the records department personnel work with the requesting department to create and develop the file.

Records Maintenance

The records of an organization are of little value if they are inaccurate or unlocatable. Properly maintained files can provide the essential information that business executives, managers, and owners need to make decisions concerning the organization. Poorly maintained files not only waste space, time, and money, but they provide the potential for poor decision making on the part of management.

The first step in developing a workable record maintenance system is to conduct a files analysis. This activity determines a number of things about the records that presently exist in the organization's files. A files analysis usually includes inventory, maintenance, retention, and disposition activities.

Files inventory. The files inventory activity is a physical inventory of the existing files and produces a master list of all files by title, such as the one shown in Figure 4.3. This master list is then used to conduct maintenance activities such as combining common files, discovering duplicated files, and spotting unused files. Managers are often surprised at the condition of their files.

Files maintenance. The files maintenance activity is a series of activities conducted by the records personnel to maintain the existing files of the organization. After the files inventory, many organizations

FIGURE 4.3
Portion of files inventory master list

- ☐ Accounts receivable
- ☐ Agreements (employee)
- ☐ Annual reports
- ☐ Articles of incorporation
- ☐ Bank statements
- ☐ Bids
- ☐ Charge slips
- ☐ Checks (cancelled)
- ☐ Check registers
- ☐ Correspondence (general)
- ☐ Depreciation schedules
- ☐ Dividend reports
- ☐ Expense reports
- ☐ Financial statements

find it necessary to completely rethink their file organization. Many times files are in such a state of confusion because of redundancy, misfiling, and file loss that managers no longer have confidence in the filing system. In these cases, complete reorganization of the records management area is required. However, short of complete reorganization, typical file maintenance activities include:

1. assigning responsibility for each file to a manager or area;
2. combining similar files into one comprehensive file;
3. removing duplicate files;
4. separating active and inactive files; and
5. reviewing filing and refiling procedures.

Files retention. The files retention activity places a predetermined date on each file to indicate how long it should be maintained in the file area. According to certain laws, many of an organization's files must be maintained a given number of years. This requirement varies from state to state and depends on the type of file. Other retention periods are established by the organization for correspondence files, job applications, and budgets, as shown in Figure 4.4, and their dates are usually determined by company policy.

Files disposition. The files disposition activity provides an organized procedure for controlling the proliferation of files and eliminating unneeded files within an organization. The strategy for disposing of records must address the legal requirements of each file, which are found on the file retention schedule, as well as the value of the file to the organization. Records management personnel prepare a records disposition schedule such as the one in Figure 4.5 to document the useful life of each file. Each file is then marked with a disposition date that indicates the date that the file is to be pulled from the records area for

FIGURE 4.4
Portion of file retention schedule

File	Retention (Years)
Accounts payable	5
Accounts receivable	5
Agreements (employee)	permanent
Annual reports	permanent
Articles of incorporation	permanent
Bank statements	7
Bids	3
Correspondence (general)	3
Job descriptions	until changed

FIGURE 4.5
Files disposition schedule

Quarterly Disposition Schedule

File	Disposition Date
Delivery schedules	1/30/87
Charge slips	1/30/87
Bank statements	2/28/87
Bids	3/31/87

disposition, as is illustrated in Figure 4.6. It is ultimately the responsibility of management to give authorization to destroy any file, and thus a formal request form for destruction of a record, like the one in Figure 4.7, should always exist within any records disposition program. An effective records disposition program solves many problems for the records management area. Valuable and expensive storage space is made available through a well-managed records disposition program.

Records Storage

The records of an organization are stored for various lengths of time and in numerous ways. Active files, which are used in the day-to-day operation of the organization, are usually stored in file folders and placed in metal filing cabinets. Inactive files, which are no longer used for the day-to-day operation of the organization but are not marked for destruction, are usually boxed in cardboard cartons and placed in the records center. The records center can either be a designated area within the organization or a commercial records storage center which rents storage space to organizations. In a manual storage system, records are stored in file folders that are labeled by some predetermined filing system, such as alphabetic, numeric, or alphanumeric, as shown in Figure 4.8. This system seems to be effective as long as each person that works with the files follows the file manual and index every time a document is filed. This procedure allows for only one user of the file at a given time.

Files can also be stored electronically on magnetic disks within an office computer system. In addition to the alphabetic, numeric, and alphanumeric schemes, electronic files can be cross-referenced in

FIGURE 4.6
Coding files for disposition

File Name: Delivery schedules Creation Date: 1/3/84
Retention Period: 3 years
Scheduled Disposition Date: 1/30/87
Manager/Supervisory: Mr. James Madison

FIGURE 4.7
Request to destroy a record

THE Arizona BANK

RECORD RETENTION/DESTRUCTION REQUEST

BR/DEPT NAME	NUMBER	DATE	
		YEAR	MONTH

COMPLETE ALL INSTRUCTIONS:

1. Write the description of contents, forms, date of contents, numbers and destruction date.
2. Contents and destruction date **MUST BE VERIFIED** by an officer of your branch or department. **FORMS & SUPPLIES SERVICES PERSONNEL WILL NOT VERIFY CONTENT.**
3. Items for storage must be in proper storage boxes with a record retention label affixed on the end of the box.
4. Forms & Supplies Services will not pick up any retention improperly boxed or labeled. Refer to Policy & Procedures #1559.

Forms & Supplies Services Use Only — BOX CODE	BOX #	DESCRIPTION OF CONTENTS	DATE OF CONTENTS	DESTRUCTION DATE	Contents and Destruction Date Verified By (Initials)

My initials above hereby acknowledge the verification of the destruction date(s) and description of contents listed.

Completed By ______________________ ______________________ Officers Signature

01019009 (3-84) ORIGINAL Branch/Department Copy DUPLICATE & TRIPLICATE Send to: Forms & Supplies Services #250

Courtesy of the Arizona Bank

numerous ways by utilizing computerized records management programs. For example, managers can code a file by name, social security number, years of service, and number of dependents. The manager can then access the file by using any one or more of the file codes. Each user of the computerized filing system can call up a copy of the file from the system without actually checking out the file folder. This allows for a much more effective means of file use, storage, and maintenance. Records storage plays an important and costly role in most organizations, and modern computer systems are playing a greater role in records management than ever before.

THE COMPUTER AND RECORDS MANAGEMENT

"Perhaps the most important contribution the computer makes to records management is the function of control" (Klathoff and Lee). Most of

FIGURE 4.8
Filing systems

- ☐ Alphabetic
- ☐ Numeric
- ☐ Alphanumeric

the problems associated with records management involve the function of control. Records personnel must control the proliferation of files (files creation), the daily changes to the existing files (file maintenance), and the numbers and types of records (file storage and disposition).

Most records management applications are ideally suited for computer processing. However, many organizations still attempt to control the records management process manually. The remainder of this chapter provides an overview of computerized records management techniques, along with some general advantages and disadvantages of computerized records processing.

Data Base Management

The basic problem associated with most manual or computerized records systems is the duplication of files. This duplication usually develops as the result of a nonresponsive or nonexistent central records center, security considerations, laziness, mistrust, and any other reason that people can think of to keep control of their files.

Data base management is the term used to describe the pooling of files from an organization. A centrally located computerized master file library is created that contains company-wide information from and for all of the major departments or units of the organization. The data base files are created, maintained, stored, and disposed from this source. Some obvious advantages of this type of system are the elimination of duplicate files and the central accessibility of data. Figure 4.9 illustrates a data base management structure.

Most manually operated records systems have a central files area

FIGURE 4.9 *Data base management structure*

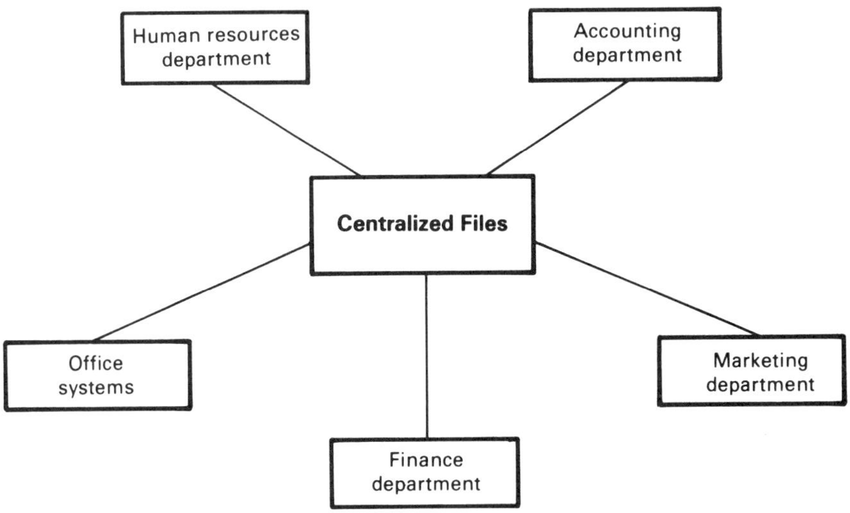

which, in theory, is supposed to be the only legitimate location for the organization's records. However, in practice, duplicated sets of files usually exist throughout the organization. The computerized data base system illustrated in Figure 4.10 eliminates the need for most file duplication. It allows the different departments to have easy access to the organization's files.

Advantages of computerized records systems. The control over the proliferation of files is only one advantage of a computerized records management system. File maintenance is much less of a chore when an organization's records are computerized. Records can be added, deleted, or changed by the various users throughout the organization without pulling a single file folder from the central file area. The change can be made quickly and efficiently at the computer terminal

FIGURE 4.10 *Data base management system*

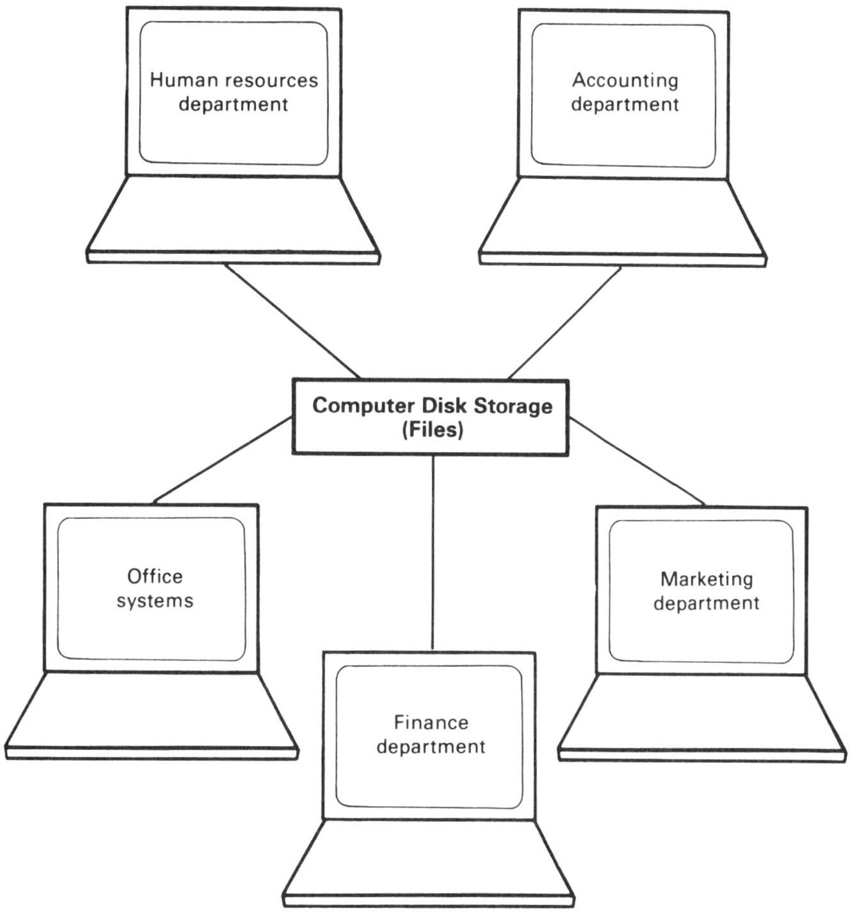

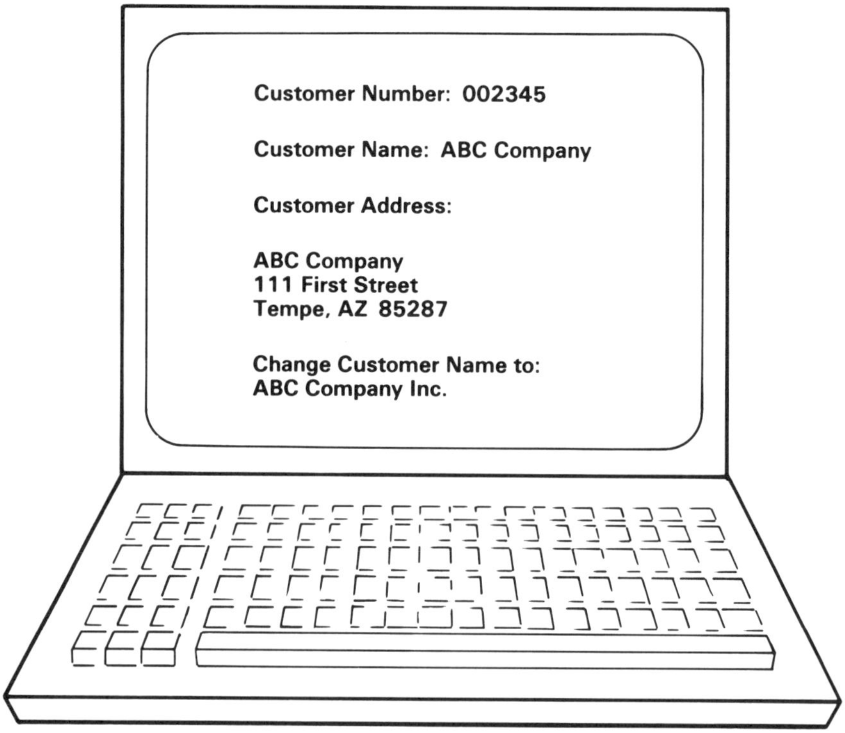

FIGURE 4.11 *Computerized maintenance function and records retrieval system*

screen; this increases the opportunity for office workers to update files more often and with fewer errors. Therefore, the computerized maintenance function, shown in Figure 4.11, provides users with more current information.

One of the most obvious advantages of computerized records systems is the tremendous reduction in storage space. Computerized records stored on magnetic disks in a central computer area eliminate the need for most of the metal filing cabinets which presently clutter business offices. Another advantage of computerized records systems is easy records retrieval. Finding a file in many organizations that use manual records systems is a time-consuming and sometimes futile task. Many times the retrieval problem is the direct result of difficult access to records storage space. Retrieving records from a computerized system merely requires that the office worker call up the file on the computer terminal screen, as shown in Figure 4.11.

Most records systems contain many unused, unneeded, and often unknown files. The utilization of a well-planned records disposition program is an effective means of controlling the records area. Although many office workers are aware of the importance of records

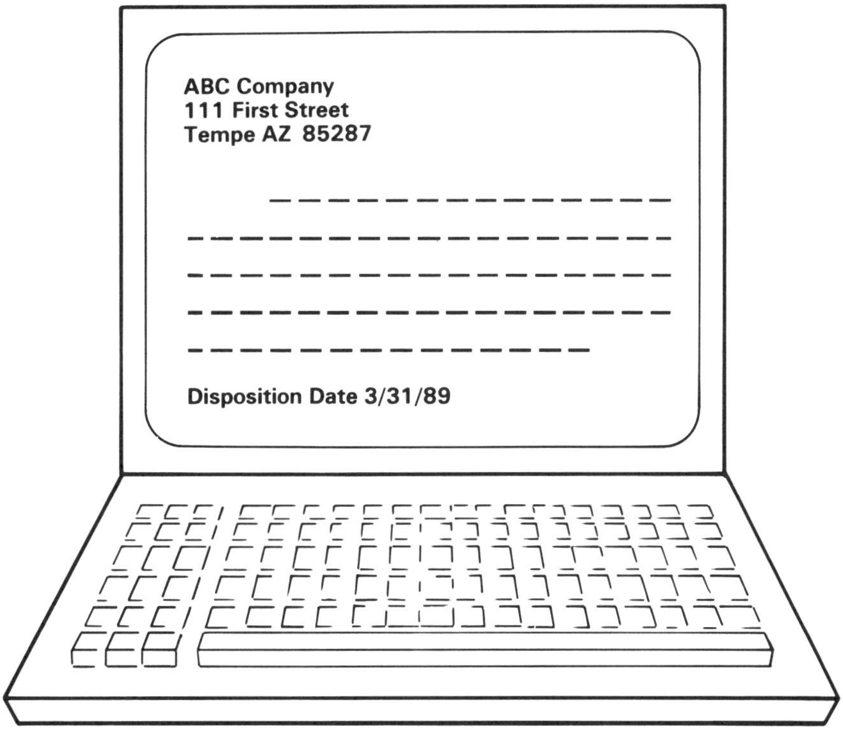

FIGURE 4.12
Records disposition prompt

disposition, few actually practice it because of the difficulty associated with the physical manipulation of large numbers of file folders. Computerized records systems provide the user with a means for effective records disposition programs. The user can be prompted of the disposition date of a given record as he or she works with the record on the computer terminal, as shown in Figure 4.12. The predetermined disposition schedule is built into the record at the time that it is created. Action taken concerning the disposition of the record is then much easier to conduct.

Disadvantages of computerized records systems. Most of the disadvantages associated with computer use in records areas are unwarranted. Time and cost savings and quality of information considerations are well-documented in many computerized records management centers. However, valid criticisms do exist. The most obvious disadvantage is the potential for computer fraud within the organization. Even properly designed computer systems are subject to fraud or misuse by criminals either outside or within the company. In addition to the computer fraud issue, another disadvantage of most computerized records systems lies in the basic design of the systems. Few organizations take the time and spend the money that is necessary to properly design an effective computerized records system. One final disadvantage of this system is the need for the organization to create and constantly maintain a back-up disk system in the event of loss or damage to the primary storage medium; this is a time-consuming and costly process.

SUMMARY

1. Records management involves creating, storing, retrieving, and disposing of documents in an organization.
2. Records management is important because it is essential to furnish accurate and complete information, to efficiently process recorded information, and to provide information, when needed, at the lowest possible cost.
3. Files should be created only with the records manager's approval and only after a records creation policy has been followed.
4. Records maintenance involves files analysis, which consists of records inventory, retention, and disposition procedures.
5. Records are stored either actively or inactively. They can be stored manually in file folders and identified alphabetically, numerically, or alphanumerically.
6. Records stored electronically on computers can be easily cross-referenced in numerous ways and accessed by more than one person at a time.
7. Data base management is a form of computer processing that allows for the pooling of files for use by numerous individuals throughout the organization.
8. A computerized records system eliminates file redundancy, improves records maintenance procedures, reduces storage space, and improves record retrieval. Computerized records systems are, however, vulnerable to computer fraud.

STUDENT ACTIVITIES

Active Orientation

As a class, brainstorm all of the kinds of records and information that are needed by your instructor for this course, such as registered students, grades, and assignments. Based upon the types of microprocessors that you have available, divide the class into sections, one for each brand of microprocessor and one for traditional records management applications (file folders). Develop a records management system that will:

- ☐ furnish accurate and complete information;
- ☐ efficiently process information;
- ☐ allow you to call up all information on a given student;
- ☐ allow for the removal of all data on an individual student if he or she drops the course; and
- ☐ protect records from tampering.

You may use any and all software available to you.

Independent Problems

1. Using a personnel file on Sidney Cycle, take his file through all of the steps in the records management cycle. Sidney began working for the company in February 1982 and was terminated last November. Be logical and rational in your process. Don't bother to work up legalities relating to particular issues; just describe when and where you would have to do such an activity.

2. How would you determine the length of time that certain records should be kept on file?

3. Write a policy for the creation of new files for a company that has only five people who would ever be in a position to create files.

4. As the new assistant office manager for XYZ Enterprises, your first assignment is to "get those darn files organized!"

- ☐ Where do you start?
- ☐ How do you progress?

5. The computer can *control* records. What does this statement mean? Is it good or bad?

REFERENCES

Klathoff, Robt. J. and Col. (Ret.) Leonard S. Lee, CRM. *Productivity and Records Automation*. Englewood Cliffs, NJ: Prentice-Hall, Inc., 1981.

5 Micrographics, Reprographics, and Forms Control

OBJECTIVES At the conclusion of this chapter, you should be able to:

1. Define the terms *micrographics* and *reprographics.*
2. Identify the various types of microforms.
3. Describe the procedures that are used to decide when to use micrographics.
4. Explain the terms *COM* and *CAR.*
5. Describe the criteria that are used to determine whether an office manager would purchase or lease reprographics equipment.
6. List several strategies for controlling costs in the micrographics and reprographics area.
7. Identify the criteria for designing effective business forms.
8. List several criteria for effective forms management.
9. List several strategies for controlling the cost of business forms.

INTRODUCTION

Every year, there is an increase in the number of documents that a business needs in order to operate efficiently. This situation has caused many companies to consider alternatives to the traditional process of storing papers in large files that take up valuable operating space. Business organizations have developed three specific applications to help control the growth of paper documents: micrographics, reprographics, and forms.

MICROGRAPHICS

Micrographics is the process of photocopying selected business documents in a miniaturized form called *microforms*. Although microfilming is the term that is most often associated with this process, other microforms, such as microfiche, micro-jackets, and microfilm in reel and strip form are also popular. These microforms are illustrated in Figure 5.1. At first, only large organizations could justify the relatively high cost of microform equipment. Now, however, smaller firms can obtain microforms from microform service companies at a fraction of the cost of purchasing the equipment themselves.

Although microform processing equipment is now available to smaller business organizations, a systematic evaluation of the docu-

FIGURE 5.1
Common microform media

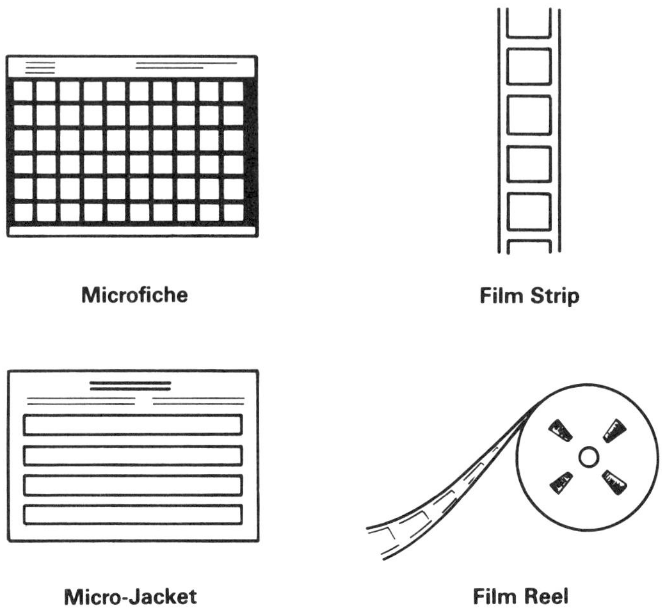

ments of a business should be conducted before commitments are made to a microform system. Most of the business records that are stored in filing cabinets and desk drawers are of little value. Organizations and office administrators should be wary of spending valuable dollars microforming worthless pieces of paper. Micrographic applications that are designed properly can significantly reduce the storage space required for business documents, provide an indexed system for filing large numbers of documents, and provide a more efficient means for document retrieval from large records areas.

A micrographics application is feasible when:

1. a high number of record requests in a large records system exist;
2. there is a need for records storage beyond the capabilities of most business computer systems; and
3. there is a need for a records system requiring duplicate files.

Computerized Micrographic Applications

Two of the newer micrographic techniques that are available today are computer output microfilm (COM) and computer-assisted retrieval (CAR). These techniques significantly reduce the time needed to build and retrieve a microrecord. (A microrecord is any business document that has been reduced through a microform process.) Computerized procedures such as COM and CAR also reduce the amount and cost of human input.

Computer output microfilm (COM). The computer output microfilm process shown in Figure 5.2 utilizes computer output as the source document, or original data, for the photographic process prior to reducing the image to miniature size. This reduction is called *microimaging*. In addition, each computer-generated microimage is coded for filing and later retrieval. This feature significantly streamlines the traditional microfilming process which required that a photograph of each document be taken before it was submitted to the microfilm process.

Computer-assisted retrieval (CAR). The computer can play the additional role of document retrieval in the microfilming process. Computer-assisted retrieval (CAR) utilizes the speed of the computer along with the code established on the computer output microfilm image to retrieve a microimage. The operator merely enters the index code of the microimage on the computer terminal to command the computer to search the index, locate the desired image, and then display the image on the terminal screen. Hard copies, or paper copies, of the image can then be generated through this process if desired.

Micrographic Services

Very few organizations can justify the high cost of purchasing their own micrographics equipment. Therefore, most businesses contract their micrographic needs to companies which specialize in business

FIGURE 5.2
Traditional microfilm process

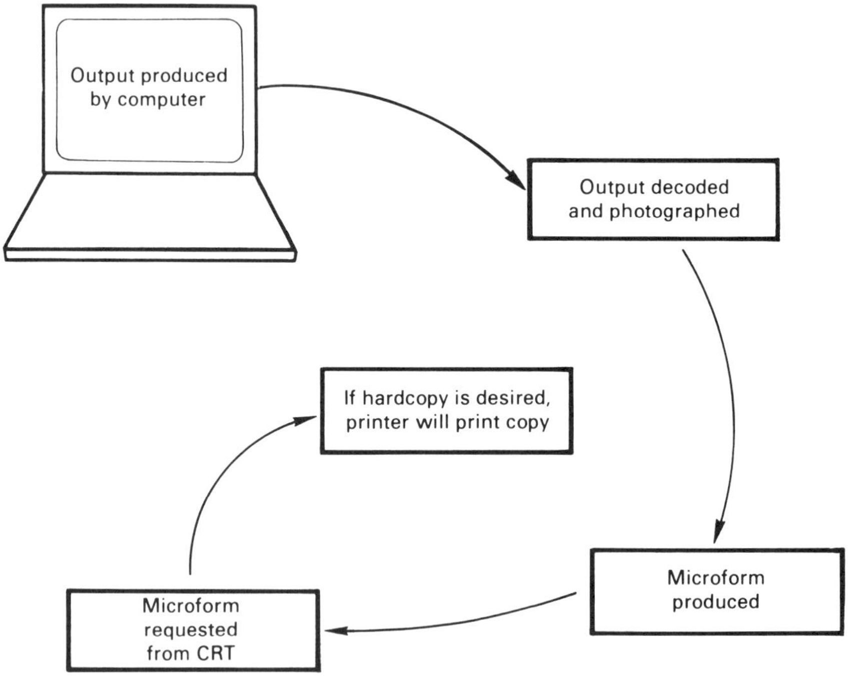

records systems analysis and micrographics. It is important for the administrative office manager to control the micrographic process through the contractor to assure the most cost-effective micrographics process possible. The following steps will aid the administrative office manager in reducing the costs of micrographic applications.

1. Conduct a complete files analysis prior to considering any micrographics application.
2. Analyze the relative worth, both long- and short-term, of each document earmarked for micrographic applications.
3. Determine the most efficient micrographic method for each document from the standpoint of cost, storage, and retrieval.

REPROGRAPHICS

Reprographics is the process of duplicating or copying the documents of an organization. There are several types of copying techniques utilized by business organizations; the most common types are stencil, fluid duplicator, and xerographic.

The stencil and fluid duplicator copy procedures provide an inexpensive means for reproducing the documents of a business. These procedures are designed to make multiple copies and the results are usually of marginal quality. Although the final product is satisfactory for internal use, it is not the type of reproduced document that most businesses would choose to send to customers or clients. The use of these two duplicating methods is declining because of the arrival of low cost xerography.

The xerographic process produces excellent copies of original business documents. Many organizations now use the xerographic process for all copies, regardless of the number needed; therefore, the stencil and fluid duplicator processes will not be addressed in this text.

Reproduction Costs

The cost of reproducing business documents is a major expenditure of the administrative office, and the management of this activity is essential. Unfortunately, because many business organizations do not keep track of the numbers of documents reproduced, it is nearly impossible to determine either the reproduction costs or strategies for controlling these costs in the future.

Business organizations have developed procedures for gathering data to track reproduction costs which include weekly copying logs, and counting devices known as machine keys—electronic "plugs" which are inserted into the copier to activate it. The key counts copies produced by that key. Often keys are assigned to each department or administrative unit. The weekly logs chart the use of the various reproduction machines throughout the business for a specified period of time. Each time a person uses a copier, he or she fills out the necessary information on the copier log. A typical weekly log is illustrated in Figure 5.3.

FIGURE 5.3
Weekly log—reproduction chart

Copier Log for the Week Ended ______

Date	Dept.	Item Copied	No. of Copies	Type of Copy

Today's Intelligent Copiers

Business copiers that are manufactured today come in a wide variety of functions and price ranges. Small or "personal copiers" can be purchased for under $1,000. These copiers are designed for small organizations that need copy services but do not require speed and multiple functions. The personal copiers' mechanical parts are usually contained in removable cartridges so that the cartridges can be removed and taken to a service center for repair or replacement.

Larger business copiers such as the Xerox 1048 shown in Figure 5.4 provide more services than some personal copiers and are designed for larger organizations. This line of copier produces forty copies per minute with copy capability on both sides of the paper. This line of mid-volume copier also staples documents when required.

Today's computerized organizations often need copies of computer-generated reports. The Xerox 1075 copier/duplicator shown in Figure 5.5 offers continuous form feeding capability. This copier contains a microprocessor and display screen for programming its various functions and will produce seventy copies per minute and thirty-five continuous printout sheets per minute.

FIGURE 5.4
Xerox 1048 copier

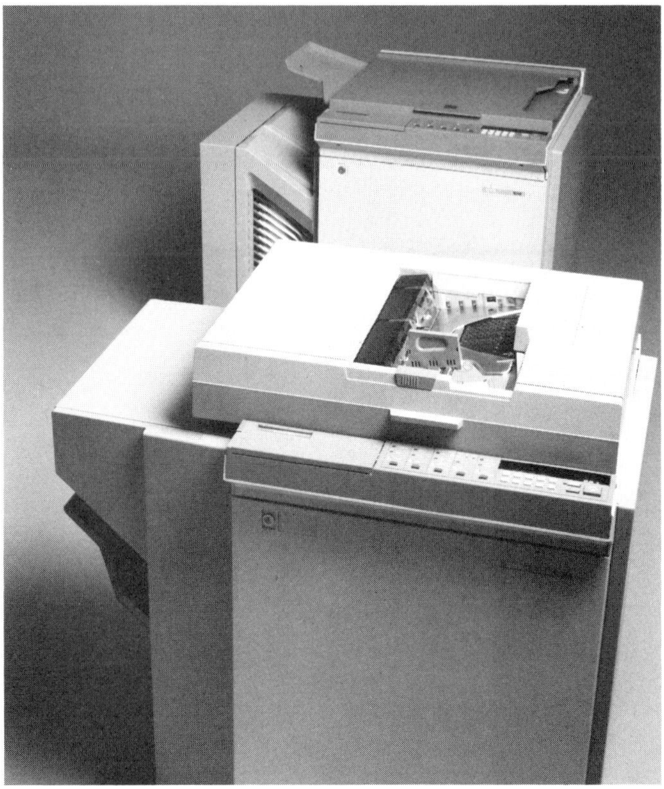

Courtesy of Xerox Corporation

FIGURE 5.5
Xerox 1075 copier/duplicator

Courtesy of Xerox Corporation

Very large business applications often need the copier capability of a state-of-the-art copier coupled with the brains of a computer. Today's intelligent copiers such as the Xerox 9900 shown in Figure 5.6 provide the user with a microprocessor-based copier equivalent to ten 64K personal computers. This copier possesses a full screen display for easy programming capability and produces copies on both sides with enlargement and reduction capabilities. In addition to printing on preprinted forms, adhesive mailing labels, and pre-drilled stock, the 9900 also makes transparencies and collates and staples documents. The 9900 will produce 120 copies per minute. Today's business copiers are truly intelligent machines. The copier industry has successfully incorporated computer technology into its copier technology.

Determining Reprographic Needs

Once specific data have been gathered concerning the reprographics process, business administrators can make informed decisions about more efficient means of reproducing business documents. The major issue associated with controlling copying costs in business organizations today is whether to purchase or lease a business copier. Leasing

FIGURE 5.6
Xerox 9900 duplicator

Courtesy of Xerox Corporation

copier equipment offers businesses an affordable alternative to the high cost of purchasing business copiers. However, the following questions should be answered before the office manager decides to lease an office copier.

1. What type of service is available?
2. Is this service done locally? Who performs the service?
3. What is the cost of leasing versus buying this model?
4. What are the tax benefits/costs of lease versus purchase?
5. What are the terms of the lease contract?
6. Is the technology changing too rapidly to warrant a purchase at this time?

The effective management of the micrographic and reprographic areas of the business office will provide cost savings to the organization. Having a more efficient means for disseminating information will also create a better decision-making environment for administrators.

FORMS CONTROL

Business forms provide a useful and often essential function for most business organizations. Although they are used to facilitate the flow of data throughout the organization, poor design and forms proliferation have reduced the effectiveness of forms in many businesses. We have all been victimized by a poorly designed form at some point in our lives. The question, "Who designed this stupid form?!!" is often asked. The answer in many organizations is "Just about anyone!" Effective forms design and utilization requires an organized plan for the creation and use of forms.

Forms Creation The procedures for creating and controlling the proliferation of forms are similar to the procedures for creating and controlling business records which were discussed in Chapter 4. One group of individuals within the organization should be given the responsibility for forms creation. Each request for a form would be sent to this group for evaluation. The group would then work with the requesting party to design the most effective form possible. This system reduces the chances of creating a duplicate or poorly designed form.

Forms Design There are a number of factors to consider in the development of an effective business form. The individuals within the organization who are given the responsibility for forms development should address the following questions regarding effective forms design.

1. Is there another form that is already available which would provide the same service?
2. What information is required from the form?
3. Who will use the data from the form?
4. Who will fill out the form?
5. How is the form routed within the organization?
6. Can this information be obtained elsewhere?
7. What is the anticipated usage level for this form?
8. What type of form is best?
9. What type of printing is best?
10. What size, grade, weight, and color of paper is best?

As a general rule, the simplest forms design usually makes for the most effective business form. Valuable aids such as line drawing functions are now available through computer-generated forms to help the office worker design a usable form. Figure 5.7 shows computer-generated forms applications.

SUMMARY

1. Micrographics is the process of copying selected business documents in miniaturized form.
2. Micrographics systems are expensive and are usually contracted out to microform service companies by all but very large companies.

FIGURE 5.7
Computer-generated forms applications

Deluxe Standard Forms are guaranteed compatible so you can count on keeping your system going without costly delays!
See The Compatibility Guide, in the center of the catalog, for a complete listing of forms.

Peachtree® Software Compatible Forms/Peachpak 4

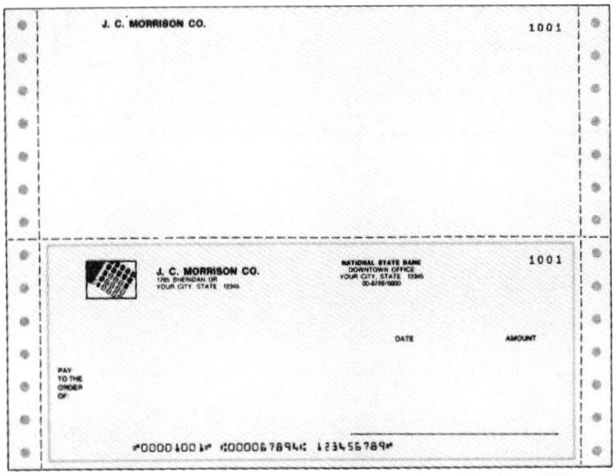

Dual Purpose Check #1013. *9½" x 7" overall, 8½" x 7" detached. Colors: Blue, Green, Yellow, Tan, Antique. Also compatible with BPI, Continental (CPA Software), Financier II, Decision Support Software and Best Programs.* **(See Grid A)**

Multiple uses—it's up to you... The Dual Purpose Check.

You can use this versatile combination check for both your payroll and accounts payable applications and you'll save money in the long run. The open voucher provides the maximum programmable area for total flexibility, even when you want to modify or update your program. It's an excellent, easy-to-work-with standard form designed to save you valuable time. That's because there's no need to change forms for different accounting functions. And, since you can cut down on your forms inventory, you'll also save valuable space. Best of all, you won't be tying up capital you could put to good use elsewhere!

GRID A

Quantity	1-Part 1013-1	2-Part 1013-2	3-Part 1013-3	4-Part —	Envelope 1500
500	$42.54	$60.38	$67.85	—	$27.63
1000	60.77	86.26	109.17	—	47.50
2000	93.00	165.22	199.86	—	79.00
5000	192.00	318.04	422.00	—	145.00

Prices valid through December 15, 1984.

PLEASE NOTE: Forms 1013 and 1319 are also compatible with State of the Art Software

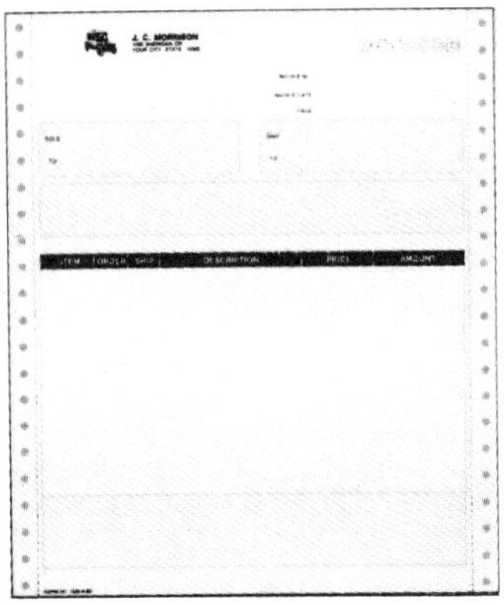

Invoice #1320. *9½" x 11" overall, 8½" x 11" detached. Color as shown.* **(See Grid B)**

GRID B

Quantity	1-Part —	2-Part —	3-Part 1320-3	4-Part 1320-4	Envelope 1503
500	—	—	$77.50	$101.95	$26.65
1000	—	—	133.20	175.25	40.10
2000	—	—	248.10	326.45	74.10
5000	—	—	579.00	761.85	176.10

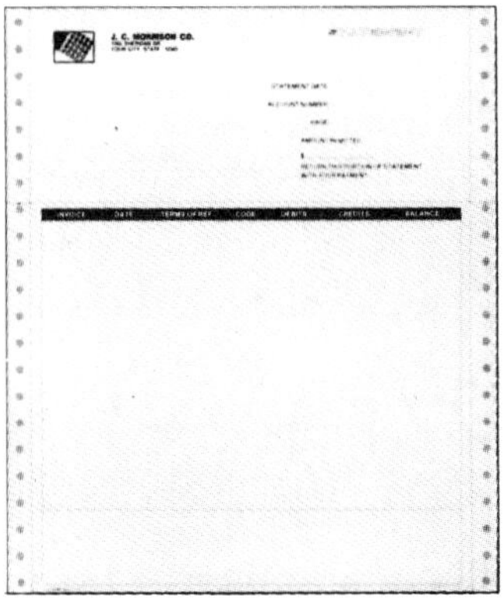

Statement #1317. *9½" x 11" overall, 8½" x 11" detached. Color as shown.* **(See Grid C)**

GRID C

Quantity	1-Part 1317-1	2-Part 1317-2	3-Part —	4-Part —	Envelope 1503
500	$45.70	$65.30	—	—	$26.65
1000	64.55	107.62	—	—	40.10
2000	108.45	191.70	—	—	74.10
5000	194.50	400.00	—	—	176.10

Multi-Purpose Form #1319. *9½" x 11" overall, 8½" x 11" detached. Color as shown.* **(See Grid D)**

GRID D

Quantity	1-Part 1319-1	2-Part 1319-2	3-Part 1319-3	4-Part 1319-4	Envelope 1503
500	$45.70	$65.30	$77.50	$101.95	$26.65
1000	64.55	107.62	133.20	175.25	40.10
2000	108.45	191.70	248.10	326.45	74.10
5000	194.50	400.00	579.00	761.85	176.10

Matching envelopes designed to fit.

All Deluxe forms are designed with companion 20# white envelopes to enhance your professional image even further. What's more, our exclusive security liner protects the confidentiality of your communications. Handy double window styles save you time by eliminating any need for addressing. Single and non-window styles are imprinted with your firm name, address and logo. For your convenience, we've matched companion forms and envelopes. Simply refer to the ordering grids on each page or The Compatibility Guide.

Please state color choice, where applicable, on the order form.

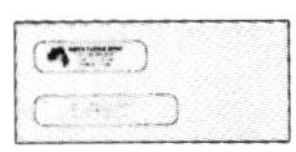

Double Window Envelope #1500. 8⅝" x 3⅝".

Single Window Envelope #1503. 9½" x 4⅛".

(See grid for compatibility.)

Courtesy of Vanier Graphics Corporation

3. Computer output microfilm (COM) is a fast and accurate process for building a microrecord.
4. Computer-assisted retrieval (CAR) can significantly reduce microrecord retrieval time and cost.
5. Because of the cost of micrographic services, it is essential that the administrative office manager conduct a files analysis and a cost analysis prior to committing the office to such a system.
6. Reprographics is the process of duplicating or copying the documents of an organization. The most common reprographics process is the xerographic process.
7. Machine keys or weekly copying logs are typical devices used for xerographic copy control.
8. Costs, service, tax benefits, and the state-of-the-art technology should be considered before deciding to either lease or purchase a copier.
9. Forms facilitate the flow of information throughout the organization. Control procedures for the creation and design of forms must be developed.

STUDENT ACTIVITIES

Active Orientation

1. Contact a local copier vendor. Gather information concerning the costs of leasing and purchasing a copier.

2. A large firm has decided to purchase a micrographics system. The marketing department of the firm feels that this purchase will be a detriment to them because they like to work with their clients' files "at their desks." As the person who must "sell" the micrographics system to the marketing department, how would you go about changing their minds?

Independent Problems

1. When and why should a company use micrographics?

2. Give an example and a use for at least three types of microforms.

3. Can CAR be used with a COM system? Explain.

4. What would be the least frustrating method of determining who was using the copier? Explain.

5. As the forms control person in your company, you must come up with a justification for your decision regarding a department's request for a new form that will combine the data from three forms into one.

- ☐ What is your decision?
- ☐ What is your justification? (Use the forms design questions from this chapter.)

6 Telecommunications

OBJECTIVES At the conclusion of this chapter, you should be able to:

1. Define the term *telecommunications.*
2. Discuss various types of office telephone systems.
3. Define the term *data communication.*
4. Describe the two types of teleconferencing.

INTRODUCTION

One of today's burgeoning industries is the telecommunications industry. Telecommunications can be defined as the transmission of all sounds, pictures, and data by wire, fiber, or satellite. The recent divestiture or break-up of AT&T as the monopoly or exclusive control agent of communications systems has opened the entire telecommunications area to new competition. In the United States, the market for communications equipment is expected to double from $75 billion annually to $150 billion annually in the next five years.

Recent technological advances have vastly expanded telecommunications beyond mere telephone service. The term *telecommunications* now includes all electronic communication, from teletypewriters to computers, including telephone systems. Telecommunications, at this time, represents one of the most diverse aspects of high-technology industries.

Advances in laser technology and fiber optics promise faster and more reliable telecommunications service in the near future. United States space shuttle flights have recently launched several communications satellites. Each year, new and more sophisticated telecommunications technology reaches the marketplace. The most relevant telecommunications components for office managers are telephone systems, data communications, and teleconferencing. This relatively short chapter is designed to acquaint the reader with the components of a telecommunications system. Chapters 11 and 12 will identify procedures for establishing telecommunications using the Information Center concept.

TELEPHONE SYSTEMS

The telephone systems used in business offices today are substantially different from those of just a few years ago. Today's business telephones transmit not only voice, but also pictures and data.

Automated Features

Automatic dialing and call forwarding features are popular with business organizations. These features significantly reduce the time needed to place a call or have a call sent to the appropriate person or area (see Figure 6.1).

Switching Systems

It has been many years since the switchboard operator fought with the octopus-like apparatus known as the switchboard. Today, automated switching systems utilize computer technology to receive, hold, override, and queue multiple incoming calls. These systems also possess the capability for conference calls between two or more parties. Popu-

FIGURE 6.1
Automated telephone systems

Courtesy of AT&T Information Systems

lar switching systems are the PABX (private automatic branch exchange) and the CPBX (computer-based private branch exchange) that are shown in Figure 6.2. Both switching systems provide electronic switching capabilities which enable organizations to receive and route more calls. The CPBX system, which is computer based, provides automatic redialing and conference calls; these are features that the PABX system does not have.

WATS Lines

Many organizations conduct daily business over great distances. In an effort to control the potentially enormous long-distance telephone charges, many organizations have rented WATS lines (wide area telecommunications service). This service establishes a fixed rate charge to the company for a given number of long-distance calls per month. WATS lines can save organizations fifty percent and more on their monthly long-distance phone bills.

At the present time, final legal questions are being resolved concerning the AT&T divestiture. These legal questions promise to have a tremendous impact on long-distance telephone rates in the United States. The administrative office manager can merely speculate as to

FIGURE 6.2
Electronic switching systems

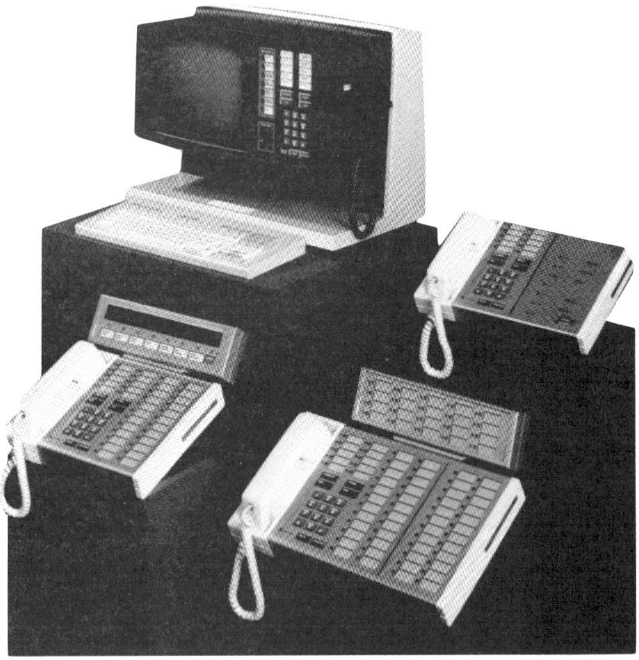

Courtesy of AT&T Information Systems

the changing nature of telephone costs and service in the coming years. It would appear that specific budget considerations and long-range planning should be given to office telephone systems during this period of uncertainty.

DATA COMMUNICATION

Transferring data through telephone systems has been a common practice for many years. Recently, organizations have been coupling the computer with existing telephone systems and using the telephone network to link computers together to allow them to communicate. Because of this technological advancement, data communication can now be defined as the ability to link computer systems together through telephone systems for the purpose of entering, processing, retrieving, storing, and transmitting information.

A typical data communication system consists of computer terminals/PCs and data conversion equipment called *modems* (modulator/demodulator) that are located at two or more sites, as shown in Figure 6.3. Modems are needed because computers operate in a digital format

FIGURE 6.3
Modem—modulation/demodulation/modulation

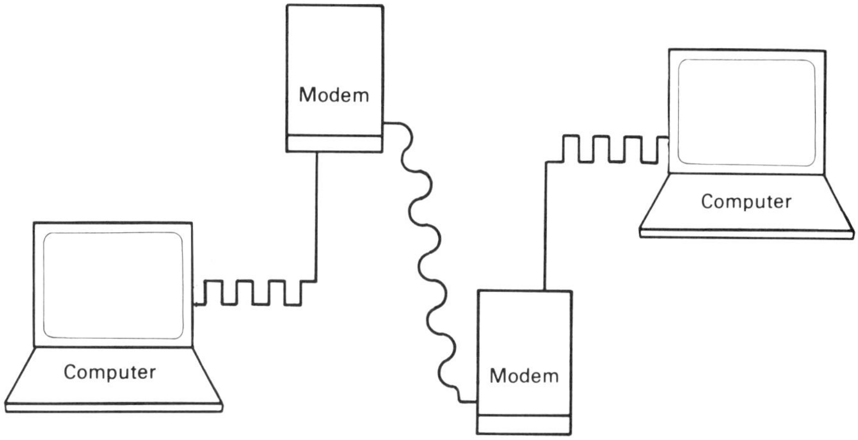

and telephone systems operate in a wave format, as shown in Figure 6.4. Modems are electronic devices which convert the digital format of the computer to a wave format for data transfer along telephone lines. The modem on the receiving end converts the wave format back to a digital format for entry into the computer at the receiving end.

The vast majority of computer systems in business organizations are utilizing telephone systems to "network," or link computer systems together utilizing the existing telephone system. Data communication capability is also available on most home computers. However, the type of data communication structure developed by business organizations is much different from the data communication network shared by millions of American home computer users. Popular data communication service companies such as The Source and CompuServe provide general, public interest data base features such as newspaper and journal articles, stock market information, and electronic bulletin board applications to any user who wishes to subscribe. This is not the type of security arrangement most business organizations would choose.

TELECONFERENCING

Bringing people together face-to-face has always been an effective means of enhancing communication, and therefore, understanding. In today's world-wide economy and market structure, the face-to-face concept can become quite expensive. Teleconferencing is a technique which utilizes the telephone to transfer voices, or voices and pictures to individuals located at different sites. This concept allows for at least a simulation of the face-to-face idea without the time and expense of long-distance travel.

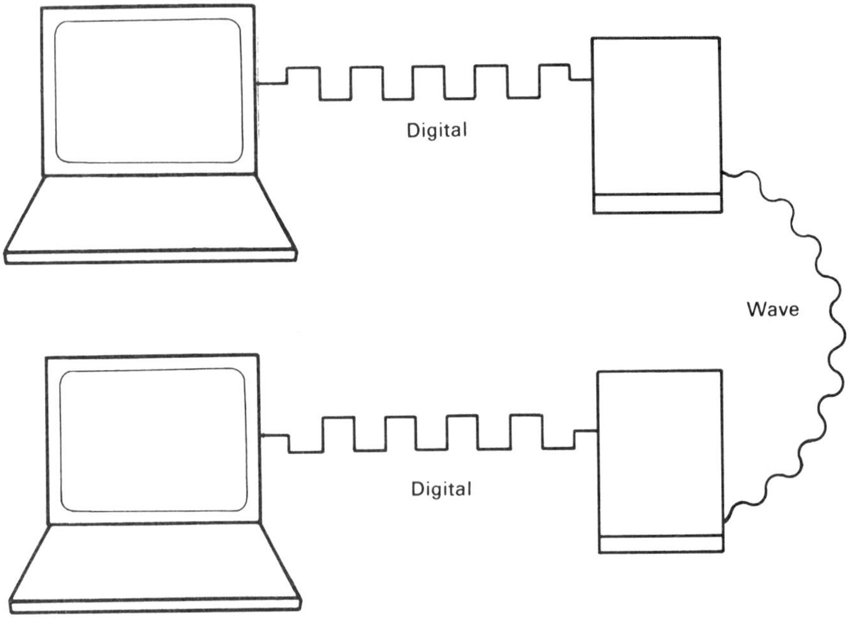

FIGURE 6.4
Modem communication

Audio Teleconferencing

Audio teleconferencing, illustrated in Figure 6.5, is the least expensive teleconferencing concept. It merely requires telephones and/or speakerphones at the various sites. However, this approach lacks the face-to-face or product review feature that is often desired.

Video Teleconferencing

Video teleconferencing, as shown in Figure 6.6, provides two features that are not available through audio teleconferencing: freeze-frame and full-motion video. The freeze-frame video feature allows conference participants to receive still pictures which change approximately every thirty seconds. The full-motion picture feature operates in a manner similar to a closed circuit television transmission.

Video teleconferencing is significantly more expensive than audio teleconferencing. Of course, the cost must be compared with the expense of sending several people to one location for a meeting. The expense of air travel, hotels, meals, and lost work time often far exceed the cost of a one or two hour teleconference. Presently, video teleconference costs are approximately $1,600 per hour. This represents a thirty percent reduction in cost in the past two years.

SUMMARY

1. Telecommunications is the transmission of all sounds, pictures, and data by wire or satellite.

FIGURE 6.5
Audio teleconferencing

Courtesy of AT&T Information Systems

2. Telephone automated switching systems like PABX and CPBX utilize computer technology to receive, hold, override, and queue multiple incoming calls.
3. Data communication is the ability to link computer systems together through telephone systems for the purpose of entering, processing, retrieving, storing, and transmitting information.
4. Modems allow the digital-based computer to be linked with the wave-based telephone system.
5. Teleconferencing uses the telephone system to transfer voices, or voices and pictures to individuals located at different sites.

STUDENT ACTIVITIES

Active Orientation

1. Visit your local telephone company and review the types of office telephone systems that are available. Prepare a list of your findings, including the costs of each system.

2. Valerie Geller, a social psychologist at Bell Labs, has found that people do not like to use their computer terminals for "important" work. As a group, discuss this problem. Do you feel that a computer or

FIGURE 6.6
Video teleconferencing

Courtesy of AT&T Information Systems

computer-linked teleconferencing capability depersonalizes a meeting to the point of uselessness? Set up pro and con groups to debate this issue.

3. How much would it cost to get a telecommunications satellite into space? How many channels would it provide? In groups of approximately five students, research these questions in the current literature and present this information to the class.

Independent Problems

1. What is meant by the term *telecommunications*? What is the role of the computer in this process?

2. How has an office telephone system changed since the days of a switchboard operator?

3. Why do we need a modem to link computers to telephones?

4. Does teleconferencing really do what it's advertised to do? Do you think that an audio-video hook-up to every home would be a good idea? A marketable idea? Why?

7 Budget Analysis

OBJECTIVES At the conclusion of this chapter, you should be able to:

1. Discuss the importance of budget analysis.
2. List the objectives of budget analysis.
3. Compare and contrast zero-based budgeting with traditional budgeting methods.
4. Discuss various ways of controlling office costs.
5. Explain the role of the computer in the budget analysis process.

INTRODUCTION

All forms of organizations—public, private, business, government, and educational—base their operations on some level of budgeting. A budget can be defined as a financial plan for conducting the affairs of an organization. The financial objectives of an entire organization, which are known as the master budget, are usually subdivided into smaller budgets and distributed to the various units or departments of the organization. Without continual analysis, the budgeting process will fail to provide the organization with valuable financial information.

OBJECTIVES OF BUDGET ANALYSIS

Budget analysis, if conducted properly, provides managers with the information needed to predict future revenue and expense levels within the organization. The budget analysis effort should strive to meet the following objectives:

1. to provide a blueprint of the financial structure of the organization for the next budget period;
2. to monitor various expense items throughout the organization;
3. to communicate the management objectives for the coming budget period;
4. to coordinate the various expense centers of the organization with the master budget;
5. to assign responsibility for the budget to specific individuals throughout the organization; and
6. to allocate financial resources to the various departments throughout the organization.

TYPES OF BUDGETS

There are several types of budgets. Figure 7.1 shows three common budget types: capital budgets, operating budgets, and financial budgets.

The Master Budget

The master budget consists of a capital budget, an operating budget, and financial budgets for the entire organization. The master budget charts the financial operation of every department for every anticipated expense within the organization.

The Capital Budget

The capital budget outlines plans the organization may have for purchasing any buildings, warehouses, or equipment during the next

FIGURE 7.1
Types of budgets

Capital Budgets

☐ used for anticipated buildings and equipment

Operating Budgets

☐ purchasing

☐ marketing

☐ personnel

Financial Budgets

☐ cash receipts and disbursements

☐ accounting functions (balance sheet and income statement)

budgeting period. Of course, building plans may transcend more than one budgeting period. The capital budget allocates those anticipated funds for the project budgeting period by budgeting period. Equipment purchases such as typewriters, filing cabinets, and office computers are also allocated from the capital budget.

The Operating Budget

Operating budgets fund the expenses that are anticipated within each department for salaries, supplies, phone expenses, and other items necessary for the day-to-day operation of each unit.

The Financial Budget

Financial budgets chart the anticipated flow in revenues and expenses throughout the budgeting period. The financial budget allows managers to analyze critical items such as accounts payable and accounts receivable during the period. Managers can thus determine if revenues need to be increased or if too much cash is on hand at a given time. Without the framework of the financial budget, management may not be able to determine the correct balance of revenues and expenses during a budget period.

STRUCTURING THE BUDGET

The manner in which budgets are structured varies from organization to organization. This fluctuation is largely a function of the size of the organization. Regardless of the size of the organization, however, the development of effective budgets requires a coordinated planning effort by the various levels of management. The following guidelines are essential to effective budget development.

Managerial Commitment

Budgets are developed, monitored, and analyzed by managerial personnel, and thus, managerial commitment to meeting budget goals is fundamental. The goals established by managers should coincide with the goals of the organization. For example, if Company A decides to expand its business into a new area of the country, it would probably have to increase the budget dollars for advertising in the new area. If the budget goals of the marketing department of Company A did not allow for this expansion, their goals would not coincide with the goals of the overall organization; thus, an unrealistic budget situation would be created.

Developing budget goals that adhere to organizational goals not only appropriates funds for official organizational needs, but also lends credibility to the budget process. Managers who believe in the budget will be more likely to support it and to encourage their workers to support the budget process also.

Employee Input

Any successful operation requires the support of the individuals who are directly responsible for the work effort. Although budgeting is certainly a management responsibility, employee input provides valuable budget-related information such as ideas on cost-saving work methods. This involvement also exposes employees to the delicate balance of organizational revenues and expenses, and thus it motivates employees to work within established budget guidelines. Employee input is a very important aspect of budget development. The cooperative atmosphere created through employee input can carry over into other aspects of the employer-employee relationship such as quality control, absenteeism, and tardiness.

Assigning Responsibility

Each department manager should be assigned specific responsibility for the department budget. Using employee input from the department, the manager can direct budget information upward through the organization. This "bottom-up" approach to budget development helps to generate a more positive employee attitude toward the budget. Furthermore, each manager is more likely to work hard to operate within the budget when he or she is directly responsible for it.

Setting Goals

The budget goals established in each department should both reflect organizational goals and be attainable. Unrealistic budgets waste resources and inhibit workers in the daily performance of their tasks. Budget goals should be established by project teams of managers and employees. The goals should be written in specific terms so that they can be easily interpreted and measured. For example, "X dollars will be allotted for the purchase of seven office microcomputer systems to be used for word processing, records management and budget analysis."

Budget Flexibility

As was stated at the beginning of this chapter, budgets are merely plans or estimates of the revenues needed to conduct the affairs of the organization during the upcoming budget period. Many times budgets need to be adjusted to account for unanticipated circumstances which occur during the budget period. Labor strikes, fluctuating interest rates, and supply shortages require rapid adjustments to the budget. If the budget is too rigid, with no opportunity for adjustment, and it has not been monitored during the budget period, the organization may not be able to respond quickly enough to make the needed adjustments.

Monitoring the Budget

Although budgets are usually established for a fiscal year time frame, budget performance needs to be monitored on a monthly basis. Each department should monitor its budget expense item by expense item to compare the actual expenditure for each item with the budgeted amount for that item during the month. Monthly budget reports such as the one in Figure 7.2 should be forwarded to top management along

FIGURE 7.2
Departmental monthly budget report

Personnel Departmental Budget Performance for the Month Ended ______

Expense Item	Budget Amount	Actual Amount	Discrepancy
salaries	$17,500	$18,300	+$800
benefits	4,500	4,500	
supplies	1,100	2,000	+ 900
word processing	750	450	− 300
filing	625	625	
telephone	75	125	+ 50
postage	310	300	− 10
Total	$24,860	$26,300	+$1,440

Variance Report (5%)

Items with Variance	Rationale for Item
supplies +81%	new supplies needed for new word processors
word processing −40%	equipment not used most of month due to training delay
telephone +66%	new employee recruitment

Comments: ______________________
Department Manager ______________________ Date ________

FIGURE 7.3
Organizational monthly budget report

Organizational Monthly Budget Report for the Month Ended _______

Department	Budget Amount	Actual Amount	Departmental Discrepancy
Marketing	$ 32,000	$ 32,500	+$ 500
Human Resources	21,000	21,000	
Accounting	28,500	25,000	− 3,500
Manufacturing	98,000	97,300	− 700
Advertising	11,500	12,000	+ 500
Admin. Services	23,900	25,000	+ 1,100
Total	$214,900	$212,800	−$2,100

Variance Report (5%)

Items with Variance	Rationale for Item
Accounting −12%	no overtime wages

Vice President Finance ________________ Date ________

with complete rationales for items that are over or under the projected budget amount. Figure 7.3 is an example of an organizational monthly budget report. Usually five or ten percent allowances under or over the projected budget are used as benchmarks for reporting budget discrepancies.

Computer systems provide efficient means for monitoring the budget. Budgetary data can be entered at the beginning of each budget period. As expenses are incurred, they are entered into the computer system. The computer program then updates each actual expense and tracks the expenditures throughout the budget period. Each department manager can receive an up-to-date report of the budget automatically at any time during the budget period by merely calling the budget program from the computer.

BUDGETING METHODS

There are numerous budgeting methods in operation today. Two common methods of budgeting are traditional budgeting and zero-based budgeting.

Traditional Budgeting The traditional budgeting approach simply provides for a percentage increase or decrease to the prior budget based on present market anticipation. For example, if Company A expects an increase in business activity during the next period, it assumes that the expenditures of each department will also increase; therefore, each department in Company A will receive a similar percentage increase in budget dollars regardless of the actual need. If there is an expected decrease in business activity, a corresponding decrease in budget dollars will be given to each department regardless of actual need. The traditional budget approach has contributed to many unrealistic budgets. Managers have simply learned to "pad" their budgets whenever possible, instead of monitoring actual budget costs.

Zero-Based Budgeting

At the opposite end of the budget method scale is zero-based budgeting. Zero-based budgeting theory requires that each budgeted item be justified every budget period. Each department manager must start his or her budget process with zero dollars. The manager lists the budgeted items, gives estimated costs per item, and writes a justification for each item. Then, the budgeted items are evaluated. The master budget is designed from the budgeted items from the various departments which best meet the needs of the organization during the next budget period.

IMPLICATIONS FOR THE ADMINISTRATIVE MANAGER

The administrative office manager stands to benefit greatly from sound budget analysis. The office manager is required to monitor a great number of expense items during any given budget period. Each year a greater share of the cost of doing business is attached to the white-collar workforce. Effective budget analysis techniques are essential for the efficient operation of today's business offices. Administrative office managers should take advantage of the computerized budget packages that are available today to help them manage the financial resources of their organizations.

SUMMARY

1. Budgets are financial plans for conducting the affairs of an organization.
2. Effective budget analysis provides useful information which can be used to predict future revenue and expense levels in organizations.
3. The objectives of effective budget analysis are:
   - ☐ to provide a blueprint of the financial structure of the organization during the next budget period;

- ☐ to monitor various expense items throughout the organization;
- ☐ to communicate the management objectives of the budget;
- ☐ to coordinate the various expense centers of the organization with the master budget;
- ☐ to assign specific personnel throughout the organization the responsibility for portions of the budget; and
- ☐ to allocate financial resources to the various units throughout the organization.

4. Elements of effective budget analysis are managerial commitment, employee input, managerial responsibility, goal setting, flexibility, and monitoring procedures.
5. Two common methods of budget analysis are the traditional budget approach and zero-based budgeting.
6. Computers allow for more efficient monitoring of the budget process during the budget period.

STUDENT ACTIVITIES

Active Orientation

1. Conduct a telephone survey of local businesses to determine the number of firms using zero-based budgeting techniques.

2. Interview an office manager in your community. Ask this individual to discuss the following topics.

- ☐ What method of budgeting is used in the company?
- ☐ What input do line personnel have in the budget process?
- ☐ What is the extent of your budget responsibility?
- ☐ How do you justify each budget item?

Independent Problems

1. Write a short report (five pages or less) justifying the conversion of a traditional budget system to a zero-based budget system.

2. Develop a list of strategies for controlling the "padding" of departmental budgets by managers in a traditional budget system.

PART 3 ADMINISTRATIVE INFORMATION SYSTEMS

Part 3 of *Administrative Information Systems: People and Technology* describes the various administrative office functions as an information system for the organization. Special emphasis is given to the role of systems analysis in developing an effective administrative information system. Part 3 contains many practical examples that are designed to aid administrators in utilizing computer systems to perform administrative tasks. Chapter 12 illustrates a popular new organizational concept called The Information Center.

8 Administrative Systems Analysis

OBJECTIVES At the conclusion of this chapter, you should be able to:

1. Define the term *systems analysis.*
2. List the major support systems of a business organization.
3. Explain the role of administrative support systems in business organizations.
4. Describe the five steps of a systems project.
5. Describe the role of the administrative office manager in a systems project.

INTRODUCTION

The term *system* is a general term that implies a host of involved activities and people performing their duties to accomplish specific goals and objectives. It is not synonymous with the term *computer*. Of course, computers efficiently process data based on systems planning; however, systems can be manual as well as computerized. Someone designed a system to create alphabets and math structures long before computers were developed, and someone else came up with a system to design and build the pyramids many centuries before the first computer became operational. Basically, systems are sets of procedures that are designed to meet particular objectives. Examples of systems can be observed everywhere in our modern society: accounting systems, educational systems, transportation systems, economic systems, and political systems.

Businesses are organized around a series of systems that are designed to meet the overall objectives of the organization. These support systems provide the administrative information necessary to make informed business decisions.

ADMINISTRATIVE SUPPORT SYSTEMS

Although the structures of business organizations vary, the majority of business organizations include most of the support systems illustrated in Figure 8.1.

Objectives of Administrative Support Systems

The administrative support systems described in Figure 8.1 provide a framework for the flow of information throughout the organization. The importance of accurate information within organizations cannot be overstated. Each support system within an organization must coordinate its function with the other support systems if useable information is to be developed. This coordinated effort requires substantial planning and cooperation among personnel from all areas.

FIGURE 8.1
Administrative support systems

The Organization

- ☐ Marketing System
- ☐ Purchasing System
- ☐ Accounting System
- ☐ Production System
- ☐ Personnel System
- ☐ Finance System
- ☐ Office Information System

The major objectives of administrative support systems are:

1. to furnish the right information to the right people at the right time so that informed decisions can be made;
2. to communicate the objectives of each support system to all employees;
3. to reduce the duplication of work efforts throughout the organization;
4. to provide automated procedures for performing routine tasks; and
5. to provide employee training and development.

DESIGNING THE SYSTEM

A *system* has been defined as a set of procedures designed to meet specific objectives. *Procedures* can be defined as specific operations or tasks that are organized to meet objectives. Each manager can develop the procedures necessary for meeting the objectives of his or her department. However, it is important to coordinate this effort with the managers of other departments to reduce the possibility of work duplication and conflicting objectives which may be counter-productive to the objectives of the organization. Therefore, a strategy must be devised to coordinate the activities of all of the administrative support systems. This strategy is called *systems analysis.*

Conducting the Systems Study

If the organization is large enough, there may be a systems staff that is organized specifically to conduct systems studies. If the organization is not large enough to support a full-time systems staff, department managers may be required to conduct systems studies. Figure 8.2 lists the steps involved in a systems study.

Systems analysis techniques have been modeled after the scientific method, in which a problem is defined, solutions are developed, one solution is selected for implementation, and the new system is evaluated for possible problems. Although many systems models have been developed, most systems studies include the following steps.

FIGURE 8.2
Steps in a systems study

- ☐ Step 1: Investigate the Problem
- ☐ Step 2: Analyze the System
- ☐ Step 3: Design the System
- ☐ Step 4: Implement the System
- ☐ Step 5: Evaluate the System

Step 1: Investigate the problem. It is important to determine the true nature of any systems problem because all efforts from this point on will be geared toward solving that problem. An inaccurate definition of the problem will result in a tremendous misallocation of resources. The data-gathering process is usually determined by the size of the organization. The most common data-gathering procedures are surveys, observations, and personal interviews.

Step 2: Analyze the system. Once the problem or problems are identified and determined to be valid, the analyst must study the present system in great detail. This process usually includes analysis of the operating procedures of the department, a study of the equipment utilized in the day-to-day operations of the department, and a review of any available operating manuals.

Step 3: Design the system. Designing alternatives to existing systems is, at best, a hit-or-miss proposition if steps 1 and 2 have not been conducted. Steps 1 and 2 provide the analyst with information concerning what has *not* worked. The analyst who is not aware of these ineffective strategies is doomed to repeat them. Alternative systems should be evaluated as to their potential for success, and the most promising design should be selected for implementation.

Step 4: Implement the system. Implementing a new system is a delicate process. The analyst must be aware that he or she may design the best system possible, but without the support of the department personnel, it is destined for failure. If the analyst has informed the department personnel of the analysis process from the beginning and has solicited their opinions and expertise during the design phase of the project, then a successful systems implementation is much more likely.

Every analyst must recognize that there may be flaws in the new system and, therefore, it is important to implement the new system under controlled conditions. There are two common methods of systems implementation: parallel implementation and crash implementation. Parallel implementation requires that the old system remain operational while the new system is being tested. Any flaws in the new system will not cause catastrophic damage because the organization can fall back on the old system while the problems with the new system are being addressed. Crash implementation is just that! The old system is discarded and the new system is implemented, with the hope that it will not crash and bring the organization crashing down around it.

Step 5: Evaluate the system. Each new system should be evaluated over a substantial period of time to ensure that the problems of the old system have been successfully solved through the implementation of the new system and to identify any new problems created by the new systems design. In other words, systems analysis is a continual process that requires constant monitoring for any chance of long-lasting success.

TOOLS OF SYSTEMS STUDIES

Systems analysts use a variety of tools to aid them in the analysis and design of systems. Of course, the types of tools used varies by the phase of the systems project and the personal preference of the analyst. However, systems charts such as workflow diagrams, work distribution charts, office layout diagrams, and employee task analysis charts are common tools used by many systems analysts.

Systems Charts

Systems charts are usually developed in graphic form. They use flowcharting symbols to depict the design of the organization and the flow of information throughout the organization, as well as specific work distribution relationships in and among departments. These are illustrated in Figures 8.3 and 8.4.

FIGURE 8.3
Common flowcharting symbols

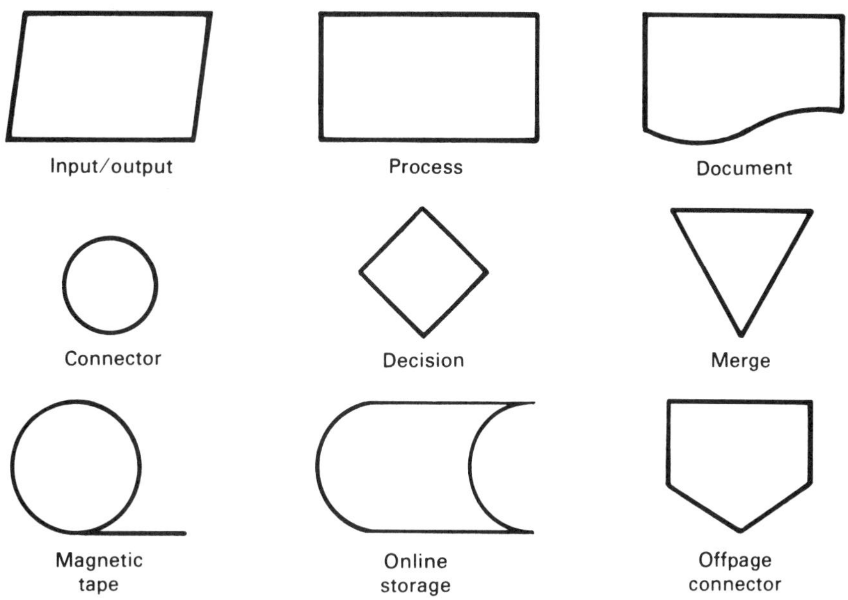

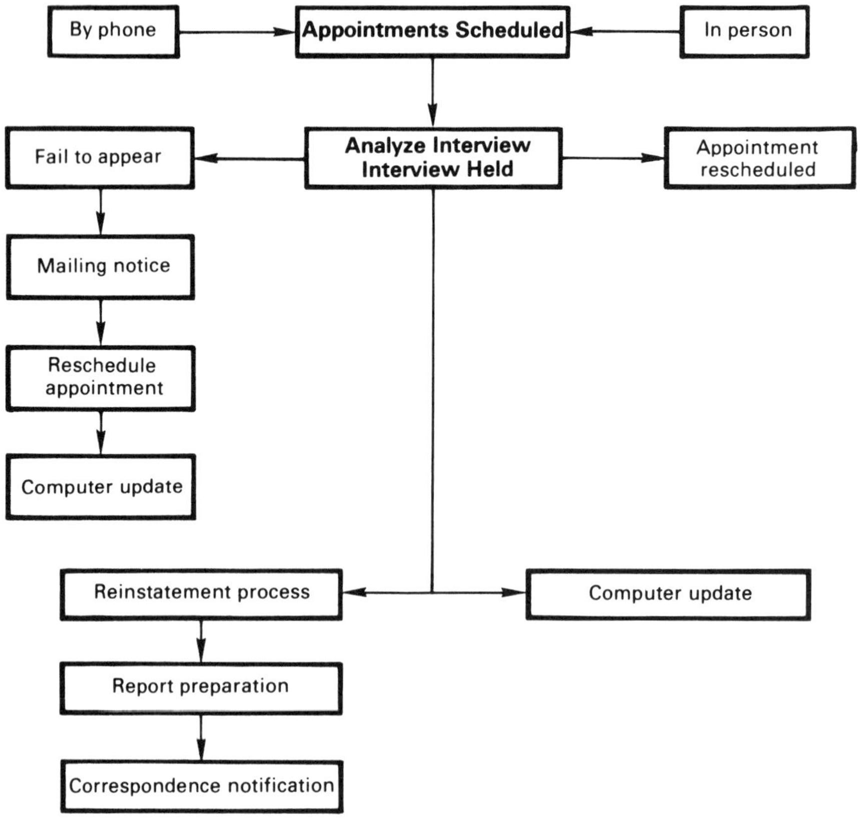

FIGURE 8.4
Workflow diagram

Systems charts are most helpful to the analyst during the first three steps of a systems project (defining the problem, analyzing the system, and designing the new system). Another common systems chart is the Gantt chart, shown in Figure 8.5. The Gantt chart is a useful tool for managing the scheduling of projects along a time line. Developed by Henry L. Gantt, Gantt charts are often used for scheduling building projects, office moves, and equipment installations. They provide the tracking structure necessary to coordinate people, events, and equipment in a realistic time frame for project completion. The time line identifies the essential components in their place in time according to the established project schedule.

Task Charts

Task charts usually provide more detailed information than systems charts because they are designed to diagram specific tasks such as work distribution patterns, office layout schemes, and employee task information.

A diagram depicting the specific job tasks of a group of individuals

FIGURE 8.5
Gantt chart

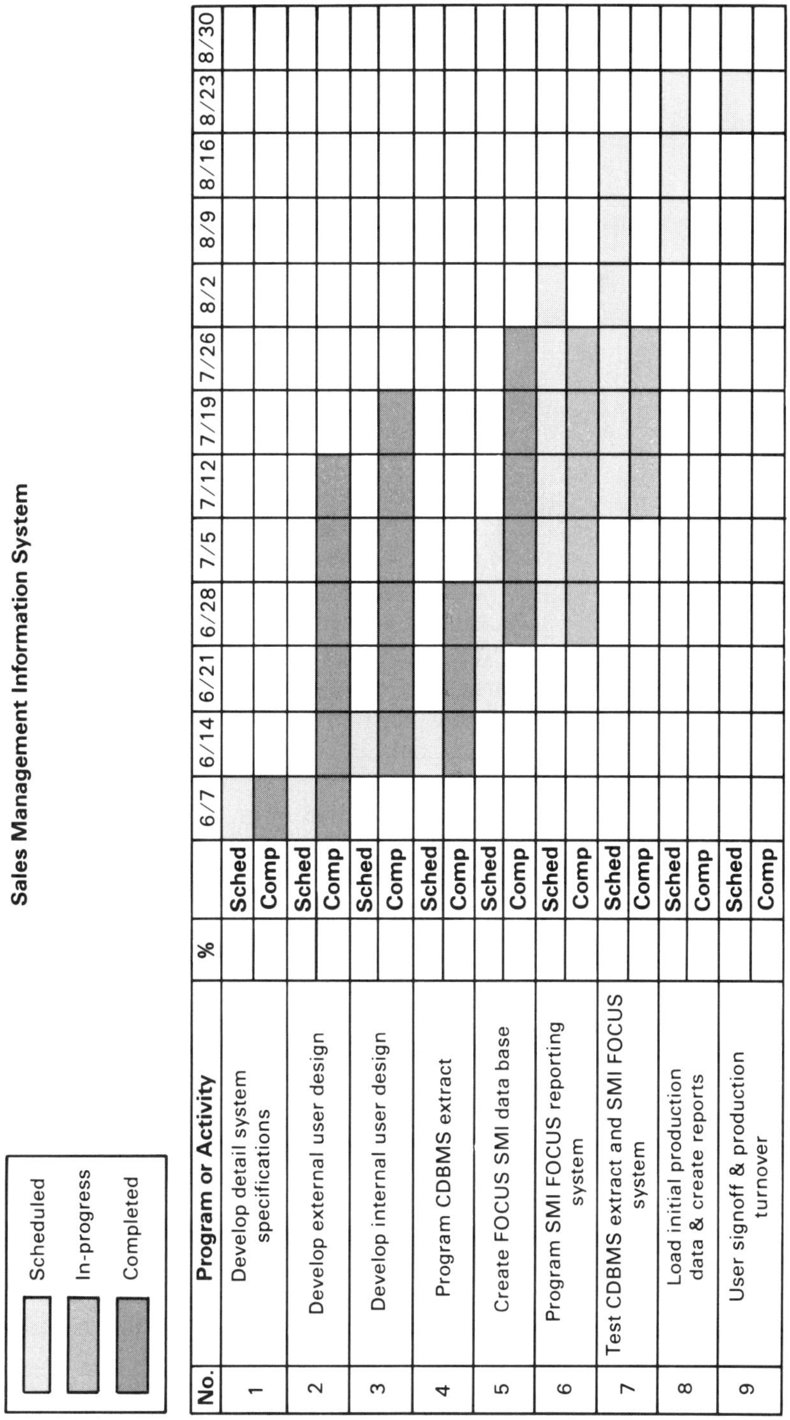

within a department or area is called a work distribution chart. A work distribution chart is illustrated in Figure 8.6. Work distribution charts help analysts determine:

1. what work is being performed;
2. who is performing the work; and
3. if the work is distributed evenly.

The information gathered from the work distribution charts can be used by analysts to document problem areas and design alternatives to present work methods.

A comprehensive analysis of an administrative area would have to include a space planning effort. Office layout charts (see Figure 8.7) are often used to diagram office workflow as well as equipment and furniture placement during the analysis and design steps of administrative systems projects.

Employee task charts such as Figure 8.8 are often the most detailed charts that are used in a systems study. These charts identify the employee by name, title, department, and supervisor. Each task performed by the employee is identified, along with a classification of the task that includes the amount of time required to complete it. Information obtained from the employee task chart can be used to document each task for the purpose of identifying efficient work methods, equipment requirements, and work duplication situations.

Systems and task charts are essential tools for analysts conducting systems studies in an administrative environment. They aid the analyst in each of the key steps of a systems study:

1. investigating problems (Step 1);
2. analyzing the system (Step 2);
3. designing new systems (Step 3);
4. implementing new systems (Step 4); and
5. providing feedback (Step 5).

IMPLICATIONS FOR THE ADMINISTRATIVE MANAGER

The development of computer systems that are designed specifically for the business office has substantially changed the way administrative office managers perform their duties. The systems analysis techniques described earlier in this chapter could be used by most office managers as tools for determining effective job methods and administrative productivity.

FIGURE 8.6
Work distribution chart

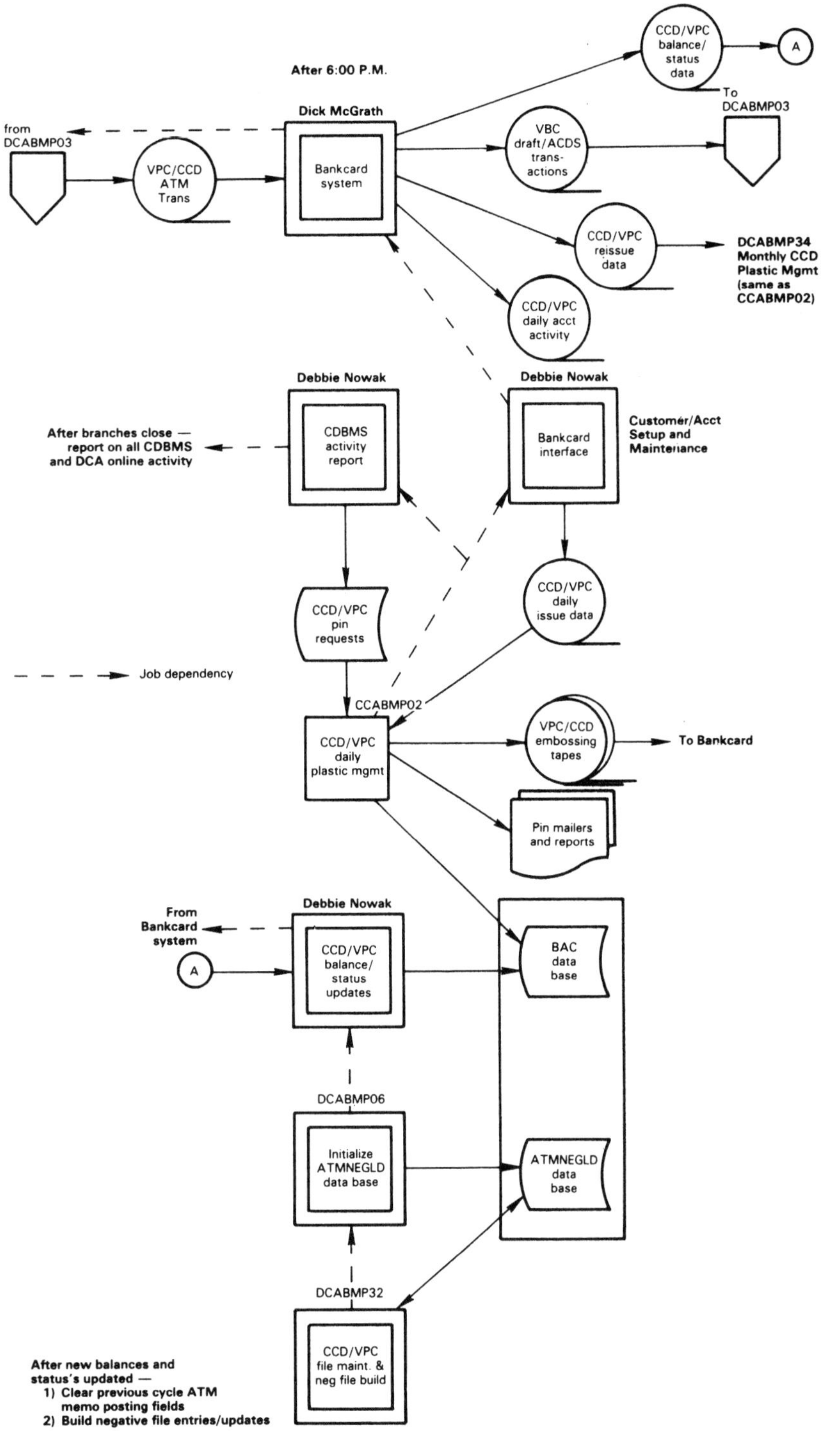

Courtesy of the Arizona Bank

FIGURE 8.7
Office layout chart

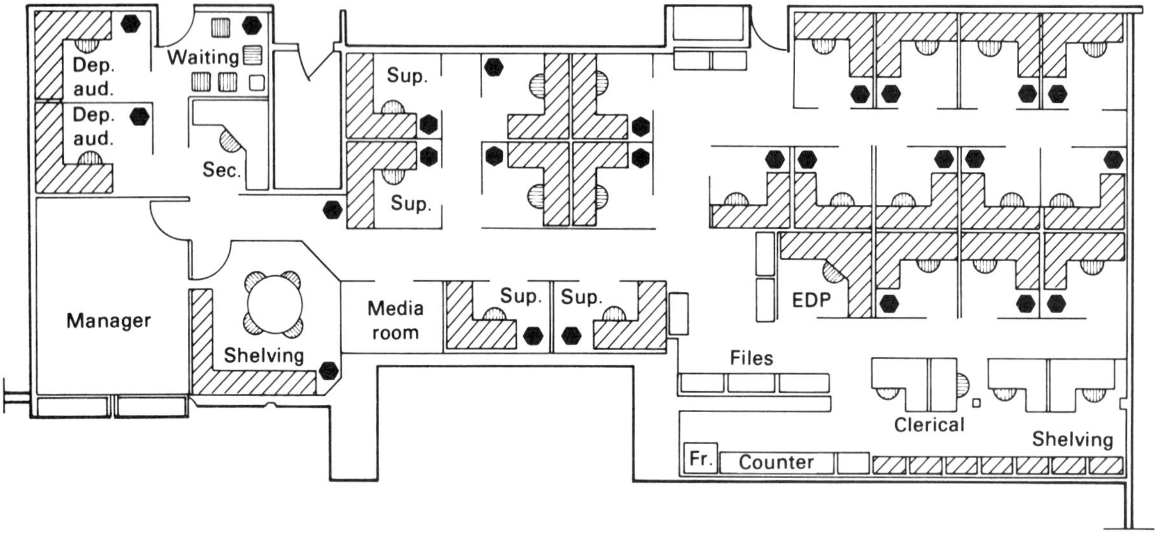

FIGURE 8.8
Employee task chart

DETAIL TASKING WORKSHEET

Project Number: ______ Project Name: ______
Task Number: ______ Task Start Date: ______ Duration (working days) ______ Date Prepared ______
Task Description: ______ Task Stop Date: ______
Task(s) Needed to be Complete Before Starting: ______ File Code: ______

Sub-Task Number	Description	Individual(s) Responsible	Start Date Plan	Start Date Actual	Stop Date Plan	Stop Date Actual	Est. Time To Complete (days)	% of Total Task	Comments

22244007 (1 82)

Courtesy of the Arizona Bank

SUMMARY

1. A *system* is defined as a set of related procedures that are designed to meet specific objectives.
2. Typical administrative support systems of business organizations are personnel, production, accounting, finance, marketing, purchasing, and office information systems.
3. The five steps in a system project are to investigate the problem, analyze the system, design the system, implement the system, and evaluate the system.
4. The administrative office manager should possess significant skills in implementing various systems in order to effectively manage today's electronic offices.

STUDENT ACTIVITIES

Active Orientation

1. Contact a systems analyst from a company in your community and determine his or her educational background and the systems analysis techniques he or she utilizes.

2. Interview an office manager whose office is automated to determine

- ☐ which office applications are automated;
- ☐ what type of equipment is used; and
- ☐ if there are any problem areas.

Independent Problems

1. Describe the difference between a system and a procedure.

2. Describe how systems analysis tools would aid the administrative office manager in purchasing an office automation system.

9 Ergonomic Designs and Productivity

OBJECTIVES At the conclusion of this chapter, you should be able to:

1. Define the term *ergonomics.*
2. Identify those ergonomic factors that often have an impact on administrative productivity.
3. List the steps necessary to conduct an effective ergonomic study.
4. Illustrate one method of determining the payback period of certain ergonomic designs.
5. Discuss the limitations of ergonomic designs on increasing administrative productivity.
6. Discuss the anticipated growth of office systems furniture and executive workstations.

INTRODUCTION

The term *ergonomics* can be defined as the study of the relationship between workers and their work environment. For years, ergonomic studies have been conducted by many European organizations seeking to increase administrative productivity. Unfortunately, in the United States, the term *ergonomics* has been misused and often ignored. Ergonomics has been used to describe everything from chairs with swivel bases to textured wallpaper. Many organizations have not taken the time to plan the design of their administrative areas; therefore, the purchase of chairs, workstations (desks), lighting, acoustics, and air conditioning systems has been completed without any consideration for the types of work performed by the employees. This nonsystematic design approach may have a negative impact on the productivity of administrative personnel.

In spite of the fact that studies in Europe, Canada, and the United States have shown that proper ergonomic designs can improve administrative productivity, most managers of computer facilities have not implemented strategies for addressing this important topic. "According to the Data Processing Management Association (DPMA) of Park Ridge, Illinois, 84 percent of information processing executives have no functional ergonomic guidelines" (*Words,* 1985). Information processing executives are not the only managers who are ignoring ergonomic factors. "Fifty-three percent of the information processing professionals said top management is unaware of the ergonomic needs" (*Words,* 1985).

This chapter is designed to provide the reader with the information necessary to identify the ergonomic factors which may be preventing maximum employee performance. A systems approach, in the form of a ten-step outline, will be utilized to illustrate how an administrative manager can design an ergonomically correct office environment. An important feature of the ten-step outline is the provision for the establishment of a productivity measurement program—a feature often overlooked by the administrative office.

WHAT ERGONOMICS IS AND WHAT IT IS NOT

Ergonomics, which is often called "human factor engineering" in the United States, is the study of human beings at work. Although environmental factors have long been known to have an effect on worker productivity, it is only recently that these factors have been considered in the administrative office. Concerns over the safety of workers exposed to computer screens, or videodisplay terminals (VDTs), for long periods of time have prompted studies into other environmental factors which may have an effect on the health and the productivity of administrative personnel. These studies have become known as ergonomic studies. Ergonomic designs should be considered an important part of an overall management strategy to increase administrative productivity. However, ergonomic factors do not provide complete solutions to an organization's productivity or personnel problems. The purchase or lease of appropriate furniture, lighting, acoustics, and air conditioning systems will not guarantee success if other management strategies are inappropriate, as is illustrated in Figure 9.1.

ERGONOMIC FACTORS

Any ergonomic factor which causes distraction or discomfort to a worker may have a negative impact on that employee's productivity. However, there are certain factors which are major contributors to office inefficiency that appear time and time again in American organizations. These ergonomic factors are inappropriately designed chairs and workstations, poorly planned lighting systems, insufficient or nonexistent acoustic partitioning, and inadequate air conditioning systems.

Chairs

The chairs employees use throughout the workday are extremely important ergonomic considerations. In recent years, office chair design features have been developed to provide greater support to the employee's lumbar (lower back) area. As shown in Figure 9.2, these ergonomically designed chairs also provide adjustment features which allow the chair to swivel, tilt, move up and down, and recline or lock in place. Ergonomically designed office chairs should include the following features.

Base features. Most ergonomically designed chairs are available in four or five pedestal models. The five-pedestal models usually allow for smoother and easier rolling action, while providing a more stable base.

FIGURE 9.1 *Ergonomics and managerial strategies*

Management Strategy	Ergonomic Factor Consideration
Increase data entry accuracy	Lighting, workstation, chair design
Reducing office reconfiguration costs	Systems furniture
Reducing glare on computer screens	Combination task/ambient lighting

FIGURE 9.2
Ergonomically designed chair

Courtesy of Haworth, Inc.

The five-pedestal models also allow for more foot room for the operator because the pedestals do not need to be as long in order to support the chair.

Armrest features. Arm supports on office chairs offer an additional support feature to the employee's back, shoulders, and neck. New support designs offer cantilevered tops for added comfort. These arm supports are also recessed so that the operator can pull the chair closer to the workstation for keyboarding and writing tasks.

Height adjustment. Chairs used in an administrative office should have a manual seat height adjustment feature. Even with standardized workstation measurements, variances in arm, leg, and torso lengths require that seat height adjustments be made. Many ergonomic chair manufacturers offer pneumatic, or gas cylinder, features for some of their models. These pneumatic features allow seat heights to be adjusted by merely touching a button that is usually found on the bottom of the seat panel.

Seat angle. Popliteal height measurements, which measure from the floor to the underside of the thigh, range from 14 inches for very small people to 19.3 inches for very large people. The seat pitch adjustment feature creates an opportunity for the operator to adjust the seat to accommodate for proper foot support on the floor, as well as for the amount of pressure exerted against the bottom of the thigh.

Back support. The back support feature is a very important aspect of an ergonomically designed chair. Lack of adequate support to the spine for extended periods of time results in back pain, shoulder and neck stiffness, and occasionally, headaches. Properly designed chairs provide a full backrest that reaches to the lumbar or lower back area. The backrest should lock in place at the upright position for use during prolonged periods of keyboarding or writing tasks. The backrest should also be able to lock in place at various reclining positions.

Workstations

The incorporation of computer systems into offices has dictated a redesign of many office desks. Managers in organizations usually discover very quickly that placing computer systems on desks that were designed for writing and typing tasks does not work. In most cases, computer keyboards cannot be adjusted to the proper height and the angle and distance of the computer screens are inappropriate when placed on most office desks.

Modern office furniture manufacturers such as Steelcase, Herman Miller, Haworth, and Westinghouse are developing modular office workstations like the one shown in Figure 9.3, which are designed for use with computer systems. These workstations are able to adjust to new office technologies. They allow for changes made to workflow designs and reconfigurations of workstations in order to better meet the needs of employees and organizations. Ergonomically designed workstations provide the user with comfort and flexibility. The following sections discuss some features that are recommended for administrative workstations.

Flexibility. "The key to designing a workstation is flexibility . . ." (Meroney, 1982). Modular furniture design allows for the entire workstation to be moved to accommodate for workflow changes. In addition,

FIGURE 9.3
Modular workstation

Courtesy of Haworth, Inc.

the workstation itself can be reconfigured to better meet the needs of the individual employee.

Electronic runways. Today's electronic offices utilize many devices, from telephones and calculators to computer systems. Obviously, these devices require a source of electric power. The modular office furniture being developed today provides a runway or channel for the electrical cables which bring the power to the workstation. These runways are usually placed in the baseboards of the wall panels. Often, the runways provide conduits to separate cables so that the possibility of electrical interference between the computer and telephone communication lines is minimized.

Panel height. The function of workstation panels is to provide a barrier to sight and sound distractions in an open office environment. Manufacturers of workstation panels provide a wide assortment of panel heights to meet the needs of each workstation. A sixty-inch panel may be appropriate for a worker who does not require any visual or verbal contact with other employees. Lower height panels may be required for employees who need to exchange information throughout the workday. Other modular panels in excess of seventy inches can be used to partition machine noises from computer printers or copying machines.

Task lighting. Although office lighting is discussed later in this chapter, task lighting is an integral part of modular workstations. Task lights are the light fixtures mounted underneath the overhead storage cabinets or shelves of the workstation. They provide the appropriate levels of light necessary to perform the reading and writing tasks common to many office workers. Task lights are usually arranged in a way that does not produce glare on computer screens in the workstation.

Adjustable keyboard panels. As was stated earlier, flexibility is the key to effective workstation design. The placement of the keyboard for computing devices is critical to the comfort of the operator. An adjustable keyboard unit such as the one in Figure 9.4 provides the operator with the flexibility necessary to remain comfortable for longer periods of time. If an employee is comfortable at the keyboard, it seems logical to assume that he or she will work for longer periods of time and produce fewer errors.

Acoustical panels. One of the purposes of workstation panels is to provide a sound barrier for the worker. Most panels made by today's

FIGURE 9.4
Adjustable keyboard unit

Courtesy of Haworth, Inc.

modular furniture manufacturers are classified as acoustical panels. This means that the materials which cover the panels are made of sound-absorbing material. Rating systems have been established to measure the amount of sound absorption, or the NRC (Noise Reduction Coefficient). Acoustical panels should be made of material which has an NRC of eighty-five or higher. This means that the panel absorbs eighty-five percent of the sound waves with which it comes in contact.

Brightness ratio. The visual comfort of an employee is affected by the amount and quality of light in his or her field of vision. The color of the objects that employees view has an effect on the function of the eye. A common example is the experience of entering into or exiting from a darkened theater. At first, it is difficult to see anything. After a few moments, the pupil of the eye adjusts and objects become easier to see. The same activity, to a lesser degree, happens when employees view writing or print on white paper when they are surrounded by a dark desk surface and/or dark wall partitions. The contrast from light to dark objects requires the eyes to work harder than they should for extended periods of time, and this results in eyestrain.

The relationship of brightness, or light contrast, between two objects in the same field of vision is known as the *brightness ratio.* To avoid excessive eyestrain caused by too much contrast in the brightness of light, a "brightness ratio of 3 to 1" (McNelis, 1985—General Electric Company) should not be exceeded.

Storage considerations. A flexible feature of most modular workstations is the different types of storage combinations which are available. Overhead storage units can be mounted on acoustical wall panels to provide readily accessible manuals, papers, and other materials. Also, pencil drawers, tub files, and file compartments can be attached to the desk surface for additional storage. These storage units can be added to or removed from workstations when necessary.

Lighting Systems

Fluorescent lighting is the most common lighting system used in recently constructed buildings. The overhead fluorescent lighting arrangement is an economical method for providing abundant amounts of light. However, these abundant levels of light may be too much light for today's electronic offices. "Virtually every office has too much lighting" (Springer, 1984).

Many offices using overhead fluorescent lighting have lighting levels that are twice as high as necessary for operators of computer equipment. The footcandle is the measurement of the amount of light falling on an observed area. Recommended levels of lighting for general office tasks such as reading, writing, and filing range from 70 to

FIGURE 9.5
Task lighting

Courtesy of Haworth, Inc.

150 footcandles (General Electric Company, 1985). However, the recommended level of light for VDT use is only 35 to 50 footcandles. The problem, of course, is that office employees usually perform reading and writing tasks as well as VDT tasks throughout the workday. The solution is to design an effective lighting system which addresses the lighting needs of reading and writing tasks without providing too much light and glare on the computer screens. This solution usually takes the form of a lighting system which utilizes task and ambient, or indirect, lighting strategies.

Task lighting. Task lighting, shown in Figure 9.5, provides the employee with lighting levels of 75 to 150 footcandles at a specific location or locations at the workstation. The task light is either mounted on an overhead storage unit or on a movable, retractable arm, like the kind used on artists' drafting tables.

Ambient (indirect) lighting. Ambient lighting is used in place of overhead fluorescent lighting units. Ambient lighting units are mounted on workstations or in stand-alone units, as shown in Figure 9.6. The light is directed at the ceiling, which reflects the light back down to the work area. This system provides a lower level of light to the work environment, which reduces the amount of glare present on computer screens. The combination of task and ambient lighting solves the problem of matching lighting levels with the different types of work performed in the administrative office.

FIGURE 9.6
Ambient (indirect) lighting

Courtesy of Haworth, Inc.

Acoustics

Like the lighting system, the acoustical system has an impact on the various types of work performed in an administrative office. Office workers are usually required to conduct reading, writing, research, analysis, and planning activities in an environment which also requires the use of various noise-producing machines such as typewriters, computer printers, and copying machines. The workers' tasks are made considerably more difficult in a noisy environment. Effective sound management requires special attention to the types of work performed and the new acoustic techniques available to managers today.

Managers can significantly reduce the impact of noise throughout the office by analyzing the work activities of employees. This work analysis may result in the placement of employees who do primarily reading, writing, and analysis tasks away from high noise areas. Acoustical panels may be strategically placed throughout the office to buffer noise-producing machines, telephones, and traffic areas. Some organizations have placed printing and copying machines in separate rooms or have purchased acoustic covers for them to eliminate much of the noise generated by these machines.

Sound management devices such as "piped-in music" or "white noise" systems have been used by organizations to mask the noises generated in most offices. These devices are most effective in controlling the transmission of voices throughout the office.

Air Conditioning Systems

Air conditioning factors include temperature, humidity, circulation, and the cleanliness of air available to employees. These various air conditioning factors have been manipulated a great deal in recent years. The energy conservation efforts of the 1970s have resulted in adjustments to the seasonal heating and cooling of office buildings. Furthermore, new "climate controlled" buildings have built-in airflow sensors to control air circulation throughout the buildings. These factors have resulted in complex systems of air control in many buildings across the United States.

Air temperature. During the workday, office temperatures should be maintained between sixty-five and sixty-eight degrees in the heating season and seventy-five to eighty degrees during the cooling season. These recommendations were established by the federal government and assume as much energy conservation as can be expected without altering employee performance.

Humidity. The temperature setting alone does not ensure body comfort. The proper combination of temperature and humidity, called *effective temperature,* is needed for true comfort. For human comfort and proper equipment function, the recommended humidity range is between forty and sixty percent. As a rule, a person will feel hotter in the summer and colder in the winter in a high relative humidity environment. Low relative humidity will result in too much static electricity, which can cause bothersome shocks to individuals and the mechanical failure of some computer equipment.

Air circulation. The amount of air circulation is dependent on the size of the environment and the number of people housed in the environment. Air circulation also includes the insertion of outside fresh air in sufficient amounts to avoid air stagnation in climate controlled buildings. Many times the outside air source is shut off or reduced during peak heating or cooling periods. This causes problems in controlling heating and cooling costs in the southwestern deserts in the summer and the northeastern cities in the winter.

As a rule, air circulation of twenty-five feet per minute with ten cubic feet of outside air per minute per employee is suggested. These levels reduce the chance for hot and cold pockets of air in an office. The air movement also reduces the chance of stagnant air without creating a chilling effect on the employees.

Air cleanliness. The cleanliness of the air is of equal importance to the issues of temperature, humidity, and circulation in the office environment. In recent years, significant safety issues have been discussed with respect to the air space that is shared by many individuals in a controlled environment. The most visible issue has been smoking on the job. Serious concerns exist for nonsmokers who must breathe the air polluted by smoking employees. Many organizations are placing bans on smoking on the job. Other organizations are providing smoking and nonsmoking areas for employees. A recent report from the Surgeon General of the United States indicates that it costs an employer $4,600 more per year to employ a smoker than a nonsmoker. This figure is based on absenteeism, productivity, and the maintenance costs associated with smoke-filled air.

In addition to the smoking issue, climate controlled buildings transmit germs, noxious fumes, pollen, and other particulates over and over throughout the building. It is important that managers and building maintenance officials address the air cleanliness issues.

CONDUCTING AN ERGONOMIC STUDY

In order for an administrative manager to address the many issues discussed in this chapter, a systems approach is required. Utilizing the systems techniques learned in Chapter 8, a manager can conduct an effective ergonomic study. The following ten-step program is designed to provide the administrative manager with a guide to conducting an effective ergonomic study.

A Systems Approach to Ergonomic Design

Step 1: Determine managerial and operational objectives. Every effective systems study requires that managerial and operational objectives be addressed. This preliminary step provides the structure that is necessary for the study to stay on course throughout the project. It also helps to ensure that the system being designed is in the best interests of the managerial objectives of the organization and is feasible given the operational objectives, or day-to-day activities, of the employees.

Step 2: Review job descriptions and operating manuals. This review provides the manager with essential information that is specific to each job being performed in the affected area. This information will be very valuable when the specifics of the new system are being designed.

Step 3: Interview employees. Interviewing employees either individually or in groups will provide the manager with additional information about specific job functions that are not found in job descriptions or operating manuals. Many times, adjustments and modifications are made to jobs without updating the manuals. Interviews with employees may also provide the manager with valuable ideas and recommendations for improving the work environment and making workdays more productive.

Step 4: Interview supervisors and managers. Supervisors and managers should not be overlooked as potential sources of ideas for improving the work environment. These individuals should have valuable insights about productivity problems ranging from employee turnover to equipment needs.

Step 5: Observe work performance. It is always important to observe work performance in an ergonomic study. The information received from steps 2, 3, and 4 can be verified and additional information not previously mentioned can be documented. Observing the "big picture" with an ergonomic perspective can be very informative.

Step 6: Analyze equipment used by employees. While observing work performance, managers may notice some equipment problems that are experienced by employees. Some of these problems may be caused by ergonomic factors such as lighting, workstation design, air conditioning, or noise generation.

Step 7: Analyze the work and nonwork environment. At this point, specific input has been received from all levels of employees, operations have been observed, and equipment has been analyzed. It is time to observe factors such as the amounts of lighting, air circulation, and noise generated in the work environment. Facility managers or building maintenance professionals should be a valuable source of help for managers during this step. The findings should be compared to government specifications and industry standards.

Step 8: Identify ergonomic factors serving as barriers to maximum employee productivity. The various ergonomic factors should be documented and discussed with employees, supervisors, and managers. Often your observations will be verified by employees; strategies will be easier to form as a result of their input. Managers should be cautious of obvious cause-and-effect relationships at this point, especially with regard to lighting and air conditioning issues. Quick fixes of these factors without substantial study can be costly. Once all factors have been addressed by employees, supervisors, managers, and industrial professionals, then strategies for designing a more ergonomically correct facility can begin.

Step 9: Develop strategies for ergonomic design. Task forces may be organized at this point to address the ergonomic roadblocks found in steps 1 through 8. The task forces should be charged with researching their areas of responsibility and reporting their strategies for solving the ergonomic problems within a certain period of time. A team should be established to coordinate the various task forces so that redundancy is eliminated and the various task forces ultimately provide a comprehensive solution to the problems at hand. PERT (Program Evaluation and Review Technique) is an appropriate level for managing this activity.

Step 10: Design/modify the environment. The reports developed in step 9 should provide management with the information needed to select plans of action for designing or modifying the existing environment. Evaluation, acquisition, and implementation of changes to be made should be carefully structured to address order processing time, workflow and project deadlines, and budget considerations. As always, a review team should be established at this time to provide a comprehensive review of the new or modified environment.

ERGONOMICS AND PRODUCTIVITY

It is clear that ergonomics is more than just buying furniture and wall coverings for the office. The modular or systems furniture market is expected to grow rapidly throughout the next decade. Over $12 billion will be spent on executive workstations by 1992. Therefore, it is important that managers accurately determine what is needed, how much it is going to cost, and the extent of the payback period for each design implementation. Ergonomic designs are too expensive for aesthetic rewards alone. It is important that ergonomic designs play a role in increased administrative productivity.

Cautions About Estimating Ergonomic Productivity

Any attempt to estimate administrative productivity always contains some subjectivity. A difficulty with productivity estimates that is associated with ergonomic designs is that there are few studies to use as references. However, the greatest difficulty is the fact that ergonomics is only one aspect of an overall managerial program which may have an effect on administrative productivity. Therefore, results from other studies should be used with caution when estimating the productivity increases associated with your ergonomic designs. Chapter 18 provides the reader with strategies for determining administrative productivity.

Estimating the Payback of Ergonomic Designs

To determine a rough estimate of the payback period associated with ergonomic designs, a number of figures must be available to a manager, including:

1. the cost of the ergonomic design;
2. the average cost of the task (employees and materials);
3. the estimated productivity increase; and
4. the number of employees in the affected area.

For the purpose of this illustration, assume that we wish to purchase $250,000 worth of modular furniture for our office. The average compensation package (salary, benefits, and percentage of actual work time) and the materials cost for the administrative office is $20,000 per employee. The estimated productivity increase found from our research is ten percent. The number of employees in the affected area of the office is 100. With this information, we have everything we need to calculate the payback period. The equation divides the product of the average cost of the activity, the anticipated increase in productivity, and the number of employees into the cost of the ergonomic design. Note that this calculation does not include depreciation or tax credits.

$$\frac{\$250{,}000}{\$20{,}000 \times .10 \times 100} = 1.25 \text{ year payback}$$

If the payback is within the acceptable limits of your organization, then some thought may be given to possibly purchasing the ergonomic design. Although this calculation is not 100 percent accurate, it will generate an *estimate* of the payback period associated with each type of ergonomic design. It should be used with caution and regarded as only one of the decision criteria.

IMPLICATIONS FOR THE ADMINISTRATIVE MANAGER

The data provided in Parts 1 and 2 of this text clearly outline the need for greater productivity in the administrative office. The insertion of computer technology into the office dictates new design structures for many administrative office tasks. The demand for greater productivity and the need for office design changes indicate that the time for ergonomics considerations has arrived.

It is important that managers understand what ergonomics is and what it is not. Ergonomics is not a solution for unsatisfactory administrative productivity in and of itself; it is only a part of the overall management strategy for increasing productivity. Ergonomics is an area which addresses the entire organization and therefore it requires a systems approach for analysis, evaluation, design, and implementation. A systems approach to ergonomic design will help the administrative manager identify ergonomic problems that prohibit maximum employee productivity and will also provide solutions to some ergonomic problems.

The time is right for managers to consider ergonomic studies of their organizations. The productivity issues are pervasive, and the equipment manufacturers have attractive and functional products available. In addition, more and more employees are demanding comfortable as well as functional work environments. Legal issues are also on the horizon. Employees and office unions are bringing litigations to the courts concerning employee health and safety issues in the office. Some state legislatures are considering laws affecting the use of VDTs and the effects of smoking on the job. Ergonomics is a management strategy whose time has come.

SUMMARY

1. The term *ergonomics* can be defined as the study of the relationship between workers and their work environment.
2. Eighty-four percent of information processing managers have no functional guidelines for ergonomics.
3. Ergonomic designs should be considered as one important aspect of an overall management strategy.
4. Ergonomic designs are not complete solutions to an organization's productivity or personnel problems.
5. Most organizations have similar ergonomic factor problems. The most common are chair design, workstation design, poor lighting design, inadequate air conditioning systems, and inadequate or nonexistent acoustic partitioning.
6. Acoustical panels should have an eighty-five or higher noise reduction coefficient (NRC).
7. The office brightness ratio should not exceed three to one.
8. Recommended levels of light for reading and writing tasks are 70 to 150 footcandles.

9. Recommended levels of light for using VDTs are thirty-five to fifty footcandles.
10. A combination of task and ambient lighting is a solution to the problems created by overhead fluorescent lighting.
11. Recommended temperature ranges are sixty-five to sixty-eight degrees in the heating season and seventy-five to eighty degrees in the cooling season.
12. The recommended humidity range in an office is forty to sixty percent.
13. Air circulation of twenty-five feet per minute with ten cubic feet of outside air per person is recommended for an office.
14. It costs $4,600 a year more, on the average, to employ a smoker than a nonsmoker.
15. A systems approach is recommended in conducting an ergonomic study. The systems approach should include the following steps:
    - ☐ Determine managerial and operational objectives.
    - ☐ Review job descriptions and operating manuals.
    - ☐ Interview employees.
    - ☐ Interview supervisors and managers.
    - ☐ Observe work performance.
    - ☐ Analyze equipment used by employees.
    - ☐ Analyze the work and nonwork environment.
    - ☐ Identify ergonomic factors.
    - ☐ Develop strategies for ergonomic design.
    - ☐ Design/modify the environment.
16. Over $12 billion will be spent on executive workstations by 1992.
17. To determine ergonomic design payback periods you must know the cost of the ergonomic design, the average cost of the task performed, the estimated productivity increase, and the number of employees in the affected area.
18. Legislation and litigation is pending on ergonomic issues in many states in the United States.

STUDENT ACTIVITIES

Active Orientation

1. Invite an office furniture salesperson to your classroom to discuss modular or systems furniture for the electronic office. The three leading manufacturers are Steelcase, Herman Miller, and Haworth. There is probably a distributor for one or more of these manufacturers in your city.

2. Contact a business lighting company in your city. Have a representative address the class on topics concerning task and ambient lighting.

Independent Problems

1. What is the difference between task and ambient lighting? How are they used in combination? Why?

2. What strategies can be used to control noise levels in the office?

3. What effects do smoking in the office have on the employees of an organization and on the organization itself?

REFERENCES

McNelis, John F. Interview, General Electric Company, April, 1985.

Meroney, John W. "Ergonomic Work Station Design Adds to Efficiency." *The Office,* December 1982.

Springer, T. J. "Remove Impediments to People Performance." *The Office,* January 1984.

Words, "Industry Briefs", April–May, 1985, p. 11.

10 Administrative Communication Systems

OBJECTIVES At the conclusion of this chapter, you should be able to:

1. Define the term *communication.*
2. List the objectives of an administrative communication system.
3. Discuss the elements of the administrative communication model.
4. Define the two basic types of administrative communication.
5. Outline the procedures for developing an effective administrative communication system.

INTRODUCTION

Communication is the transfer of information, thoughts, and emotions among people. The extent to which the communication process is effective determines the level of understanding achieved. Thus, for managers to transfer the information, thoughts, and emotions of a company to the workers, an effective communication system must be established. This communication system must be flexible enough to communicate the ever-changing goals and objectives of the organization and, at the same time, maintain control over the accuracy of the information being disseminated.

OBJECTIVES OF AN ADMINISTRATIVE COMMUNICATION SYSTEM

A well-designed plan is essential in order to establish an effective administrative communication system. This plan must address the communication needs of people who come from diverse backgrounds and who often have conflicting agendas. It is critical that the organizational objectives be considered when developing an administrative communication system.

Objective #1: To Inform The primary responsibility of any management team is to communicate the goals and objectives of the organization to supervisory and line personnel. This sharing of information can keep workers on task and motivate them to be productive, loyal, and innovative employees.

Effective information sharing implies that the information is accurate and timely. Accurate information that is disseminated in a timely fashion reduces the chances for rumors, employee morale problems, and other negative influences within the organization. A well-informed employee is more likely to be loyal to the organization during difficult times because he or she has been privy to pertinent business information.

Objective #2: To Direct An effective administrative communication system consists of channels through which managers can direct the action of supervisors and line employees. This type of communication system includes the various written communication media such as memos, letters, invoices, and budget reports.

Objective #3: To Lead All great leaders of our time in business, government, and education have been effective communicators. A most recent example is Lee Iacocca, chairman of the Chrysler Corporation. His ability to communicate within the corporation as well as to the American buying public has led the Chrysler Corporation from the brink of bankruptcy to profitability.

ADMINISTRATIVE COMMUNICATION MODEL

In order for a manager to inform, direct, and lead his or her employees, a communication process must be designed to deliver the information, direction, and leadership style. The administrative communication model illustrated in Figure 10.1 provides the framework for effective administrative communication. If managers constructed their administrative communication around this model, each of the critical areas of effective business communication would be addressed.

- **The sender.** The person responsible for starting the communication process is the sender. It is the sender's responsibility to create the message to be communicated, select the most appropriate media for transmitting the message, and provide for a method of response from the intended receivers of the message.
- **The message.** The thoughts, ideas, and emotions of the sender comprise the message. The message may be constructed for delivery in either written or oral form.
- **The media.** The media used to deliver the message is critical. In a departmental meeting, training session, or other oral presentation, a verbal message can be delivered using as few or as many words as necessary. Furthermore, the message may be repeated if more clarification is desired. The written message, however, is much more difficult to construct. Words must be chosen carefully to communicate the exact intentions of the sender so the receivers can accurately interpret the message. Managers should evaluate their written and oral communication strengths to determine whether they should utilize written media such as memos, letters, and re-

FIGURE 10.1
Communication model

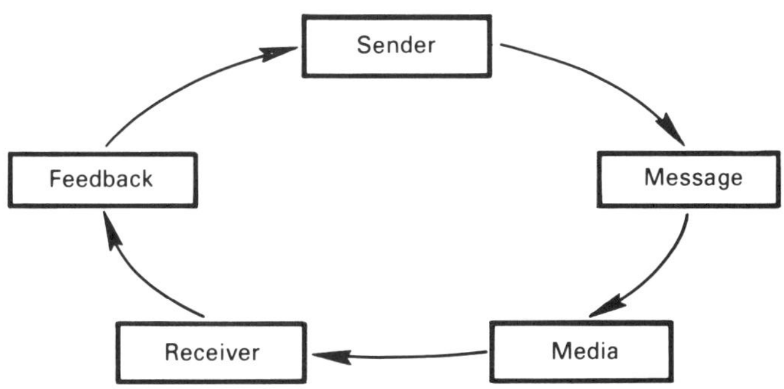

ports, or oral media such as face-to-face meetings, seminars, telephone, and teleconferencing media for their specific communication efforts.

- **The receiver.** The primary reason for sending a message is to achieve the understanding of another individual or group of individuals. Therefore, the sender of the message must understand the needs and the capabilities of the person or persons receiving the message. These are important factors when considering the various levels of expertise among employees in an administrative organization. A thorough understanding of the receivers of a message will aid the sender in developing a more direct, understandable, and therefore more effective business message.
- **Feedback.** By allowing a response from the receiver of a message, the sender can determine the extent to which his or her message has been received and understood. The feedback aspect of the communication process also provides employees with an additional opportunity to participate in the business organization. This participation will pay large dividends to the organization simply because the management recognizes the importance of feedback in the business communication process.

TYPES OF ADMINISTRATIVE COMMUNICATION

There are two basic types of administrative communication: written communication and oral communication. Although oral communication takes place much more often, official business communication is almost always conducted in written form.

Written Communication

Business reports, contracts, letters, directives, memos, operations manuals, and procedures manuals comprise the majority of written administrative communication. The amount of paperwork generated by business organizations is staggering. As was discussed in Chapter 4, the growing number of business documents kept on file within organizations has made it imperative that managers develop policies to control the proliferation of written administrative communication.

Some organizations have stringent policies for writing memos, letters, and other business documents for internal use. For example, memos may be restricted to one-half of a page, letters to one page, and business reports to five pages. Even in the absence of a company-wide policy on written communication, some managers require that their subordinates limit their written communication to specified lengths to reduce the amount of reading time necessary to understand the message. These policies force individuals to become more effective communicators.

Oral Communication The majority of the communication activities which take place every day are oral communications. These activities include informal face-to-face conversations, business meetings, training sessions, and telephone conversations. Many organizations recognize the tremendous variance in oral communication skills among their employees. These organizations provide their employees with communications seminars featuring speaking and listening skills development.

DESIGNING AN ADMINISTRATIVE COMMUNICATION SYSTEM

The communication system is the most important of all the systems within an organization. Yet very few companies thoroughly plan for their communication needs. Figure 10.2 outlines a comprehensive communication plan for a business organization.

Step 1: Determine Organizational Objectives Every administrative system must address organizational objectives. The design of the communication system should correspond to the flow of information throughout the company. These information channels will flow from top managers to middle managers to supervisors to line employees and back through the organizational hierarchy to top management again. The information channels must also reach any branch offices, factories, or plants which may exist. These information channels diagram the network of managerial reporting desired by the organization. An effective communication system will parallel these organizational objectives.

Step 2: Determine Needs Assessing the communication needs in an administrative organization includes many factors. Written and oral communication needs include memoranda, letters, reports, contracts, advertising copy, telephones,

FIGURE 10.2
Designing an effective business communication system

- ☐ Step 1: Determine organizational objectives
- ☐ Step 2: Determine needs
- ☐ Step 3: Establish organization-wide policies
- ☐ Step 4: Evaluate equipment
- ☐ Step 5: Provide cost analysis
- ☐ Step 6: Design the system
- ☐ Step 7: Purchase or lease the system
- ☐ Step 8: Implement the system
- ☐ Step 9: Evaluate the system

teletypewriters, computer-generated voice and data systems, and teleconferencing. Although not all organizations will need the most sophisticated communication equipment available, it is important to determine which communication devices will be necessary to conduct business both today and in the foreseeable future. A more detailed discussion of communication technology is found in Chapter 12.

The types of communication devices needed can be determined by tracing the information patterns developed in step 1. The combination of word processors, printers, telephones, teletypewriters, computer systems, and teleconferencing facilities can then be arranged to meet the reporting objectives of the management team.

Step 3: Establish Organization-Wide Policies

Policies should be established as to the procedures employees will follow when creating written and oral communications for internal and external use. The policies for written communication should include the format for all written documents, regardless of whether they are generated by a word processor, computer system, or typewriter. The format should identify the type of document, the maximum length of the document, the writing style, and a description of which types of communication must always be in written form.

Oral communication policies should address procedures for developing the verbal communication skills of managers, supervisors, and employees. Policies should also be established concerning procedures for communicating to people outside of the company. For example, formats for presenting press releases, advertising, and public speeches or interviews should be determined.

Step 4: Evaluate Equipment

Once organizational objectives have been determined, communication needs established, and policies written, current communication equipment can be evaluated. The communication needs identified in step 2 should be matched with the growing types of communication equipment available in the marketplace. This will provide the organization with a knowledge of the versatility, or lack of versatility, of the equipment as well as the costs associated with the various equipment.

Step 5: Provide Cost Analysis

A complete cost analysis of each type of communication device should be prepared, including a rationale for its inclusion into the new communication system. The rationale should identify the reasons why this device is recommended over other less expensive devices, provide a projection of the device's useful life to the organization, and state the degree to which it is compatible with existing or proposed equipment.

Step 6: Design the System

Now that all of the pertinent information has been gathered, the new communication system can be designed. Organizational charts, department schematics, color photos of the equipment, engineering blueprints, and related materials such as job descriptions and operator skill levels should be packaged in the new design proposal.

The design report should include the location of the proposed equipment, the individuals who will be operating the equipment, the training programs necessary to orient employees to the new system, and specific policies for utilizing the communication system created in step 3.

Step 7: Purchase or Lease the System

Communication systems are being developed at a rapid pace. Technological advances warrant a close look at the estimated useful life of state-of-the-art equipment. In such a rapidly developing industry, leasing equipment can be a wise choice.

Step 8: Implement the System

Implementing a system that has such an impact within the organization requires that systematic installation and implementation take place. In large organizations, implementation may take place department-by-department or branch-by-branch. In all companies, it is important to organize the implementation of a communication system. This includes giving advance notice to managers, supervisors, employees, and customers. Also, a copy of the implementation schedule should be given to each manager so that departmental planning can coincide with the system installation.

Step 9: Evaluate the System

The most frequently overlooked aspect of the development of a new system is the evaluation phase. It is entirely likely that, even though substantial planning has taken place, the new system has created difficult situations for some individuals within the organization.

The evaluation program should include participation from individuals at all levels of the organization. This participation will direct the company to provide the necessary changes to the communication system. It must be remembered that the communication system must be looked at as a complete package and not just at how well it works for the supervisors or the management team. An evaluation team consisting of managers, supervisors, and line employees provides the best opportunity for developing a responsive communication system.

SUMMARY

1. Communication is the transfer of information, thoughts, and emotions among people.
2. The objectives of an effective administrative communication system are to inform, to direct, and to lead.
3. The administrative communication system model includes the sender, message, media, receiver, and feedback phases.

4. The two basic types of administrative communication are written and oral.
5. Written communication includes reports, contracts, letters, directives, memos, operations manuals, and procedures manuals.
6. Oral communication includes face-to-face conversations, meetings, training sessions, and telephone conversations.
7. Almost all official administrative communications are in written form.
8. The most important of all systems within an organization is the communication system.
9. The following nine steps are recommended for designing an effective administrative communication system: determine organizational objectives; determine needs; establish organization-wide policies; evaluate equipment; provide cost analysis; design the system; purchase or lease the system; implement the system; and evaluate the system.

STUDENT ACTIVITIES

Active Orientation

1. Contact your local telephone company and have a sales representative provide a demonstration of the latest business telephone systems.

2. Visit a local company which utilizes an electronic mail system. If you do not have a local facility which uses electronic mail, write to a major corporation which does business in your city for a description of how their electronic system works.

Independent Problems

1. Develop written and oral communications policies for a fictitious company. Don't forget to provide a rationale for each policy.

2. Design an administrative communication system for the fictitious company from independent problem 1.

11 Information Processing Technology

OBJECTIVES At the conclusion of this chapter, you should be able to:

1. Trace the development of computer use in business from the mid–1950s to the present time.
2. Describe the component parts of computer systems.
3. Describe the role of the computer in the business office.
4. Describe the information processing cycle.
5. Define *distributed information processing.*

INTRODUCTION

The growth of computer technology in recent years has been truly phenomenal. Computer performance has increased significantly, and market prices have dropped to a small fraction of their costs of just ten years ago.

Since 1975, the rapid growth of the microcomputer has literally changed the way small companies, government agencies, and educational institutions conduct their daily business. The U.S. Bureau of Labor projects that by 1990, one in every four households will possess a microcomputer. IBM predicts that by the end of this decade, sixty million microcomputers will be in use in the United States; many of them will be on the desktops of executives, managers, and clerical workers.

This chapter attempts to put the computer revolution into perspective for the office worker. We will illustrate both the advantages and the disadvantages of office computing, thus providing a blueprint for managers to follow concerning office computer technology.

THE DEVELOPMENT OF BUSINESS COMPUTER SYSTEMS

Electronic computer systems were first pioneered by Dr. John Atanasoff in the 1930s and Dr. John Mauchly and J. Presper Eckert during the 1940s. These machines were experimental designs and not the type of computer system that was capable of meeting the computing needs of most businesses. Nonetheless, these early efforts were the driving force behind the development of the electronic computers of the mid-1950s—machines that truly altered business data processing techniques.

First Generation Business Computers

During the early and mid–1950s, three companies, Univac, Remington-Rand, and IBM, produced the majority of computer systems for general business use. The computer systems of this time were large and bulky by today's standards. Each machine contained more than 16,000 vacuum tubes. As shown in Figure 11.1, the machine would literally fill an average size room. First generation computers were used primarily for "number crunching" business activities such as inventory control and payroll.

In addition to being extremely large, first generation computer systems were prone to breakdowns and costly repairs. However, the stage was set for business computing, and in a few short years, promising new technology was available for the business user.

FIGURE 11.1
First generation computer—ENIAC

Courtesy of International Business Machines Corporation

Second Generation Business Computers

By 1958, transistor technology had replaced vacuum tube technology for computer systems. The Univac II and the IBM 7090 and IBM 7070 computers of this period were considered state-of-the-art transistorized computer systems. Figure 11.2 shows the IBM 7070 computer. The transistor could be mass-produced on an assembly line, which significantly reduced the cost of production as compared to the vacuum tube technology of the first generation computer systems.

Transistor driven computers were much cheaper to produce and much more reliable than their earlier vacuum counterparts. Reduced cost and increased dependability sparked tremendous growth in the business computer market. From 1955 to 1958, it is estimated that the number of computers installed in the United States increased tenfold.

Even with the reduced cost of the second generation business computers, most business organizations still could neither afford the machines nor the technicians required to operate and program them. The good news was that technology was not standing still; the third generation computer system was just around the corner.

Third Generation Business Computers

In April 1964, IBM announced its IBM 360 family of computers, which utilized integrated circuits instead of transistor technology. This an-

FIGURE 11.2
Second generation computer—IBM 7070

Courtesy of International Business Machines Corporation

nouncement has been described as the turning point in business computer use. The integrated circuit technology substantially reduced the chance for computer errors. Research indicated that one could expect more than thirty million hours of computer use without a circuit failure. In addition to increased processing speeds, the circuits could be mass-produced; this significantly reduced the cost of each third generation business computer. Figure 11.3 shows the IBM 360. However, it wasn't until the mid–1970s that the price of a business computer system dropped below $20,000. By then, the growth of the minicomputer was underway.

Minicomputers for Business

Prior to the mid–1960s, all computers were large and expensive tools called mainframe computers. Digital Equipment Company (DEC), Hewlett-Packard, and other companies saw an opportunity to develop computer systems for the small business user. They produced computers with smaller memory capacities and reduced processing speeds at lower costs. These computers became known as minicomputers. By

FIGURE 11.3
Third generation computer—IBM 360

Courtesy of International Business Machines Corporation

the time the minicomputers began to develop a hold on the low-end computer market (small business user), new technological innovation was once again promising more technology for less money.

Microcomputers for Business

Microprocessor technology was developed during the late 1960s and early 1970s. Microprocessor technology can be described as a "computer on a chip." Microprocessors are extremely small integrated circuits on silicon chips, as shown in Figure 11.4. The capabilities of microprocessors are truly amazing. More data can be sorted in smaller spaces, processed more rapidly, and manufactured for fewer dollars than any other computer technology to date. For example, "Today, the circuitry for an entire computer can be contained on a single chip at a cost of less than $25.00. These microcomputers have many times more computing power than the original ENIAC, are a thousand times more

FIGURE 11.4
Motorola's MC68020 Microprocessor

Courtesy of Motorola, Inc.

reliable, occupy 1/2,000,000 the volume, and cost 1/16,000 as much" (Shelly and Cashman, 1980).

The rapid development of microcomputers during the 1970s severely limited the growth potential of the minicomputer. By 1980, the small business owner could purchase a full-fledged business computer for under $10,000. As illustrated in Figure 11.5, the impact of the microcomputer has been so great on the entire computer industry that it has threatened the very existence of traditional mainframe computer manufacturers who had not developed microcomputer products.

Today's business computer systems consist of mainframes, minicomputers, and microcomputers. Many large businesses use all three types in some combination, while many small businesses have only one microcomputer. Before we can seriously discuss today's business computers, it is important to trace the development of office computers since the mid–1960s. Today's business computer systems are not just the data processors of the 1960s; they are true information

FIGURE 11.5
Micro—mini—mainframe market

Percentage of Worldwide Market by U.S. Manufacturers

	Mainframes	Minicomputers	Microcomputers*
1975	83%	9.5%	7.5%
1980	60%	17.0%	23.0%
1985	36%	21.0%	33.0%

*Small business computers, office word processors, and desktop computers
February 15, 1982, *Business Week*

processors. Yesterday's computers were machines that processed accounting, inventory, and budget data; today's computers are machines that process both data and words.

WORD PROCESSING: 1964 TO THE PRESENT

Prior to 1964, the clerical activities of businesses in the United States were performed on manual or electric typewriters. In 1964, IBM released the Magnetic Tape Selectric Typewriter (MT/ST) shown in Figure 11.6. The major feature of the MT/ST system was its ability to record text on a magnetic recording surface similar to a tape recording device. The MT/ST also contained an editing feature. Typists could add, delete, or edit characters, words, sentences, or paragraphs from documents stored on magnetic tape. Once the recorded document was edited, it could be typed on paper from the magnetic tape at speeds exceeding 100 words per minute.

By 1970, magnetic tape typing systems were being replaced by magnetic card systems. The magnetic card typewriter, shown in Figure 11.7, worked on the same recording principle as the magnetic tape system with the exception that the text was stored on a magnetic card.

Electronic Typewriters

The development of electronic typewriters was logical in the evolution of text processing. Electronic typewriters, like those shown in Figure 11.8, replaced magnetic tape and card systems because of their expanded memory capabilities and advanced text editing features. Electronic typewriters have suffered the same fate as the minicomputer. The rapid growth of word processors which have massive storage capability and full screen displays has severely limited the growth potential of electronic typewriters. Although substantial numbers of electronic typewriters are sold each year, they are considered poor investments when compared to the cost/performance ratios established by word processors.

FIGURE 11.6
IBM® Magnetic Tape Selectric Typewriter

Courtesy of International Business Machines Corporation

Word Processors

Low cost microcomputer-based word processors became popular purchases in business offices during the mid–1970s. Lanier, CPT, and IBM produced models with advanced text editing features and large storage capacities. Models like the ones shown in Figure 11.9 were available for less than $20,000.

As was pointed out in Chapter 3, word processors are designed for stand-alone use or for a shared-logic environment. By 1980, manufacturers of microcomputer-based data processors were offering word processing software packages for their machines. The level of word processing was not up to the standards of the dedicated word processing machines, but the price of the new information processors was significantly lower than the stand-alone word processors of CPT, Lanier, and IBM. The result was the development of integrated infor-

FIGURE 11.7
Magnetic card typewriter

Courtesy of International Business Machines Corporation

mation processors, which process both words and data, like those shown in Figure 11.10.

Word processing and data processing came from two different directions through a twenty-year period of rapid technological advancement. Now they have collided to form a vast information processing industry, which includes telecommunications. This collision has implications for the office manager with regard to office automation decisions. However, before office automation concepts are discussed, it is important to determine just how information processors actually work.

HOW TODAY'S INFORMATION PROCESSORS WORK

Today's information processors operate on the same principle as all computer systems. Hardware items are the component machine parts (i.e., disk drives, monitors, printers, keyboards, etc.) which make up the

Correcting Selectric III (1980)

Electronic 65 (1982)

Electronic 85 (1982)

Wheelwriter 3 (1984)

Wheelwriter 5 (1984)

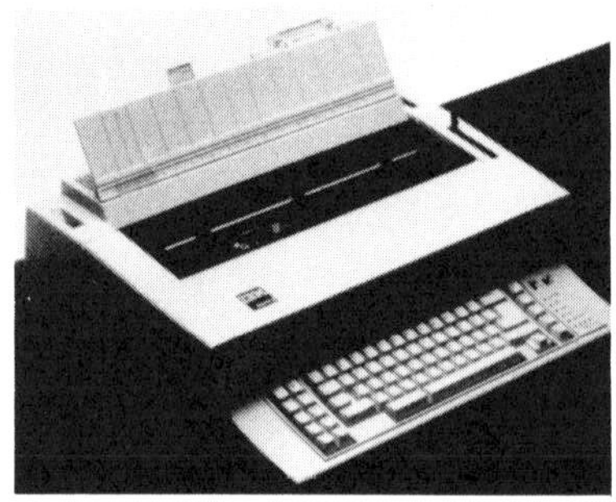

Quietwriter 7 (1984)

Courtesy of International Business Machines Corporation

FIGURE 11.9
Word processors

Courtesy of Wang Laboratories, Inc.

FIGURE 11.10
Integrated information processors

Courtesy of International Business Machines Corporation

Courtesy of AT&T Information Systems

computer system. Software items are the computer programs (sets of instructions written in various computer languages) which direct the hardware to perform certain tasks. The procedure for computer processing is called the information processing cycle.

The Information Processing Cycle

The information processing cycle consists of three phases: the input phase, the processing phase, and the output phase, as illustrated in Figure 11.11.

Input. Before data or text can be processed, it must be entered into the computer system. This is usually done by using a keyboard to type in the information. Data or text previously stored on a storage medium such as magnetic disks or tapes can also be used as input to the computer system for processing, as shown in Figure 11.12. It is important to remember that the computer can only process data or text as it is entered into the system. Therefore, if information is entered inaccurately, the output is likely to be inaccurate.

Processing. Data or text are processed by computer systems according to predetermined software packages such as word processing, accounting, records management, or spreadsheet software packages.

The computer's processor unit is called the central processing unit (CPU). As shown in Figure 11.13, the CPU is made up of three component parts: the arithmetic logic unit (ALU), the control unit (CU), and main memory cells that are used for temporary storage of data. The ALU controls all of the arithmetic functions needed to process the data and compares different values to determine which are larger or smaller. The control unit's main function is to supervise or monitor all the functions of the computer system, including the peripheral devices such as the printer and the disk drives. The main memory consists of available memory cells that are used for storing program instructions, input data, or output data until a storage device such as a disk drive is available to store the data or text.

Output. Computer-generated output can appear on several devices. The most common type of computer output is the paper document. However, output can also be sent to video display terminals (VDTs) or auxiliary storage devices such as magnetic disks or magnetic tapes, as shown in Figure 11.14.

Computer Software

There are three basic types of computer software: operating system software, applications software, and communication software.

FIGURE 11.11
Information processing cycle

Operating system software. This type of software is the critical component of any computer system. The operating system is a large and complex program which coordinates all of the hardware functions of the computer system with the specific software packages to be used with that system. As a result, if an accounting software package is written for use on a computer with a particular operating system, it will not work on a computer system with a different type of operating system.

Most computer manufacturers have developed their own operating systems for use with their computers. For example, the operating system for most Radio Shack computers is the Radio Shack TRS–DOS operating system. Apple computers run on the Apple DOS operating system and the IBM PC uses the MS–DOS operating system. The AT&T microcomputers utilize both the MS–DOS and Unix operating systems.

An emerging trend seems to be for computer manufacturers to develop computers that utilize the most popular operating systems available at the time. The reason for this is that software availability

FIGURE 11.12
Input phase of the information processing cycle

FIGURE 11.13
Processing phase of the information processing cycle

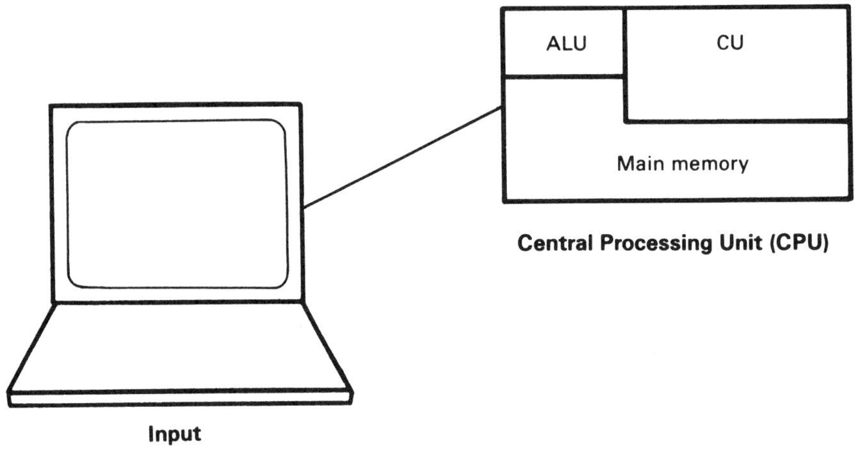

is the key to sales, and the operating system dictates the types of software that will run on the computer. An example of this trend is the new Radio Shack series of computers that use the popular MS–DOS operating system. This is a radical departure from Radio Shack's other computers, all of which used the TRS–DOS operating system.

Applications software. The programs written for specific purposes, such as accounting, word processing, records management, and financial planning, are types of applications software packages. These packages are usually written with a particular market in mind and for a particular operating system. Applications packages vary in sophistica-

FIGURE 11.14
Output phase of the information processing cycle

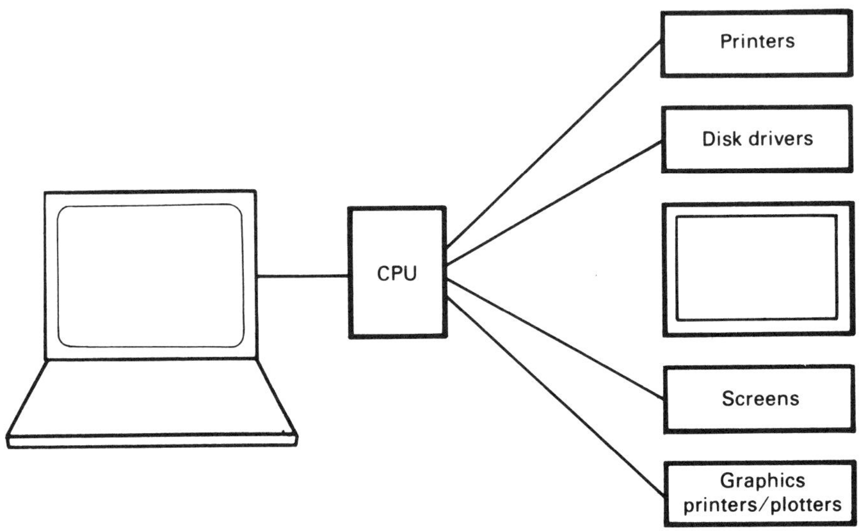

FIGURE 11.15
Computer networks

Courtesy of AT&T Information Systems

tion and price. Prior to the microcomputer explosion, applications software was developed primarily by the computer manufacturer. Today, applications software may be designed either by the manufacturer or by enterprising software companies.

Communication software. This type of software is relatively new to the computer marketplace. Communication software packages are sets of written computer codes which make it possible for the computer to interface, or work in connection with, the telephone and communication satellite systems.

COMPUTER NETWORKS

One of the most promising features of today's computer systems is computer networks. One of the objectives of administrative support systems in Chapter 8 was to get the right information to the right people at the right time. Computer networks are designed to do just that. Computer networks connect computers from various departments or office locations so that users from different aspects of an organization can all have access to the same data. Computer networks can be developed to service computer users from different departments in the same building, across town, or over great distances (see Figure 11.15). It is estimated that nearly seventy-five percent of all computer systems installed have networking features.

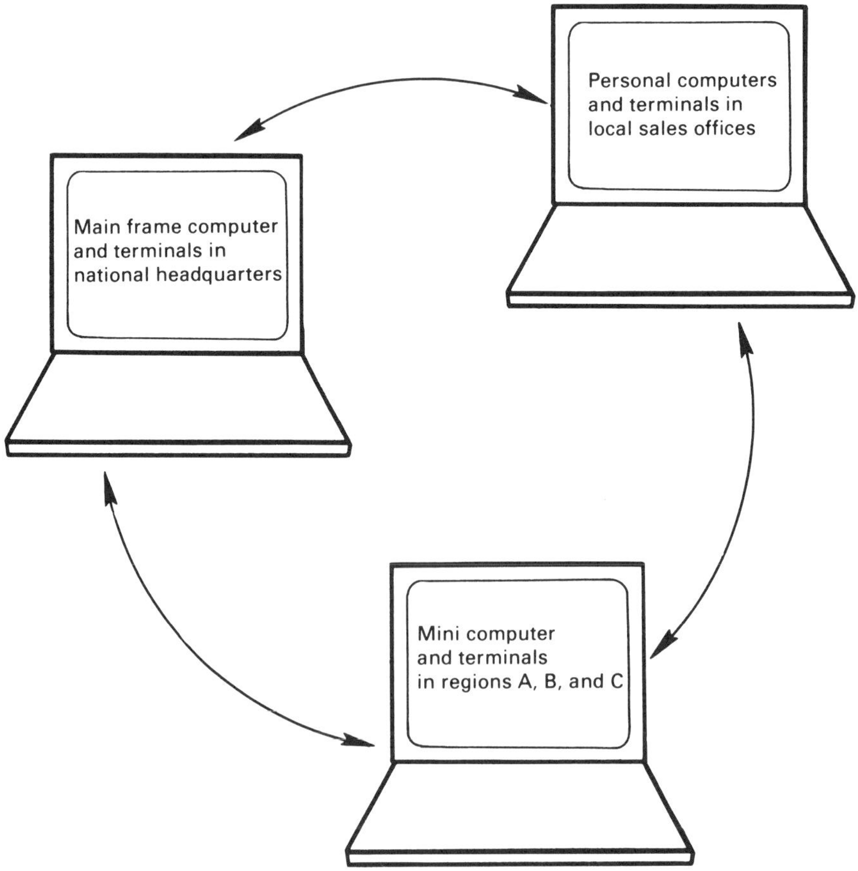

FIGURE 11.16 *Distributed information processing*

Computer networking strategies are also used to connect computers of different sizes at different locations. For example, a company may require different types of computing at various levels within the organization. This would dictate the use of a combination of microcomputers, minicomputers, and maybe even a mainframe computer. This process, shown in Figure 11.16, is called *distributed information processing*.

SUMMARY

1. The use of computers for business office applications is growing rapidly.
2. The three generations of computer development utilized vacuum tubes, transistors, and integrated circuits.

3. Today's computers, called information processors, can process both text and data.
4. The information processing cycle consists of three phases: the input phase, the processing phase, and the output phase.
5. There are three types of software: operating system software, applications software, and communication software.
6. Computer networks allow computers to communicate with each other.
7. Distributed information processing is the use of computer systems at different locations within the organization.

STUDENT ACTIVITIES

Active Orientation

1. Contact a local company which uses information processing equipment and ask for a list of the administrative activities which are automated. Share this information with the class.

2. Use the information processing cycle model to diagram the activities of a company's purchase order process.

Independent Problems

1. What role does networking play in the electronic office?

2. Describe the advantages of distributed computer processing over centralized computer processing.

3. List the major functions of the CPU.

REFERENCES

Shelly, Gary B., and Cashman, Thomas J. *Introduction to Computers and Data Processing*. Fullerton, CA: Anaheim Publishing Co., 1980.

12 The Information Center

OBJECTIVES At the conclusion of this chapter, you should be able to:

1. Describe the objectives of the Information Center.
2. List the various tasks performed by Information Center personnel.
3. Describe the duties of the Chief Information Officer.
4. Prepare strategies for developing an Information Center.
5. Identify the implications of the Information Center for the administrative office manager.

INTRODUCTION

In recent years organizations have come to understand both the value and the cost of information. Information is now viewed as an asset that must be managed like other organizational assets. John J. Connell of the Office Technology Research Group describes information as ". . . an increasingly important corporate asset which should be managed with the same concern and attention as other key corporate assets—people, money, materials, and facilities." Even the federal government has identified the relative value of information. In 1977, the Commission on Federal Paperwork reported to Congress that:

> Information is not a free good, any more than pure drinking water or clean air are free goods. Government must come to regard its information flows and holdings as valued but costly assets that must be managed in the same way it manages human resources, physical assets and even natural resources.

As the United States rapidly shifts from an industrial society to an information society, organizations will continue to search for the most efficient means of processing data into information so that effective business decisions can be made. This chapter will discuss the latest organizational structure that has been developed to harness the information explosion—the Information Center.

INFORMATION MANAGEMENT

In recent years, companies in the United States have been maligned for having relatively low levels of productivity. Numerous reasons have been offered to explain this situation, including government regulations, obsolete physical plants, poor labor relations, and the decline of the work ethic. Arnold Judson of Gray-Judson, a Boston-based consulting firm, suggests that these excuses have no validity. Furthermore, he claims that "management ineffectiveness is by far the single greatest cause of declining productivity in the United States."

During the past two decades, organizations have made attempts to manage information by computerizing as much of the information flow within organizations as possible. However, the results have not always been satisfactory.

Data Processing and MIS

As companies computerized their business records, departments of data processing were established. These departments were managed by computer professionals who had high levels of technical skill but little management expertise. The results, in many cases, were ineffective management reporting procedures, which became known as the "garbage in—garbage out" syndrome.

The organizational reaction to this situation was to reorganize the data processing department (DP) into a new department known as Management Information Systems (MIS). The goal was to find individuals who had both technical and management skills to manage the information needs of the organization. The MIS function works well for many of the large data processing applications of organizations such as payroll, inventory control, accounting, and billing. However, as organizations desired to utilize the word processing and spreadsheet applications that were popular with smaller computer systems, the MIS centers were either unable to supply the service on their mainframe computers or reluctant to allow the proliferation of microcomputer workstations throughout the organization.

Peter J. Nofel describes the manager's frustration: "Waiting for DP or MIS people to develop the applications programs managers need to manipulate data in certain ways can take months, even years in extreme cases. Why the delay? Because DP and MIS are not designed to support end-user computing."

Managers who found the inflexibility of the MIS structure unacceptable have embarked upon a new concept to facilitate the flow of information within their organizations. This new concept is the Information Center.

WHAT IS THE INFORMATION CENTER?

The Information Center is an area within an organization where employees can go to learn how to use the computing resources of the company. The Information Center concept recognizes the expertise of the employee within his or her field and merely instructs the employee as to how he or she may use the company's technology more efficiently.

There is more to the Information Center concept than just the provision of computer instruction to potential users, however. The Information Center is usually designed to coordinate computing services, acquisitions of new technology, and training and development of potential users of the organization's technology.

Herb Jacobson and John Cardullo describe the two major functions of an information center as end-user computing and technical assistance.

End-user computing includes:

- ☐ training and education;
- ☐ assisting in applications development;

- ☐ developing prototype programs;
- ☐ assisting in debugging;
- ☐ consulting with the user to determine if a particular application is appropriate for end-user development;
- ☐ providing a formal means of communication between management and the traditional data processing staff;
- ☐ working with the data administration group to develop ways to make the best use of a shared-data resource; and
- ☐ generating a catalog of existing applications for future use.

Technical assistance includes:

- ☐ guiding the selection of hardware and software systems;
- ☐ helping with the selection and evaluation of applications packages;
- ☐ assisting in the choice of interactive packages;
- ☐ helping with the set-up and use of hardware;
- ☐ assisting in the set-up and use of communications;
- ☐ providing data base (or file) back-up, recovery, and archive guidelines;
- ☐ serving as a resource to answer questions from employees about the best way to proceed with a computerized application;
- ☐ determining the compatibility of equipment;
- ☐ setting standards for industry; and
- ☐ integrating equipment and long-term planning.

INFORMATION CENTER STRUCTURE AND PERSONNEL

Jacobsohn and Cardullo's description of the Information Center implies a wide variety of duties that must be performed. It also raises many questions that must be answered. How should the Center be staffed? What skills should the Center employees possess? Where does the Information Center fit in the company's organizational structure?

Structure

The structure of an Information Center, of course, will vary according to the needs and designs of each organization. Figure 12.1 illustrates the organizational structure of the Salt River Project of Arizona. The Information Center at the Salt River Project (SRP) is depicted as a line function within the Information Systems Division and provides the coordination of training and development services to SRP employees in conjunction with the data processing department, planning and control, and user support services. The SRP chart is clearly a departure from the traditional data processing or MIS organizational structures, which usually illustrate only the data processing area.

Many large organizations possess automated applications in addi-

FIGURE 12.1
Organizational structure —information center Salt River Project

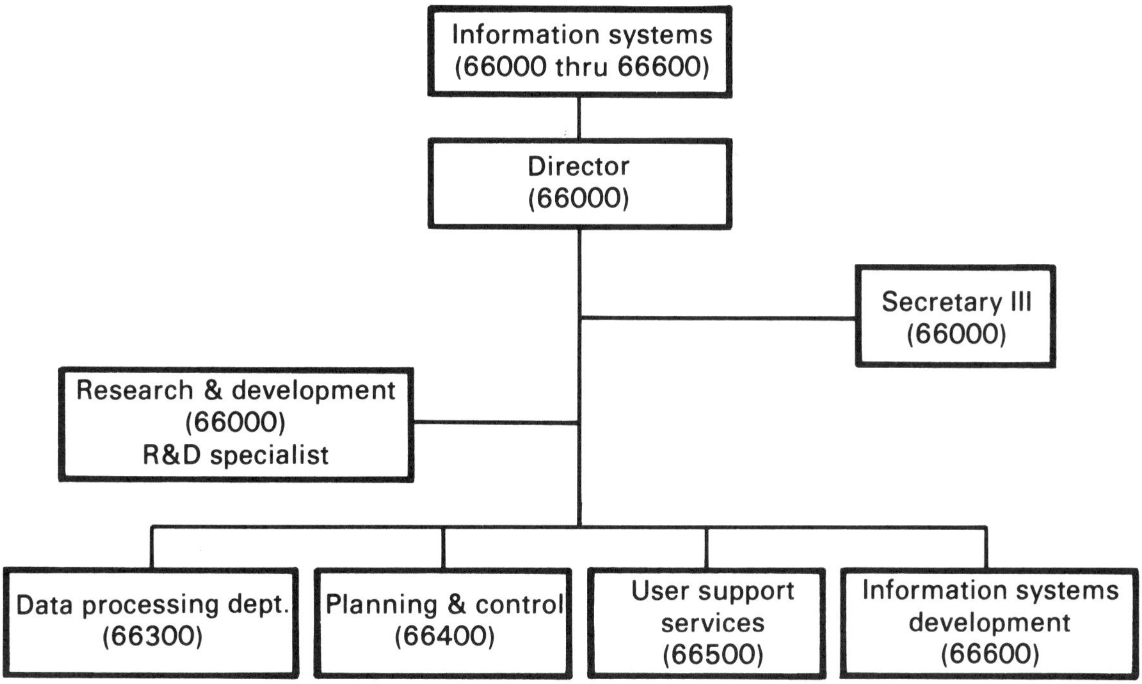

Courtesy of the Salt River Project

tion to the traditional data processing functions. These may include word processing, electronic records management, voice and image processing, and computer-output microfilm. A primary focus of an Information Center is to manage the integration of all of these technologies. Figure 12.2 illustrates the Salt River Project's fully integrated information system. The integrated nature of SRP's information system provides nearly every employee in the organization with access to many forms of technology. As a result, Information Center personnel must have an understanding of not only the technology base, but also the business policies and procedures of the company.

Personnel

Where does an organization find people with both technical and managerial skills? Recent issues of *The Wall Street Journal* and *Management Technology Journal* describe this most difficult task. Usually organizations that are frustrated by unsuccessful attempts to find someone from outside the company begin internal searches for man-

FIGURE 12.2
Fully integrated information system Salt River Project

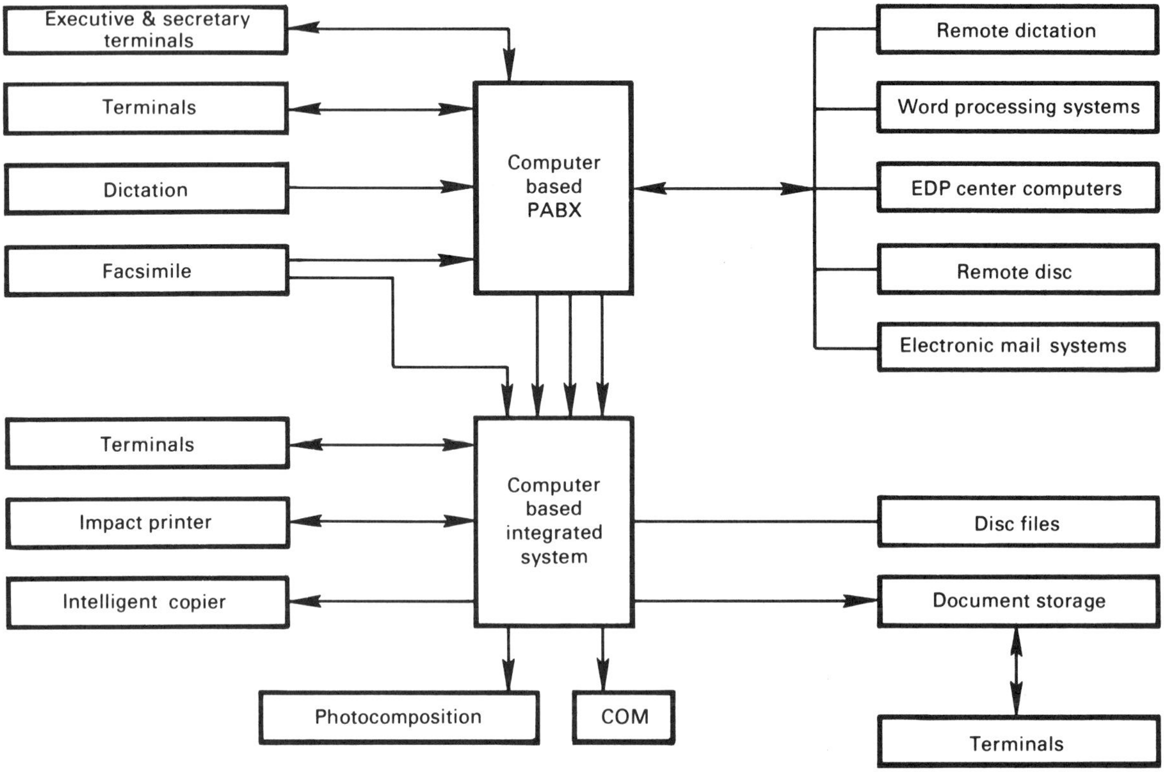

Courtesy of the Salt River Project

agers who have the potential to learn the technical skills necessary for a position in the Information Center.

E. Ward Stearns of GrandMet USA, a holding company in Montvail, New Jersey, suggests that "the chief information officer would need to both relate to management and its functions, and have enough technical knowledge to translate management's ideas into the kinds of systems they want." Stearns also recommends that the Chief Information Officer (CIO) report directly to the chief executive officer as a vice-presidential officer of the organization.

William Synott and William Gruber describe the duties of the CIO as:

> The CIO of the firm will be responsible for establishing corporate information policies, standards, and procedures for information resources management in the corporation and will

identify, coalesce, and manage information as a resource. Because information is a necessary and important ingredient in corporate and business planning, decision support systems, and control activities, the CIO will necessarily be involved in these activities with senior managers throughout the firm.

Specific responsibilities of the Chief Information Officer include:

- ☐ selecting and acquiring equipment;
- ☐ selecting and acquiring systems software;
- ☐ selecting and acquiring applications software;
- ☐ conducting feasibility studies;
- ☐ requesting software development;
- ☐ negotiating contracts for hardware and software acquisition and maintenance;
- ☐ using consultants;
- ☐ maintaining security of data, sites, equipment, and software;
- ☐ overseeing system and program implementation, documentation, controls, testing, and changes;
- ☐ establishing backup and recovery of data files;
- ☐ acquiring insurance of hardware/software and data;
- ☐ establishing data communications protocols;
- ☐ planning and installing voice and data communications;
- ☐ maintaining corporate data standards;
- ☐ ensuring data privacy; and
- ☐ using computers (non-business-use policies attempt to avoid misuse of company systems).

Patricia LaRosa of Arizona State University suggests that ". . . the CIO need not have a technical grasp of all of these areas. However, he/she must be familiar enough with them to communicate intelligently with the individual managers who have these responsibilities."

The Information Center staff. The size and specific duties of the staff will vary, depending on the objectives of the organization. However, staffing needs can be addressed by using the Salt River Project fully integrated information system model shown in Figure 12.2.

Technical support. This staff is essential to the development of an effective Information Center. Individuals with technical expertise in mainframe and microcomputer systems hardware, dictation systems, facsimile and copier systems, photocomposition, computer-generated microforms, and impact and nonimpact printer devices will be required to adequately support the automated functions of the Information Center. It is likely that qualified personnel will possess expertise in more than one of these areas.

Software support can be classified under technical support. Personnel who are responsible for developing, evaluating, and providing additional support to applications, systems, and communications software will be required. These individuals will be instrumental in coordinating the needs of management with the available company data base for making decisions.

Training and development. The members of this staff hire from various departments within SRP personnel who have both knowledge of the objectives of the organization and a desire and potential to learn the technology necessary to be of service as a trainer in the Information Center. Developing a center to coordinate the technology and training needs of an entire organization is an ambitious undertaking. It can be done, however, but it requires substantial planning and commitment from top management.

STRATEGIES FOR DEVELOPING AN INFORMATION CENTER

This section describes some strategies for developing an effective Information Center. As with all projects of this size and scope, absolute commitment from the organization's top management is required.

Step 1: Define the Scope of the Project

The goals and objectives of the Information Center should parallel the goals and objectives of the organization in terms of commitment to technology uses, the value and dissemination of information, and the continual training and development of organizational personnel.

The scope of the project should include the following information if top management support is to be expected:

- ☐ personnel requirements and costs;
- ☐ equipment requirements and costs;
- ☐ software requirements and costs;
- ☐ developmental plans;
- ☐ estimated impact on other departments (DP/MIS); and
- ☐ anticipated benefits to the organization.

Step 2: Acquire Commitment from Top Management

It is critical that top management support the concept of the Information Center. The nature of the Information Center is such that it touches, and therefore impacts on, literally every department in the organization. Top management must be made to understand that its commitment must extend to the considerable amount of financing that will be required to establish the Information Center.

Step 3: Articulate Objectives with DP/MIS

It is essential that the Information Center proponents articulate their goals and objectives with the existing data processing and/or MIS areas. The short- and long-term objectives of both groups should be discussed and agreements should be reached as to the direction both parties will take. Both groups should agree in writing how they will support each other. There are numerous opportunities for each area to share resources and personnel.

Step 4: Staff the Center

Any time an organizational system is modified, the staffing impact is critical. Individuals should be selected first for their ability to work with others in a training and development atmosphere and second for their technical abilities. Based on the assumption that present employees already possess an understanding of the goals and objectives of the organization, recruitment from within may produce more favorable results.

Step 5: Develop the Implementation Plan

The areas within the organization that are considered to be prime candidates for inclusion in one or more of the automated functions should be identified. That group should be targeted for initial action, and then a complete course of action for other groups in the organization should be developed. Figure 12.3 illustrates this course of action.

INFORMATION CENTER EVALUATION PROGRAM

The rationale for the development of an Information Center is to provide a more efficient means for supplying management with the information needed to make effective decisions. Top management should

FIGURE 12.3
Course of action

Office Systems Strategy—Course of Action
Salt River Project
PROFS/OASIS Product Expansion

	Organization	Date of Introduction
Short-Range	Remaining Service Group	10/84
	Planning and Resources	10/84
	Power Group	4th. Qtr. '84
Mid-Range	Water Group	1st. Qtr. '85
	Remainder of Company	1st. Qtr. '86
Long-Range	Next Generation	1st. Qtr. '87

Courtesy of the Salt River Project

FIGURE 12.4
Distribution of usage—PROFS study

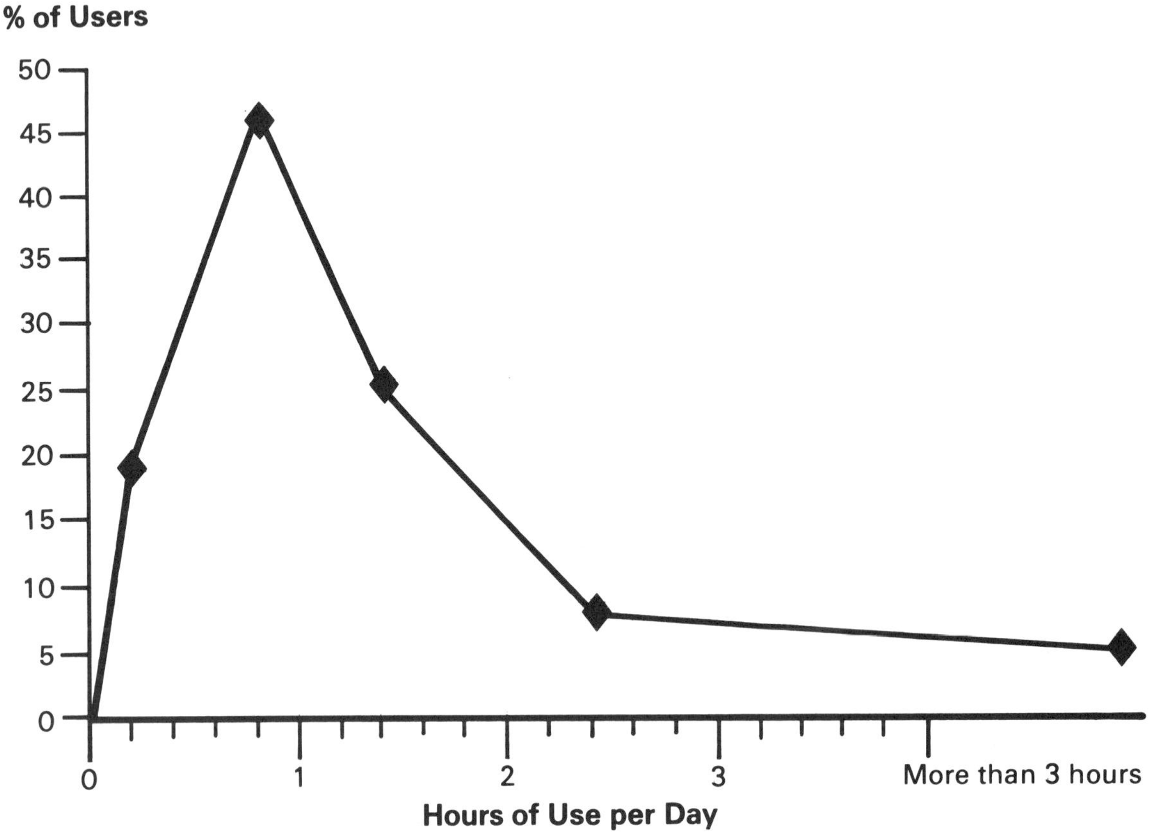

PROFS—Professional Office System from IBM
Courtesy of the Salt River Project

require that every proposed program include a method for evaluating the success of the various aspects of that program.

All systems projects, including the Information Center, should be viewed as neverending, or evolutionary. Systems must continue to evolve to meet the changing needs of the organization. Therefore, in order for systems projects to be of real value to the organization, they must contain effective evaluation programs. Figures 12.4, 12.5, and 12.6 illustrate three evaluation measures of the office automation aspect of the Salt River Project's integrated system.

FIGURE 12.5
PROFS time savings by function

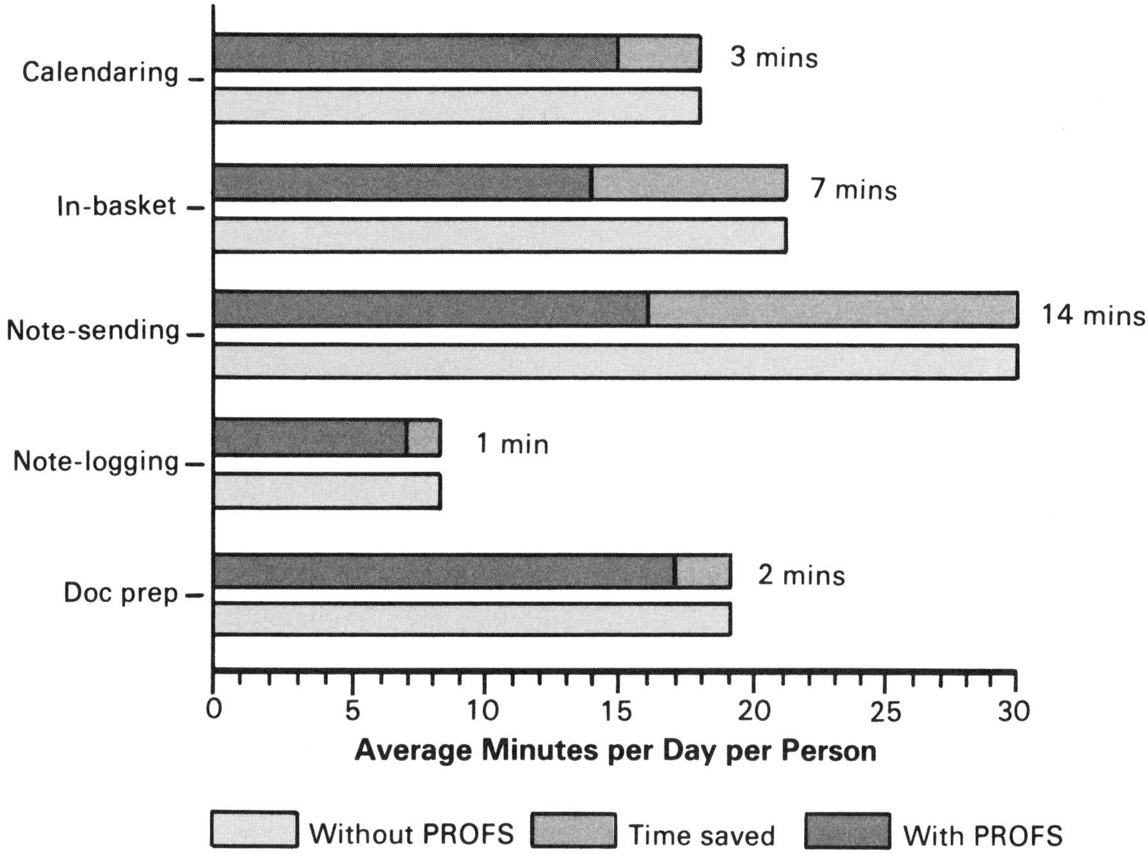

PROFS—Professional Office System from IBM

Courtesy of the Salt River Project

IMPLICATIONS FOR THE ADMINISTRATIVE MANAGER

The systems approach to developing an effective Information Center described in this chapter has numerous implications for the individual charged with managing the Center. This person will surely be severely challenged by both the wealth of technology and heavy-handed company politics. However, the rewards will be great in terms of organizational power and monetary compensation.

FIGURE 12.6
Average time savings—PROFS

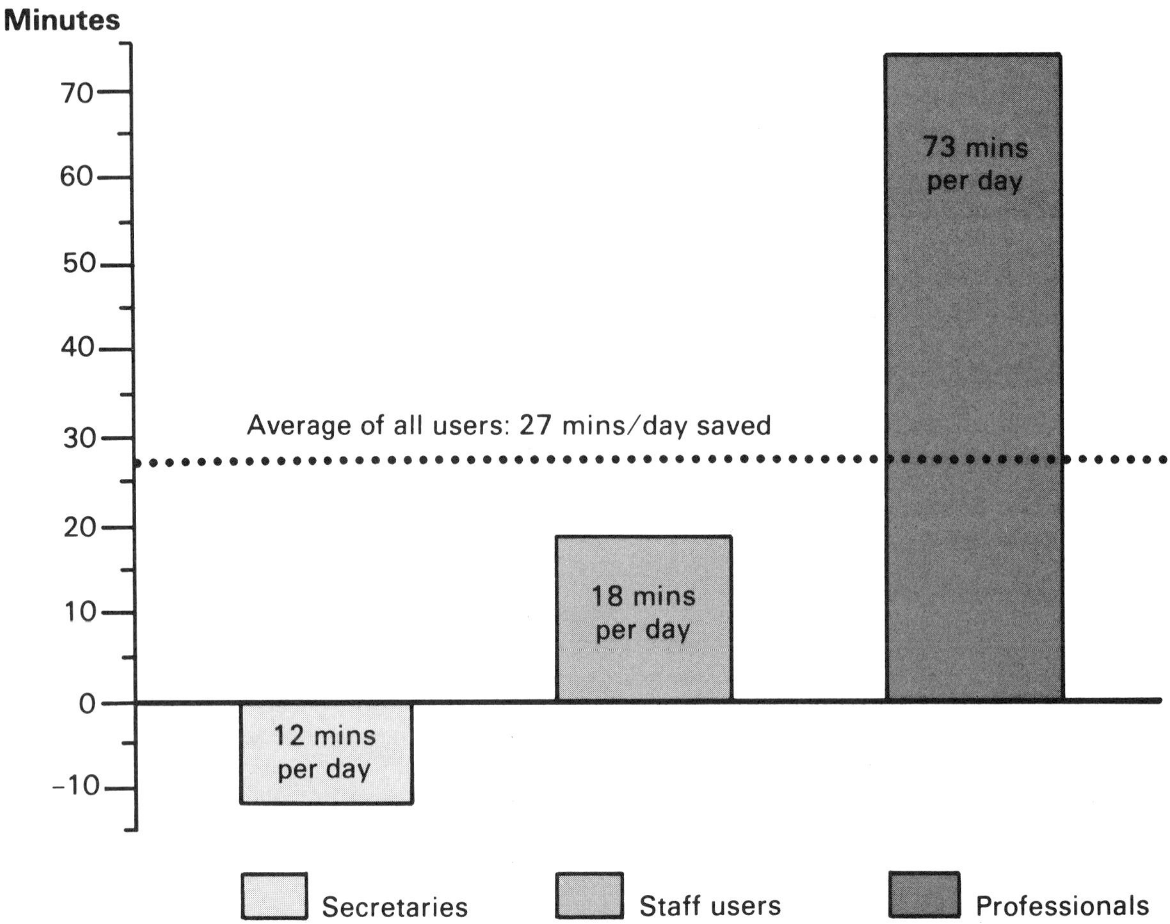

PROFS—Professional Office System from IBM
Courtesy of the Salt River Project

The administrative office manager is uniquely qualified to assume the position of Chief Information Officer in the Information Center. LaRosa suggests "the lines differentiating the administrative manager from the CIO appear blurred. If administrative services include data processing, systems and procedures, records management, office services, and standards . . . then administrative management can be considered information management." Administrative office managers should be encouraged to take up the challenge offered by the Information Center concept and seek to establish a Center in their organization.

SUMMARY

1. Management ineffectiveness is the single greatest cause of declining productivity in the United States.
2. The Information Center is an area within an organization where employees can go to learn how to use the computing resources of the company.
3. The Information Center is usually designed to coordinate the computing services, acquisitions of new technology, and the training and development of potential users of the organization's technology.
4. The two major functions of the Information Center are end-user computing and technical assistance.
5. The Chief Information Officer needs to both relate to management and its functions and have enough technical knowledge to translate management's ideas into the kinds of systems they want.
6. The Chief Information Officer will be responsible for establishing corporate information policies, standards, and procedures for information resources management and will identify, coalesce, and manage information as a resource.
7. The Chief Information Officer may not need to have a technical grasp of all areas; however, he or she must be familiar enough with them to communicate intelligently with the individual managers who are responsible for the areas.
8. A technical support staff is essential to the development of an effective information system.
9. Training and development personnel are key people in the Information Center.
10. The extent to which the Information Center is successful depends directly on the effectiveness of the training and development personnel.
11. The steps in developing an effective Information Center are:
    - ☐ define the scope of the project;
    - ☐ acquire commitment from top management;

- □ articulate objectives with DP/MIS;
- □ staff the center; and
- □ develop the implementation plan.

12. Top management should require that every systems project contain a procedure for evaluating its effectiveness.
13. The person chosen to lead the Information Center will be challenged by the wealth of technology and volatile internal company politics.
14. The administrative office manager is uniquely qualified to assume the position of Chief Information Officer in the Information Center.

STUDENT ACTIVITIES

Active Orientation

1. Invite an Information Center Director to speak to your class. If one cannot be found, contact a local office manager and ask him or her to discuss the relative merits of the Information Center concept.

2. Write to the following companies for information on their Information Centers. Ask specifically for organizational charts and evaluation program information.

- □ The Salt River Project
  Phoenix, AZ
- □ Petro–Lewis Corp.
  Denver, CO
- □ Mervyn's Stores
  Haywood, CA

Independent Problems

1. Is the administrative office manager uniquely suited for the position of Information Center Director? Why? If not, who is best suited for this position?

2. What one specific skill will best serve the Information Center Director in his or her role? Why?

REFERENCES

Jacobson, Herb, and Cardullo, John. "Information Centers: Boon or Bane." *Management Technology,* September, 1983, pp. 45–50.

Judson, Arnold S. "The Awkward Truth About Productivity." *Harvard Business Review,* September–October, 1982, pp. 93–97.

LaRosa, Patricia. "Corporate Information Executives: Preparations Regarding Roles, Responsibilities, and Job Preparation." Doctoral Dissertation, December, 1985.

Management Technology, February, 1984, cover story.

Nofel, Peter J. "Information Center." *Modern Office Technology,* February, 1984, pp. 75–77.

Stearns, Edward. Quoted in Nofel, Peter J., *op. cit.*

Synott, William R., and Gruber, William H. *Information Resource Management: Opportunities and Strategies for the 1980's.* New York: John Wiley & Sons, Inc., 1981.

13 Evaluating and Acquiring an Administrative Information System

OBJECTIVES At the conclusion of this chapter, you should be able to:

1. Describe the importance of utilizing a systems approach to purchase or lease an administrative information system.
2. Describe the process necessary to purchase or lease an administrative information system.
3. Develop a set of hardware and software specifications for office automation equipment.
4. Prepare guidelines for hands-on user evaluation of proposed office automation hardware and software.
5. Describe the importance of developing managerial and operational objectives before considering an administrative information system purchase or lease.

INTRODUCTION

Certain problems are inevitable when computer technology is brought to the administrative office. The most common concerns of managers who seek administrative information systems seem to be:

1. What equipment is available?
2. How much does the equipment cost?
3. Who will service the equipment?
4. Am I buying obsolete equipment?
5. How will our employees learn to use it?
6. Will the equipment really make us more productive?
7. Am I buying from a company that will survive?
8. What about upgrading the system at a later date?

If managers are unable to get the answers to these questions, at least two situations may occur. First, managers may ignore these important questions and purchase a system on faith from a known vendor. This process can result in the purchase of too much or too little computer system for the users' needs. Second, managers may fail to take any action at all. This decision may result in continued low productivity and employee morale and turnover problems.

This chapter provides the administrative manager with procedures for evaluating and acquiring a complete administrative information system. The procedures outlined in this chapter have been used to purchase numerous information systems for businesses, government agencies, and educational institutions. They are designed to match the needs of the users with available technology while maintaining control of the purchase process.

WHERE TO START

Chapter 11 illustrated the importance of organizational involvement in the development of computer systems. It is essential that organizational involvement begin during the evaluation and acquisition process. Thus, the first step in evaluating and acquiring an administrative information system is to identify the individuals within the organization who are in a position to provide input to the process at all functional levels of the company. Figure 13.1 illustrates this identification process.

Selecting Team Members

A project such as the acquisition of a computer system eventually touches all levels of the organization. Therefore, team members should be selected from the levels of the organization where the greatest im-

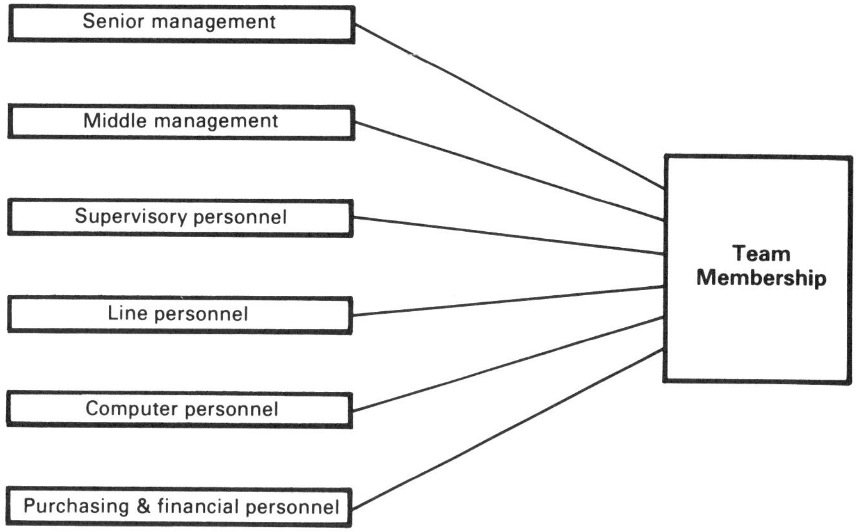

FIGURE 13.1
Team members

pact of the system will occur. For example, organizational and operational objectives must be identified if an effective information system is to be selected. This means that upper-level and middle-level managers should be selected as team members to articulate the objectives of the organization.

Supervisory and line personnel can provide operational input to the evaluation and acquisition process. These individuals are the key people in the evaluation phase because they represent the majority of potential users within the organization. Obviously, any individual with a knowledge of computer systems should be included as a team member. If your organization does not employ anyone with these skills, an individual from outside the organization should be contacted to provide this service on a consulting basis. Other important individuals to include as team members are the purchasing agents and financial managers of the organization. These people can provide the team with information concerning the writing of bid specifications and contracts with potential vendors.

THE EVALUATION AND ACQUISITION PROCESS

The following outline, which is also illustrated in Figure 13.2, represents a procedure for evaluating and acquiring an administrative information system for an organization after the team members have been selected.

FIGURE 13.2
Evaluation and acquisition process

- ☐ Step 1: Determine organizational objectives
- ☐ Step 2: Analyze the present method of operation
- ☐ Step 3: Match software
- ☐ Step 4: Select hardware
- ☐ Step 5: Develop bid specifications
- ☐ Step 6: Hold a bidders' conference
- ☐ Step 7: Evaluate bids
- ☐ Step 8: Hold a user evaluation session
- ☐ Step 9: Hold a team and user evaluation meeting
- ☐ Step 10: Make recommendations to senior management

Step 1: Determine Organizational Objectives

Team members should identify the organizational and operational objectives which will be affected by the establishment of an electronic information system. This effort will give team members the opportunity to search for an information system which closely matches the established goals of the organization.

Step 2: Analyze the Present Method of Operation

Managers should be asked by team members to analyze the existing methods of operation within their respective areas. Often, departmental operations manuals are outdated and this misinformation could be misleading to team members who are seeking automated systems to replace the current work system. Thus, it is extremely important to document the present methods of operation throughout the entire organization before the team proceeds to step 3.

Step 3: Match Software

The key aspect of any information system is the software. As stated earlier, software are sets of instructions written in various computer languages which direct computers to perform specific operations. Team members should search for software packages for accounting, word processing, records management, budget analysis, and any other applications which parallel the present methods of operation documented in step 2.

This software matching process insures that only software packages that match or come close to matching business practices are identified for use in the organization. Software should always be identified before considering hardware, or computer equipment, because without the appropriate software the information system is not functional. In addition to applications software such as accounting and word processing packages, operations software for operating systems and communications software for networking should be identified at this time.

Step 4: Select Hardware

Once the software considerations have been researched, the team can then concentrate on the hardware factors. These factors include the number of workstations, types of keyboards and screens, number and type of disk drive units, number and type of printers, modem features, network cabling, and the ergonomic design of the various workstations.

Step 5: Develop Bid Specifications

At this point in the process, organizational and operational objectives have been determined, methods of operation have been documented, and software and hardware features have been researched. Now it is time to put the information system needs of the organization into writing in order to communicate with the vendors of different computer systems models. This written communication is usually referred to as *bid specifications* or *requests for proposal* (*RFP*). The bidding process is usually required of government agencies, educational institutions, or other public organizations on capital items that cost more than $4,000. However, given the competitive nature of the computer industry, it is recommended that even organizations from the private sector consider using the bidding procedure to communicate their information system needs to the vendors.

The bid specifications should include all aspects of the intended purchase or lease of the information system. These aspects usually include:

1. hardware and software specifications;
2. delivery and set up costs;
3. training of personnel on the new system;
4. conversion assistance from the old system to the new system;
5. maintenance agreements; and
6. procedures for submitting bids.

Step 6: Hold a Bidders' Conference

Many times bid specifications that are mailed to vendors need clarification. The vendors usually have a number of questions about specific features of the bid specifications. A bidders' conference is an efficient way of handling the many questions that come from the various vendors. The conference should be held at least one week after the bid specifications have been received by the vendors and at least two weeks before the vendors must submit their bids for evaluation. This time frame will give the vendors sufficient time to review the specifications and prepare their bid packages.

The purpose of the bidders' conference is to clarify the bid specifications for the vendors. Vendors are invited to an open meeting with the organization's team to ask questions and make sure that they understand all the needs of the organization. It is important that the team appoint a spokesperson to answer the questions to avoid the confusion of potentially inconsistent responses to the vendors' questions. The spokesperson should respond as completely as possible to all questions except those inquiring about how much money the organization is willing to spend on the project. It should also be made clear that this will be the only official time when responses will be made to any vendor prior to the submission of bids. The bidders' conference will save the team many hours of time clarifying details on the telephone. It also provides the vendors with a clear picture of their competition and encourages them to submit competitive bids.

Step 7: Evaluate Bids

Once the bids have been submitted, the team should begin to evaluate them based on two key factors:

1. Does the bid meet the minimum specifications? and
2. Is the bid within the designated budget guidelines of the project?

If the bid does not meet these two criteria, it should be rejected. If none of the bids meet these criteria, the project should be halted until new budget guidelines or new project parameters can be established.

It is possible to receive very confusing bids because vendors have many models of information systems to market. An evaluation instrument like Figure 13.3 would help to place the bids in a side-by-side fashion for comparison purposes. This type of an evaluation grid will aid the team members in identifying specific items from the original bid specifications for comparison among vendor bids. The bids which meet the specifications and cost criteria should be further analyzed by user groups in a "hands-on" session.

Step 8: Hold a User Evaluation Session

A representative group of employees from the organization should be called on to try out the equipment that was proposed by the vendors who met the specification and cost criteria. This trial session will provide the organization with valuable input from the people who would actually be using the system if it were purchased from the vendor. It is important that vendors supply the same models of equipment that were proposed in their bids and not more advanced versions of the equipment.

Step 9: Hold a Team and User Evaluation Meeting

Following the user evaluation session, the team members should meet with the users to document their reactions to the vendors' hardware and software packages. The time spent at this meeting will be invaluable to the team as it prepares to make its recommendation to senior management.

FIGURE 13.3
Evaluation Grid

	VENDOR						
Specifications	**Vendor A**	**Cost**	**Vendor B**	**Cost**	**Vendor C**	**Cost**	
Hardware							
input devices:							
processor:							
printer:							
up/compatability:							
Software							
operating system memory requirements:							
compilers:							
Software applications							
accounting package:							
W/P package:							
others:							
Program support							
consulting (tech.):							
training:							
maintenance:							
security:							
local contacts:							
Financial							
lease, purchase, l/p:							
delivery cost(s):							
delivery time:							
standard/add-on chgs.:							
other:							

Step 10: Make Recommendations to Senior Management

At this point, the team should be able to recommend the purchase or lease of an information system to senior management. If, for some reason, none of the bids were acceptable to the team, then they should recommend that further study of this project be conducted at a later date.

IMPLICATIONS FOR THE ADMINISTRATIVE MANAGER

The incorporation of an electronic information system into an organization affects every individual in the company even if he or she is not an actual user of the equipment. The information system does not work in isolation any more than any individual in the organization does. Therefore, the implications for managers are numerous.

Managers must have some assurance that the proposed system is immediately available, that it won't be obsolete in the near future, that the organization's employees can learn to use it with minimal training time, and that it is cost-effective. These assurances are not easy to come by in these days of rapid technological development. Thus, it is imperative that managers consider a systems approach similar to the one described in this chapter when evaluating and acquiring an information system.

SUMMARY

1. Managers seeking to purchase or lease an administrative information system need to determine what equipment is available, how much it costs, who will service the equipment, how employees will be trained to use the equipment, and the anticipated productivity increases resulting from the new equipment.
2. Evaluation team members should come from all levels of the organization.
3. Upper-level and middle-level managers can provide the organizational objectives input to the evaluation process.
4. Supervisory and line personnel can provide operational input to the evaluation process.
5. An outside computer consultant should be hired if no internal expertise exists.
6. Purchasing agents and financial managers can provide important procedural information to the evaluation process.
7. The incorporation of an administrative information system into the organization affects every person in the organization even if he or she is not an actual user of the equipment.

8. The steps recommended to evaluate and acquire an effective administrative information system are:
   - ☐ determine organizational objectives;
   - ☐ analyze the present method of operation;
   - ☐ match software;
   - ☐ select hardware;
   - ☐ develop bid specifications;
   - ☐ hold a bidders' conference;
   - ☐ evaluate the bids;
   - ☐ hold a user evaluation session;
   - ☐ hold a team and user evaluation meeting; and
   - ☐ make recommendations to senior management.

STUDENT ACTIVITIES

Active Orientation

1. Contact a local computer vendor. Arrange to have the vendor make a presentation to your class regarding his or her office automation systems. Critique the presentation during the following class period. Discuss the following points.

- ☐ What was the vendor's marketing strategy?
- ☐ Was training discussed in depth?
- ☐ Did the vendor sound knowledgeable?
- ☐ Was software demonstrated or just talked about?
- ☐ Did the vendor bring software documentation?

2. Contact two office managers whose offices are automated. Determine the evaluation and acquisition procedures used by both managers.

Independent Problems

1. Should computer systems training be part of the purchase or lease process or should it be contracted with the vendor at a later date? Why?

2. Should the data processing manager or the administrative office manager be responsible for the purchase or lease of the administrative information system? Why?

14 The Office of the Future

OBJECTIVES At the conclusion of this chapter, you should be able to:

1. List the major challenges to be faced by managers in the future.
2. Describe the anticipated technological changes that will impact the administrative office.
3. Describe how office employees can work at home instead of at the office.
4. Identify the projected job market for secretaries, clerks, and administrative managers.
5. Discuss the importance of developing programs to evaluate administrative productivity.

INTRODUCTION

Administrative costs are increasing at an annual rate of twelve to fifteen percent, and managers and office professionals account for seventy-five percent of all administrative costs; thus, the rush to automate the administrative arena seems justified. However, many problems remain unsolved for managers seeking to automate their offices. This chapter discusses the productivity, technological, and human resource challenges which need to be addressed by management as the office automation industry continues to expand.

THE PRODUCTIVITY CHALLENGE

According to U.S. Bureau of Labor Statistics, 786 billion dollars were paid out to workers in the form of wages and benefits in 1985. Office workers received sixty percent of this pool of money. The implication is clear—the major cost of doing business in the United States can now be found in the administrative office instead of in the factories and warehouses. It is only a matter of time before administrative productivity programs begin to receive greater emphasis in companies.

Productivity Measurement

Although administrative productivity has been thought of as being more difficult to measure than factory or assembly line productivity, recent efforts by university researchers and private sector companies such as Booz, Allen, and Hamilton indicate that productivity statistics can indeed be gathered for administrative jobs. The specific job functions of managers and office professionals can and should be documented, along with the amount of time spent on each function in order to determine the cost to the company. As a greater share of the cost of doing business moves from the industrial plant to the administrative office, more emphasis will be placed on the productivity measurement of costly administrative jobs.

George Plotzke, marketing manager for AT&T's Technology Communications Group, emphasizes that "an executive typically devotes 94 percent of the workday to communications-related activities. Oral communications account for 69 percent of that time—53 percent in face-to-face meetings, 16 percent on the telephone. Twenty-five percent of the workday is consumed by written communications or mail." Plotzke also indicates that only three percent of the executive's workday is spent on "management functions" such as problem-solving, conceptualizing, and long-range planning, as shown in Figure 14.1.

It is likely that today's executives are spending too much time attempting to communicate by ineffective means such as the telephone

FIGURE 14.1
Manager's workday

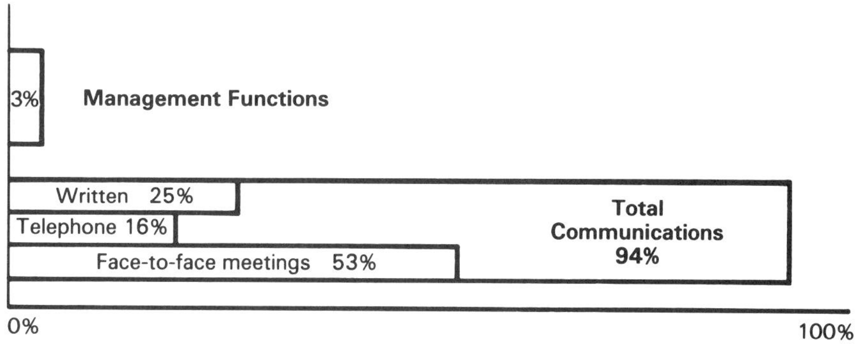

or by traveling to meetings. This wasteful effort leaves managers with too little time and energy to execute the tasks for which they were hired. Administrative productivity studies will identify these ineffective methods and illustrate their enormous costs to the organization. Managers in offices of the future will probably use electronic mail to communicate to employees within the organization.

Business organizations in the United States spend over 300 billion dollars annually in travel-related expenses. Some estimates indicate that over one-half of all business meetings in which travel was required could have been conducted more effectively through teleconferencing. Furthermore, for every dollar spent on teleconferencing, one to thirty travel dollars can be saved. At the present time, few teleconferencing sites exist around the United States. However, as the telecommunications industry continues to grow, the need for business travel as it is conducted today should decline sharply.

As companies begin to address the matter of administrative productivity, they will search for the technology which will aid them in increasing the productivity levels of administrative personnel. The following section will discuss the new office automation technology which will be available in the near future. The real promise of this technology is its ability to be integrated into a comprehensive electronic administrative network consisting of computers, printers, copiers, and communication devices.

THE TECHNOLOGY CHALLENGE

Although individual electronic workstations are currently available to administrative personnel to perform word processing, spreadsheet analysis, budget forecasting, and other functions, few office automation applications are "networked." As described in Chapter 11 and illustrated in Figure 14.2, networking allows the electronic connection

FIGURE 14.2
Local area network

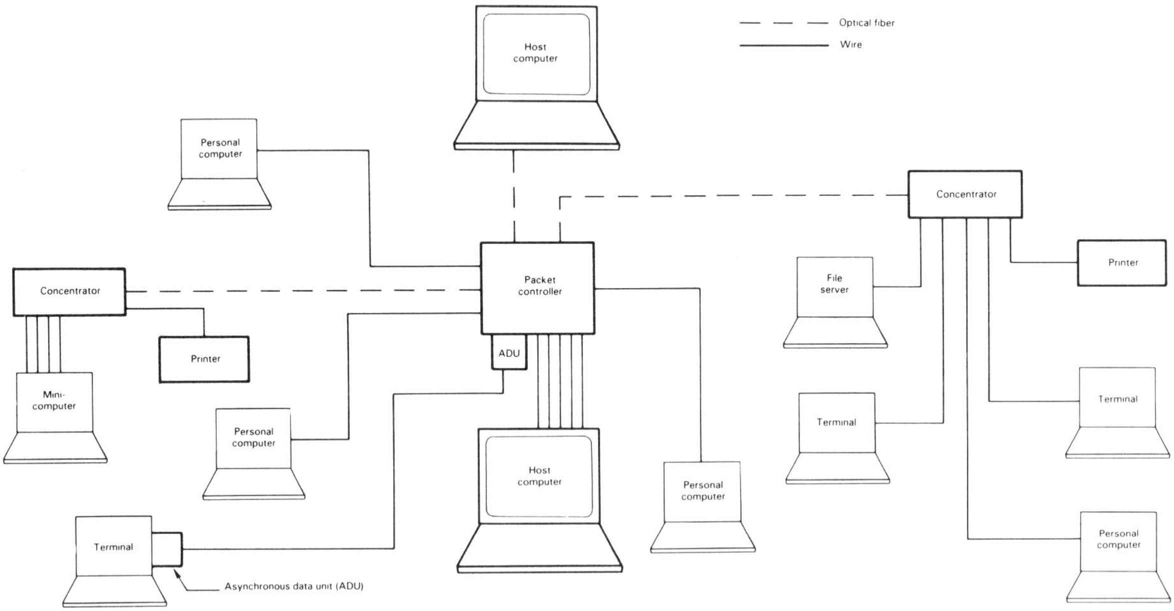

Courtesy of AT&T Information Systems

of various workstations throughout the organization for optimum communication and data sharing capabilities among administrative personnel. These networks, presently called LANS (Local Area Network Systems) represent excellent opportunities for administrators to automate many of the administrative tasks which are now performed in isolated areas of the office. This isolation often results in the duplication of work and hidden information.

Technology Integration With local area networks as the vehicle for office automation expansion, the effective integration of the various administration functions is now possible. As shown in Figure 14.3, administrative activities such as word processing, data processing, micrographics, reprographics, and electronic mail can be integrated into the same electronic system that will be used by individuals throughout the organization.

Barriers to Integration It should be noted that some organizations have been more successful at integrating their administrative technology than others. The biggest obstacle to integration at this time seems to be the failure on the part of management to handle the proliferation of personnel computers which may not be compatible to networking. Victor Poor, an executive

FIGURE 14.3
Integrated information system

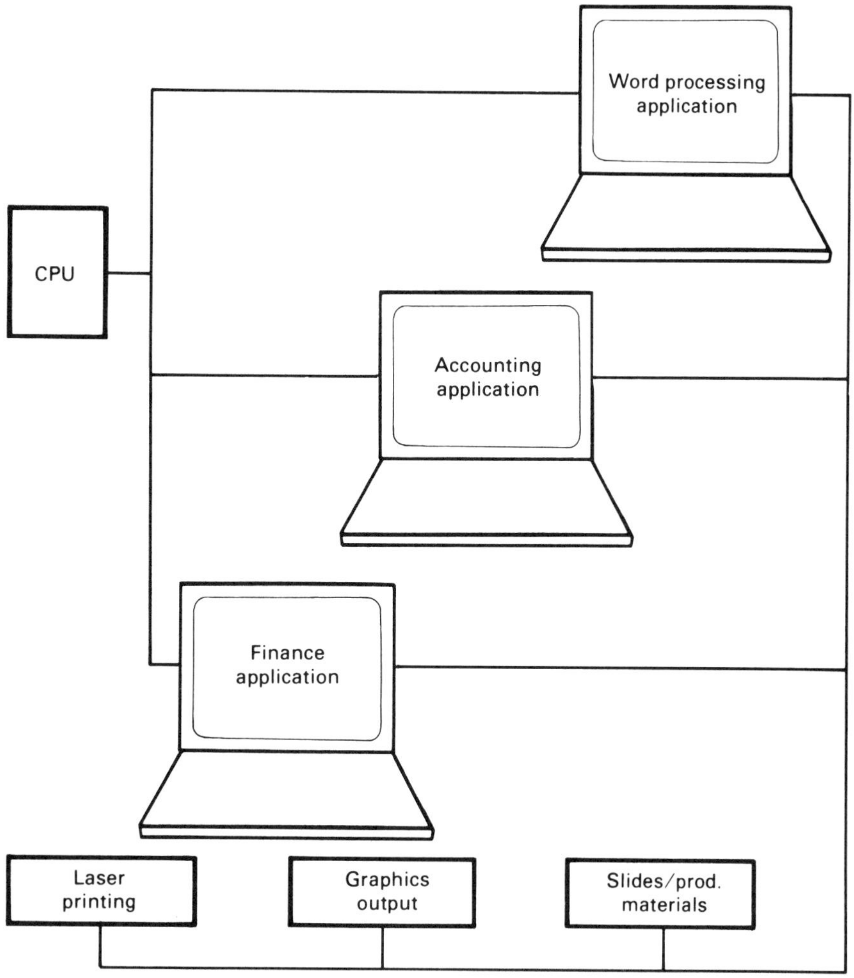

vice-president for research and development at Datapoint emphasizes this point. "God help the user who tries to link up disparate equipment."

Not all the blame should be placed on managers for failing to properly equip their companies. The computer industry has not been able to produce a clear winner in the networking race. Although Datapoint's ARCNET and Xerox's Ethernet networks have been leading the way, AT&T and IBM networks are looming on the horizon. Administrative offices will surely use local area networks in the near future, but as of this writing companies are proceeding slowly and cautiously.

The key to the development of an effective administrative information system will be the management personnel. If the management team is truly interested in administrative productivity and controlling the cost of doing business, then technology will be sought to aid them in meeting their efficiency goals. The techniques described in Part 3 of this text give the manager insight into identifying and acquiring an effective administrative information system. The extent to which managers succeed will be determined more by the skills of the management team than by the technology itself.

THE HUMAN RESOURCES CHALLENGE

The human resource challenge for the office of the future is a most interesting one. There are at least two major human resource factors to be addressed by administrative managers:

1. How will present workers deal with the changes associated with the expanding information processing technology?
2. How will administrative managers hire new and retain old employees in the face of a shrinking labor pool and an increasing job market?

Dealing with Change

Joseph McKendrick, assistant editor of *Management World,* describes the anticipated change in the administrative office as follows: "The workforce and work environment of the typical office in 1990 will be the product of perhaps the most dramatic upheaval in work relationships and demographics in North American history."

Training. As automation takes place in tomorrow's offices, considerations will have to be made for the needs of the employees. At the present time, programs designed to train office personnel on new computer equipment are rare or at best inadequate. The results of these poorly designed training programs are usually low productivity, employee turnover, and dissatisfaction with the computer system.

Environmental conditions. Ergonomic factors, which were discussed in Chapter 9, are just beginning to receive notice in companies in the United States. Ergonomically designed workstations provide a viable answer to many of the problems of productivity and health which contribute to administrative costs. In addition to the design of the workstation, health concerns are surfacing about the consequences of working at a computer screen for eight hours per day. Few conclusive studies have been conducted in the United States to determine the effects of long-term computer screen exposure.

Work scheduling. New strategies for performing administrative tasks will be considered in the future. For example, computer communications capabilities have made it possible for many workers to perform their tasks away from the office. Some employees may prefer to work at home instead of to commute to the office each day. They may choose to prepare and transmit their work from their computer terminals at home to the computer system at the office. This concept represents a substantial change in the performance of office duties, which will have a tremendous impact on the hiring and promotion practices of administrative managers.

Job scheduling. Although flexible hours and job sharing are not new concepts, they will play a greater role in work performance in the administrative office of the future. Little emphasis has been given to this concept or any other work arrangement except for the routine nine to five method of operation in most business offices. The extent to which these change factors are handled by administrative managers will determine the effectiveness of the production effort of office workers in the future. A failure to recognize the needs and concerns of the office employees presently working in the administrative office will produce increasing employee turnover problems, especially as the growing need for office workers provides new opportunities for experienced personnel.

WHERE WILL THE NEW WORKERS COME FROM?

The U.S. Bureau of Labor Statistics predicts that by 1990, seventy-five percent of the labor force will be engaged in information occupations. Furthermore, 685,000 new office jobs will be available annually through 1990. Nearly half of these (305,000) will be secretarial positions. The remaining 380,000 openings will be for bookkeepers, file clerks, receptionists, stock clerks, office machine operators, and cashiers. Overall, during the period from 1978 through 1990, more than sixty-six million jobs will become available in the United States. More than one-half of these will be in white-collar occupations.

The total number of available administrative office positions tells only part of the story. By 1990, it is anticipated that women will comprise more than sixty percent of the United States workforce. McKendrick suggests that this fact, coupled with "raised consciousness about their potential" will provide a definite pressure on management to provide women with interesting and rewarding positions in the administrative office.

By 1990, the largest portion of the workforce will be between the ages of twenty-five and forty-five. The number of entry-level workers will be significantly less, creating a substantial labor shortage for entry-level office positions. Experienced office employees will begin to understand their relative worth in the marketplace. This understanding is likely to lead to demands for increases in salaries and benefits, more flexible work schedules, more management responsibility, and a more pleasant and productive working environment.

It seems clear that administrative managers in the future will be competing for experienced workers from a shrinking labor pool. The major source of these experienced workers will probably be other companies. Therefore, managers will have to provide attractive job packages to compete successfully in the administrative job market.

IMPLICATIONS FOR THE ADMINISTRATIVE MANAGER

Administrative managers must face the fact that the administrative office is no longer the place where women are hired to perform routine office tasks with outdated equipment at wages which represent only sixty percent of those earned by male counterparts. Technological and demographic alterations have redefined the office of the future to include a complete rewriting of the definition of the term *human resource*.

Managers in offices of the future will be required to use systems skills to design jobs which not only meet the needs of the organization but also incorporate the latest technology to address productivity quotas. Of equal importance will be the ability of the manager to provide job packages which are attractive to the limited number of available experienced employees. These packages will undoubtedly include substantial salary and benefit adjustments from present levels, office automation training and development programs, management responsibilities, ergonomically designed workstations, and flexible work schedules. Part 4 of this text was designed specifically for the manager who recognizes the importance of the human resource.

SUMMARY

1. Administrative costs are increasing at a rate of twelve to fifteen percent annually.
2. Managerial costs represent seventy-five percent of all administrative costs.
3. Office workers received sixty percent of the 1.3 trillion dollars paid in the form of salaries and benefits in 1980.
4. The major cost of doing business in the United States is associated with administrative expenses.

5. An executive devotes ninety-four percent of his or her day to communications-related activities.
6. Only three percent of a manager's day is spent on problem-solving, conceptualizing, and long-range planning.
7. Business organizations in the United States spend over 300 billion dollars annually in travel-related expenses.
8. For every dollar spent on telecommunications, one to thirty travel dollars can be saved.
9. LANS (Local Area Network Systems) represent excellent opportunities for administrators to automate various tasks.
10. Administrative activities such as word processing, data processing, micrographics, reprographics, and electronic mail can be integrated into the same electronic system that will be used by individuals throughout the organization.
11. The key to developing an effective administrative information system will be the management team.
12. At the present time, programs designed to train office personnel on the use of new computer systems are rare, or at best inadequate.
13. Ergonomically designed workstations provide a viable answer to many problems of productivity and health which contribute to administrative costs.
14. Flexible hours and job sharing will play a greater role in work performance in the administrative offices of the future.
15. By 1990, seventy-five percent of the workforce will be engaged in information occupations.
16. By 1990, 680,000 office jobs will be available annually.
17. By 1990, the largest portion of the workforce will be between the ages of twenty-five and forty-five.
18. By 1990, over sixty percent of the American workforce will be comprised of women.
19. Managers in offices of the future will be required to use systems skills to design jobs which not only meet the needs of the organization but also meet the needs of the employees.

STUDENT ACTIVITIES

Active Orientation

1. Contact a local company and interview the administrative manager to determine the following:

- ☐ Have they considered automating any of the office functions? If not, why not?
- ☐ What problems have they encountered? Do they have any solutions?

2. Contact a local office automation vendor and determine the problems encountered in trying to sell office automation to administrative managers.

Independent Problems

1. What implications do the U.S. Bureau of Labor Statistics projections have for you as a future worker?

2. Given the projected job market for the administrative office area, what possibilities are there for unionization of office employees? Discuss your opinions with others in your class.

REFERENCES

McKendrick, Joseph. "The Office of 1990 Human Resources." *Management World,* January, 1982, pp. 15–17.

Plotzke, George T. "New Technology Creates 'The Office of the Future'." *Management Review,* February, 1982, pp. 8–15.

PART 4 HUMAN RESOURCES MANAGEMENT

Part 4 of *Administrative Information Systems: People and Technology* presents a practical approach to managing the most important organizational resource—the *Human Resource.* Special emphasis is given to strategies for acquiring, supervising, and motivating administrative personnel. Guidelines are presented for developing job descriptions and specifications for today's administrative workers. In addition, strategies are listed for measuring administrative productivity and compensating administrative personnel.

15 Acquiring Office Employees

OBJECTIVES At the conclusion of this chapter, you should be able to:

1. Describe the procedures for acquiring office employees.
2. List possible sources of employees for the business office.
3. Identify important legislation concerning the hiring process.
4. Describe the features of an effective employee orientation program.

INTRODUCTION

In Chapter 14 the growing need for administrative office workers was discussed. Because of the tremendous rate at which these jobs will become available, it appears that there will be too many jobs, and not enough people to fill them. This set of circumstances creates a very demanding situation for business organizations. Finding qualified personnel will continue to be a major problem for business office managers. Therefore, an effective office employee acquisition program should be a high priority item for business organizations.

In recent years, increased government regulations in the areas of tax reporting, compensation and retirement programs, and affirmative action have created needs for larger office staffs. As stated earlier, sixty cents out of every dollar spent for wages, salaries, and benefits in the United States goes to office workers. Consequently, business organizations are faced with the task of finding expensive office workers at a time when the office labor pool is small.

WHERE TO LOOK

Assuming office managers have conducted effective job analyses, and are therefore well aware of the specific type of employee needed, the candidate search can begin. Office administrators should become familiar with the available sources of labor in their geographic area. Typical sources of labor are:

- ☐ internal listings of employees in the personnel department;
- ☐ temporary help agencies;
- ☐ educational institutions;
- ☐ public employment agencies;
- ☐ private employment agencies; and
- ☐ job advertisements in local papers and professional journals.

Internal Referrals

An often overlooked source of qualified, dedicated employees is the organization's own human resources department. Many well-managed human resources departments keep track of information for each employee concerning skills and job aspirations. It is possible that employees who are presently holding other positions within the organization are qualified for employment in the office and desire an internal transfer. If the human resources department doesn't keep track of this type of employee information, the posting of job openings in various departmental locations could result in applications from interested individuals from within the company. Some organizations which are caught in desperate situations such as the nursing shortage have gone to "bounty hunting" programs. Here, employees of the hospital are paid a "bounty fee" of several hundred dollars for finding qualified candidates.

Finding employees from within the organization provides office administrators with some unique opportunities. Individuals who are presently employed in the organization have:

1. current knowledge of the organization;
2. a job history specific to the organization; and
3. recommendations from the company's own supervisors.

These factors provide the office administrator with employee data which should be somewhat more reliable than employee data from outside sources.

Another source of qualified candidates can come from within the organization. Employees can be encouraged to refer people they know personally as potential employees of the company. This practice can add to the prestige of the employee because that person feels that he or she is an important part of all aspects of the company. However, if an employee refers a person who is not suitable or qualified for the job, it could cause embarrassment to everyone involved.

Temporary Help Agencies

Temporary help agencies such as Kelly Services and Manpower provide the business office manager with temporary or short-term sources of office employees. Employers normally pay a fee to the temporary service, which in turn provides an employee who is qualified to perform the position outlined by the employer. The business organization benefits from the hiring of temporary employees in several ways. There are:

1. reduced employee costs for recordkeeping;
2. no expenses for payroll taxes;
3. no expenses for vacation, sick leave, and fringe benefits; and
4. no expenses for worker compensation.

Business organizations should proceed with caution when dealing with temporary help agencies. Business office administrators must know the type of skills required for the job to be filled by the temporary person. Although this is an important factor in hiring anyone, whether they are temporary or permanent, it is especially important when trying to request personnel from a temporary agency. The following is a set of procedures that is recommended for conducting employee searches with temporary agencies.

1. Determine the specific job requirements and provide the temporary agency with an up-to-date job description.

2. Determine the length of time that the temporary person will be needed.
3. Calculate the cost of the temporary placement.
4. Check the credentials of the temporary agency.
5. Prepare the present office staff for the arrival of the temporary person.
6. Prepare a proper orientation for the temporary person, which includes a complete work assignment sheet and the assignment of an "office buddy."

Educational Institutions

Many public and private secondary and post-secondary educational institutions provide excellent sources of office employees for business organizations. Some schools provide placement services for their students, and many have work study, co-op, or internship programs. These programs not only provide students with real life experiences but also give business office administrators an opportunity to cultivate prospective employees. The educational market should not be overlooked as a source of office employees. Many of these students have both the applications and computer skills necessary to work in the business office.

Public Employment Services

Most states have local or regional employment offices known as the Job Service, which provide employee information at no charge to either the employer or the prospective employee. In recent years however, a lack of funds has severely handicapped these agencies.

Private Employment Agencies

Private employment agencies also provide business organizations with potential employees. They are commonly used by small and medium sized companies to do the initial screening of applicants. In the long run, this type of arrangement saves both time and money for the applicants. The agencies usually charge a fee to either the employer or the employee for their services. This fee is either a flat fee or a percentage of the employee's first year salary.

Some private employment agencies specialize in a certain type of employee placement, such as executive placements or engineering and high-tech placements. In all cases, the business organization is encouraged to check out the employment agency with the local chapter of the Better Business Bureau.

Advertisements

Advertising for employees in newspapers has been used for many years as a means of attracting applicants to jobs. However, the major disadvantage of this type of blanket advertising is the number of applicants that may apply or attempt to apply for a job. During the present recession, a factory in the Midwest advertised in a local newspaper for

50 job openings and had more than 5,000 requests for applications. Although these numbers are indicative of the recession, newspaper advertisements generally produce more unqualified applicants than they do genuine candidates. A common way to solve this logistical dilemma is through the use of blind ads, where the applicant writes to a post office box number. This process simplifies the screening process immensely.

Recent job discrimination legislation concerning how jobs can be advertised makes advertising a job opening even more complicated. For example, it is illegal to describe a job in an advertisement which indicates a preference in terms of age, sex, race, or religion.

Despite the disadvantages of job advertisements, many organizations continue to inform the public of their occupational needs through printed media such as professional journals. Many professional organizations provide their own placement service through their journals. Other business publications such as *The Wall Street Journal, Barron's,* and *Management World* provide specific reader groups with employment information.

A recent development with respect to the growth of the home computer market has produced an interesting approach to job hunting. A number of private employment agencies are providing computerized data bases of job information which can be accessed by the employer and the prospective employee directly through a home computer network. This type of employment information exchange appears to be quite promising for both the employer and the prospective employee.

PERSONNEL ACQUISITION PROCEDURES

Procedures for acquiring office employees will vary depending on the size and resource availability of the organization. However, as in most endeavors, structure aids the organization in completing a given task. Therefore, the following guidelines are suggested to any business organization seeking office personnel.

The Application Process

After prospective employees have been notified of a job opening, they are asked to submit an application. This application form is usually the official application form of the organization. The application form generally asks for information concerning the applicant's personal information, educational background, work experience, and professional references.

The Interview Process

In addition to reviewing application information, employers usually require one or two personal interviews with prospective employees.

The interview is used to verify application information, to view the personal appearance of the applicant, and to gather additional information about the applicant that could not be obtained in an efficient manner on an application form. During the interview the interviewer should ask only questions that relate directly to the occupational qualifications of the position for which the candidate is interviewing. Questions about intimate subjects such as a person's age, marital status, sexual preferences, or religious practices are out of order in an interview. Therefore, in order to prevent discrimination under the fair employment practices regulations, an interviewer should only ask questions that produce data that is useful in predicting job-relevant behavior.

There are several types of job interviews. The three most common types are the direct interview, the indirect interview, and the patterned interview.

The direct interview. The purpose of the direct interview is to ask specific questions concerning the skills and job preferences of the candidate. Questions such as

- ☐ What is your work shift preference?
- ☐ Have you used a word processor before? and
- ☐ Do you take shorthand?

are typical of the questions of a direct interview process.

The indirect interview. The purpose of the indirect interview is to get the applicant to open up. Questions asked in an indirect interview are usually open-ended. The following are typical indirect interview items.

- ☐ What are your positive and negative qualities?
- ☐ What position do you expect to hold five years from now?
- ☐ Why do you want this job?

The indirect interviewer must be a good listener as well as a good facilitator so that as much pertinent information can be gathered about the candidate as possible without wasting valuable time by allowing the applicant to ramble.

The patterned interview. The purpose of the patterned interview is to allow one or more interviewers to screen large numbers of people for a number of jobs. A standard printed form containing a series of key questions is used by each interviewer. The following are typical patterned interview questions.

- ☐ When could you begin work?
- ☐ How many years of experience do you have?

- ☐ What are your salary requirements?
- ☐ What is your past salary record?
- ☐ Are you willing to work overtime? If so, when?

Questionnaires can be gathered and reviewed by the Personnel Department. This type of interview can free upper-level personnel from the time-consuming task of initially interviewing multitudes of prospective employees.

EMPLOYMENT LEGISLATION

Substantial employment legislation has been passed in the last twenty years. It is extremely important that administrative office managers be aware of these legislative actions. The following is a listing of the most significant employment legislative actions.

- ☐ **Fair Labor Standards Act and the Equal Pay Act (1963).** The Equal Pay Act of 1963 amended the Fair Labor Standards Act to forbid employers to discriminate with respect to wages and salaries on the basis of the sex of the employee.
- ☐ **Civil Rights Act (1964).** The Civil Rights Act of 1964 and the amendments of 1972 prohibit employers from excluding job applicants from employment or from discharging employees for reasons based on race, color, religion, sex, or national origin. The Equal Employment Opportunity Commission (EEOC) was created under Civil Rights Act guidelines as an enforcement agency to seek compliance with employment law.
- ☐ **Age Discrimination in Employment Act (1967).** This legislation prohibits employment discrimination based on the age of the individual worker. The law prohibits discrimination against individuals who are between forty and sixty-five years old.
- ☐ **Special Group Employment Legislation.** This legislation, which is commonly known as Affirmative Action, is designed to prevent employment discrimination to specific groups of individuals such as women, minorities, handicapped workers, and veterans. The Rehabilitation Act of 1973 is designed to eliminate employment discrimination to qualified workers because of physical or mental handicaps. The Vietnam Era Veterans Readjustment Act of 1974 requires employers to take "affirmative action" to employ veterans of the Vietnam war.

EMPLOYEE ORIENTATION

An often overlooked aspect of a personnel acquisition program is employee orientation. A proper orientation program can be both informative and comforting to the new employee. An effective office employee orientation program means more than showing the employee his or her parking space and the direction to the lunch room. This section outlines a comprehensive office employee orientation program.

Materials

The office manager or department supervisor should gather the necessary materials before the new employee arrives for work on the first day. These materials may include an employee handbook, company policy statements, company and departmental organizational charts, and a company history brochure. In addition to this information, a complete set of working supplies should be made available at the employee's workstation so that the employee can begin work with all the necessary materials at hand.

Notifying Other Workers

The office administrator should inform other workers in the area about the arrival of the new employee. Attempts should be made by the co-workers to welcome the new employee and to offer their help and support during the first few days of employment. Depending on the number of employees in the area, it may be possible to have a breakfast/coffee greeting on the first day in honor of the new employee. This type of effort will make the new employee feel welcome and offer an opportunity for the workers to get to know one another in a less formal setting.

The "Buddy System"

A popular practice in some office settings is to assign a "buddy" to the new employee for a one or two week period. This buddy should be familiar with the workload of the new employee so that specific guidance, as well as general company information, is available to the new employee during the transition period.

Because of staff shortages or company policy, the office supervisor

FIGURE 15.1
Office orientation checksheet items

- ☐ Provide workstation materials.
- ☐ Notify co-workers.
- ☐ Assign an "office buddy."
- ☐ Arrange appointments with payroll and personnel.
- ☐ Arrange end-of-first-week meeting with new employee.
- ☐ Schedule a "get acquainted" breakfast or coffee break.
- ☐ Arrange appointments with area supervisors.
- ☐ Supply office and company policy statements.

may serve as the buddy in a much more structured type of orientation. Some organizations even have a one or two week orientation checksheet, like the one in Figure 15.1, that must be completed and signed by appropriate managerial personnel to ensure a comprehensive employee orientation. When using this type of office employee orientation, it is important to ensure that the new employee and the office buddy interact on a daily basis so that problems or questions can be worked out or answered.

SUMMARY

1. The U.S. Bureau of Labor indicates that the administrative office jobs are one of the fastest growing areas of employment in this country.
2. Presently 60 percent of all wages, salaries, and benefits are paid to office workers in this country.
3. Common sources of office labor are workers employed in other capacities within the organization, temporary help agencies, educational institutions, public employment agencies, private employment agencies, and local advertising.
4. Office employee personnel acquisition procedures include the application process, interviews, legal and affirmative action considerations, and employee orientation.

STUDENT ACTIVITIES

Active Orientation

1. Contact a local office manager to determine his or her sources of office employees. Discuss the particular problems this office manager has in finding qualified office personnel. Report your findings to your class.

2. Contact a local temporary help agency to determine the types of requests that are made of agencies from local business organizations. Discuss any problems the agency encounters in trying to find qualified office personnel. Report your findings to your class.

Independent Problems

1. Research the average salaries of local office personnel. Compare these data with national data from sources such as the American Management Society.

2. Contact personnel directors from local business organizations to determine the interview method most often used in interviews with candidates for administrative office positions.

16 Supervision and Motivation of Office Employees

OBJECTIVES At the conclusion of this chapter, you should be able to:

1. Define and discuss the terms *supervision, leadership, motivation, attitude,* and *behavior.*
2. Categorize and describe the three main characteristics of leadership behavior.
3. List and define the seven functions of supervision.
4. Identify the human factors of supervision.
5. Synthesize Maslow's Hierarchy of Needs with Herzberg's Motivation/Maintenance model.
6. List and describe five individual behaviors relating to attitude.

INTRODUCTION

In order for a leader to be effective in today's world of work, he or she must be aware of the forces operating in that world. Leaders should have a good understanding of leadership, the functions of supervision, and the human factors and attitudes that make up and affect leadership.

A general overview of how individuals interact with and in an organization is graphically illustrated in the model developed by Getzels and Guba shown in Figure 16.1. This model can also be found in Chapter 1, but it is used in a different context here. Getzels and Guba believe all social systems have two dimensions: an organizational, or nomothetic, dimension and a personal, or idiographic, dimension. The interaction of these two dimensions results in observed behavior. In the nomothetic perspective, the social system consists of organizations with prescribed roles, goals, or objectives which are based upon certain expectations and result in an observed behavior such as productivity. In the idiographic perspective, the same social system is made up of individuals who have distinct personalities, needs, or dispositions. The result is an observed behavior such as praiseworthiness, which could be turned into productivity.

The challenge for the supervisor in this model is to deal with social behaviors in an organizational setting. This is important because the achievement of organizational goals and fulfillment of individual needs depends upon the leader's ability to balance the demands of the organization with the needs of the individual staff members. Obvi-

FIGURE 16.1
Getzels/Guba interactive model

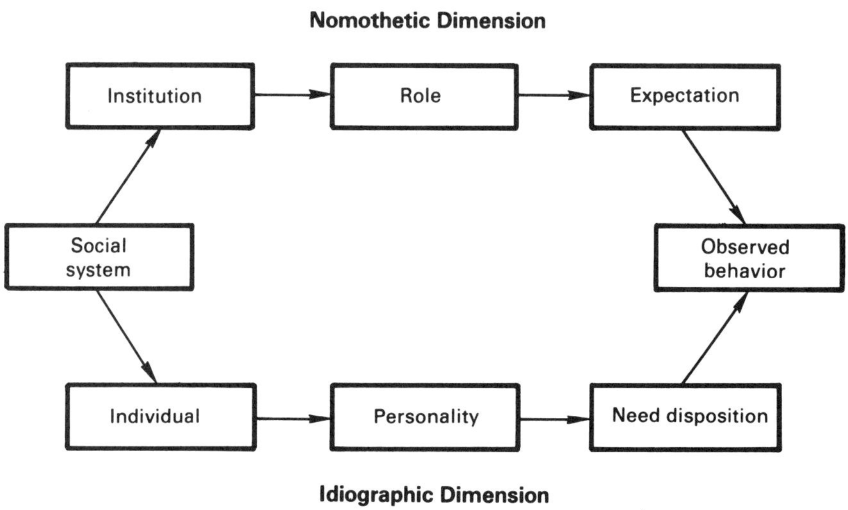

ously, no social system exists for very long if either the nomothetic or the idiographic dimensions are religiously followed. As in real life, the model shows that a great deal of give and take, or transaction, takes place between the dimensions.

LEADERSHIP

Leadership is an elusive term that connotes different mental images to all of us. Great military men like MacArthur and Eisenhower were considered leaders. Martin Luther King and Robert Kennedy were also categorized by this term. In business and industry, a good operational definition of a leader may be "someone who can effect change, and initiate and implement the goals and objectives of the organization." Change is essential in our definition because, to use an old cliché, "if we're not moving ahead, we're falling behind."

A leader will probably have administrative duties, but this does not always have to be the case. Many people in the informal organization exert leadership. Leadership can be said to be either trait or situationally oriented. Trait leadership suggests that leaders possess certain characteristics such as a positive self-image, poise, intelligence, and plenty of energy. This theory is not given much credence throughout the profession because it looks at one dimension of an individual's behavior over a given time. Situational leadership, on the other hand, is a well-respected theory. It focuses upon the observed behavior of an individual in different settings. Typically, the resulting profile of the leader is two-dimensional, reflecting the leader's concern for the organization (nomothetic) on one axis and the leader's concern for the individual (idiographic) on the other axis. If you tried to plot a point on a graph which represented the ideal position for a leader, you would find it impossible because the point would change with every situation. That is why this theory is called situational leadership. If this concept seems too abstract, think about the behavior of the office manager on the morning that a very big quotation has to be sent out, as compared to that person's behavior at three o'clock in the afternoon when the quotation left the office at two.

Leadership behavior can also be categorized. The most common way of doing this is to classify the behavior into the types of autocratic, democratic, and/or laissez-faire. In reality, the classification falls somewhere between the first two types because a laissez-faire (do whatever you want to do) leader will not be a leader for long. Tannenbaum and Schmidt developed a continuum of leadership behavior that clearly depicts the broad range of leadership styles within the democratic/autocratic types. Their model is illustrated in Figure 16.2.

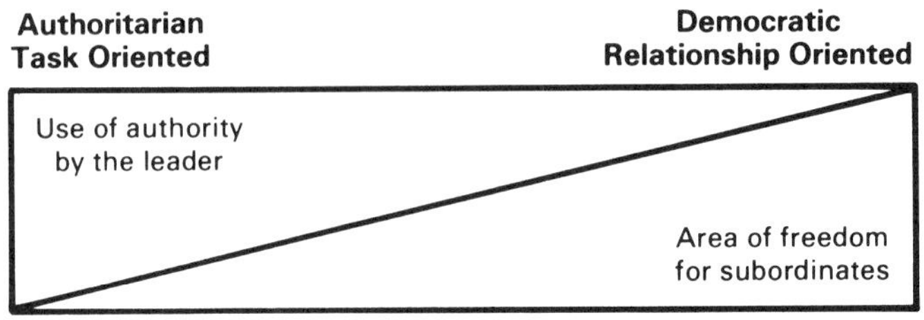

FIGURE 16.2 *Continuum of leadership behavior*

As can be seen from Tannenbaum and Schmidt's model, the more authoritarian a leader is, the more task-oriented he or she becomes. We all know someone who fits into this classification: the never-smile company crusader who eats, breathes, and lives work. On the other side of the model is the democratic leader; this person tries to give the workers all the freedom that they can tolerate. At this extreme, work may seem like a "country club" environment when compared to the "trenches" of the authoritarian style. Unfortunately, most hard-core democratic leaders have difficulties with worker productivity. This brings us back to the situational leadership concept; sometimes a leader must be autocratic, while at other times the leader can be democratic. When there is a fire in the building, the leader is autocratic; when the office manager is working on a special project with three or four senior office personnel who have a history of productive behavior, he or she can be democratic. For the most part, however, leadership behavior seeks a middle ground between autocratic and democratic styles.

SUPERVISING EMPLOYEES

An office supervisor should be a leader who can fit comfortably into the transactional role. That person should be able to combine the best method with the best person to achieve the best results for the good of the organization. To effectively meet this challenge, a supervisor should understand the functions of supervision and the human factors involved in leadership.

Functions of Supervision

What does a supervisor do? This question has been discussed for years because of the diverse nature of the job of supervisor. Most people agree that supervisors typically staff, direct, coordinate, and report. A closer look at each of these functions follows.

Staffing. This function, which traditionally is the responsibility of the human resources department, includes the various phases of recruitment, hiring, familiarizing, training, and maintaining a favorable work environment.

Directing. This process includes constantly analyzing and synthesizing activities relating to the goals and objectives of the organization or the department; developing specific directions, instructions, and orders; and acting as the responsible agent of the enterprise.

Coordinating. Typically, supervisors have responsibility for managing only a part of a much larger system. The meshing of these subsystems into the whole system and the logistical manipulations within each subsystem require coordination.

Reporting. Supervisors must inform individuals who are in superior and subordinate positions about organizational information through records, research, and inspection.

Other functions that require input from supervisors but are typically the responsibility of superiors are planning, organizing, and budgeting. The key to determining functions rests with the allocation of responsibility.

Planning. This includes the development of an outline in which the goals to be established and the means to accomplish those goals are stated.

Organizing. This function includes the establishment of a formal organizational structure to accomplish the goals and subsequent objectives of the organization.

Budgeting. Fiscal planning, accounting, and controlling are aspects of the budgeting function.

Human Factors That Affect Leadership

A leader must become aware of a number of human factors that relate to his or her leadership position. Wenig and Matthews identify nine human factors that affect leadership. According to Wenig and Matthews, a leader has the ability to communicate well, has highly developed interpersonal relationship skills, is able to motivate and challenge people, finds time to listen, gets people to accept leadership responsibility, fosters and maintains high morale, gives credit to others, develops positive attitudes toward new ideas, and promotes the profession.

A leader has the ability to communicate well. A leader must be able to use a communication process that operationalizes the model

FIGURE 16.3
Communication model

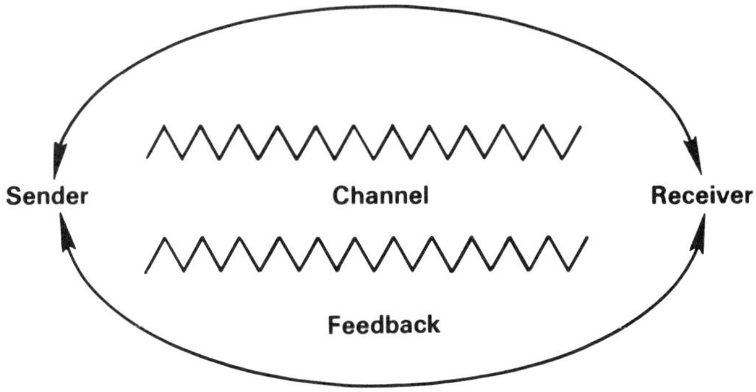

shown in Figure 16.3. The *sender* (leader) must be familiar with any and all *channels* (modes of communication, such as speech, interoffice memos, telex, and microcomputer) that will allow the *receiver* (superior, peer, subordinate, or client) to clearly understand the message. You can't possibly know if what you said, wrote, typed, or presented through your body language was what the receiver understood unless you have *feedback*. Feedback is essential in order to confirm that "what I said is what you heard."

A leader has highly developed interpersonal relationship skills. A leader should be perceived as being able to see where others "are coming from." This perception should not be mistaken for agreeing with others. In fact, when a person understands what has been said, but doesn't agree, interpersonal relationship skills become more relevant and necessary.

A leader motivates and challenges. A leader should organize tasks and duties for subordinates that are perceived as being rewarding and meaningful most of the time. Everyone must do ordinary and routine activities as part of his or her job. However, unmotivating and unchallenging activities lead to unhappiness and frustration. The leader must remember that dignity can be found in all work and should be sought after in all people.

A leader finds time to listen. A leader should not only receive feedback but also be a good receiver. What are superiors and subordinates really saying? This shouldn't become a paranoid trait, but rather a healthy dialogue characteristic. Good counseling skills are particularly important for supervisors.

A leader gets people to accept leadership responsibility. A leader can't do it all alone; he or she must be able to delegate responsibility to people who are willing and able to accept that responsibility. This sometimes involves the use of teaching skills such as demonstrating and explaining in order to bring someone "up the ladder."

A leader fosters and maintains high morale. Happy people are more productive. High morale lends itself to good company or unit teamwork, which also helps productivity. A friendly, professional team environment is a benefit to both management and workers.

A leader gives credit to others for accomplishments. A leader must recognize the efforts of others. Teams, companies, and corporations are not built upon the accomplishments of one individual but rather upon the accomplishments of all members. Recognition is a high mileage human factor for leaders.

A leader develops positive attitudes toward new ideas. As mentioned earlier, forward thinking is essential in the business and industrial world. A good leader quickly recognizes that his or her perspective is only one of many ways to view innovation. Therefore, a leader can't afford to become rigid or intolerant.

A leader promotes the profession. A leader recognizes that the field of expertise at his or her disposal is broad and consists of many leaders with differing philosophies and perspectives. Healthy personal and professional growth results from interactions with other professionals for the good of the profession.

Another human factor that every leader must be concerned with is fairness. Much like the teacher who has "pets," leaders who have favorites can cause the fabric of the organization to tear. Fair and equitable policy implementation across the board is essential to the accomplishment of many of the nine human factors already mentioned.

MOTIVATING EMPLOYEES

"Show me a person who has a good attitude about his or her job and I'll show you a good employee." Most employers agree with this statement, but it is a prime responsibility of the office manager to create the kind of environment which supports worker motivation and enthusiasm. This is no small challenge! An understanding of worker attitudes and individual behavior is essential to the accomplishment of this goal.

Work values, work attitudes, and work habits, or affective work competencies, account for the majority of dismissals and job action disputes in business and industry today. The problem with the term *attitude* is its measurement difficulty; it's an abstract concept. Most experts feel that the best way to measure attitude is through the observation of behavior. Two categories of behavior relating to attitude are group behavior and individual behavior.

Group Behavior

The term *group behavior* provides the foundation for the examination of motivation, needs theory, and cognitive dissonance theory. Each of these topics will be discussed briefly.

Abraham Maslow formulated a theory of motivation based upon a hierarchy of needs. The theory states that a person must satisfy a lower-level need before any major effort can be given over to satisfying a higher need; as one need is satisfied, the next higher need is dealt with. The five significant needs according to Maslow are:

1. Physiological needs, such as shelter, food, and clothing. These needs are virtually guaranteed to most people in the free world.
2. Safety needs, such as freedom from the hazards of life: accidents, war, and disease. This includes job seniority and security, health and accident insurance, and retirement benefits.
3. Love needs, such as attention and social activity. People tend to want to be around people that are similar to them and to engage in informal group membership.
4. Esteem or recognition needs meet the motives of prestige and power. Prestige is the ability to command admiration or respect from others. Power is the ability to induce or influence behavior.
5. Self-actualization needs are for an individual to be what he or she wants to be. This need meets the motives of competence and achievement. Competence is the ability to control environmental factors. Achievement reflects high task orientation and the ability to work to capacity.

If, in fact, lower-level needs must be satisfied before the higher-level needs are considered, it would be logical to assume that a reasonably well-satisfied need is no longer an active motivator of behavior. For example, if a full-time employee feels that he or she has job security and a fairly good pay/benefit package, chances are very good that the lure of more money or added dental coverage will not motivate that employee toward greater productivity. However, the opportunity for greater interaction with others or a shift in job title or responsibility that resulted in greater recognition might serve the production purpose in a very positive manner.

This idea is supported by Fredrick Herzberg, another expert on the subject of needs theory and motivation. He feels that people have two categories of needs called *motivation* and *maintenance factors*. Motiva-

FIGURE 16.4
Hersey and Blanchard model; Maslow/Herzberg overlay model

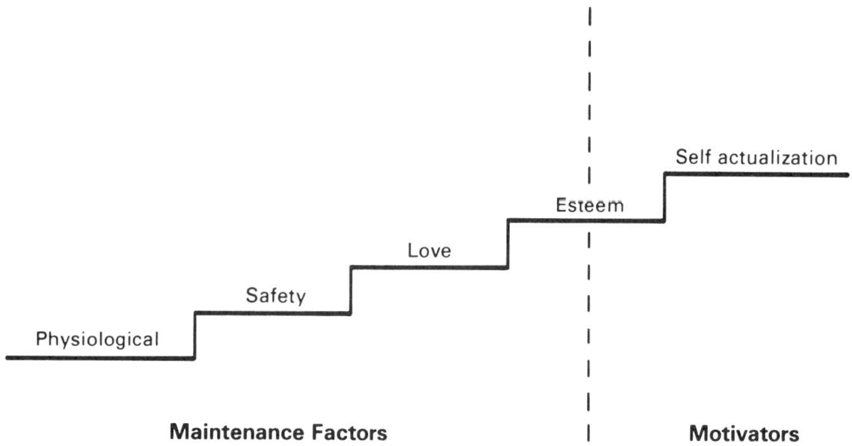

tion factors are directly related to intrinsic matters that come from the work itself; examples are achievement, recognition for accomplishment, challenge, increased responsibility, and growth and development. Maintenance factors are directly related to extrinsic matters that come from the conditions or the environment of the work; examples are policies, supervision, working conditions, interpersonal relations, money, status, and security.

Maslow's and Herzberg's theories complement each other to the point that they can be overlaid on each other, as demonstrated in the Figure 16.4 model developed by Hersey and Blanchard. Both Maslow's and Herzberg's models advocate a participative style of management that is utilized by many administrative office managers. This style, called the *Theory Y* style by Douglas McGregor, is based on the assumption that a worker's needs are never totally fulfilled. McGregor lists six observations regarding this type of worker.

1. The expenditure of physical or mental effort in work is as natural as play or rest.
2. People will exercise self-direction and self-control in the service of objectives to which they are committed.
3. Commitment to objectives is a function of the rewards associated with their achievement.
4. The average human being learns, under the proper conditions, not only to accept but to seek responsibility.
5. The capacity to exercise a relatively high degree of imagination, ingenuity, and creativity in the solution of organizational problems is *widely* and not narrowly distributed in the population.
6. Under present working conditions the intellectual potentialities of the average person are only partially utilized.

McGregor's Theory Y style was developed in contrast to the assumptions that he perceived some managers held about people, which he called *Theory X*. Those assumptions are:

1. The average person has an inherent dislike for work and will avoid it whenever possible.
2. Most people must be coerced, controlled, directed, or threatened with punishment in order to get them to put forth adequate effort toward the achievement of the organization's efforts.
3. The average person prefers to be directed, wishes to avoid responsibility, has relatively little ambition, and wants security above all.

William Ouchi takes the concepts of Theory Y one step further by presenting *Theory Z,* which emphasizes team effort, the generalization of duties and responsibilities, and a coordinated effort to have employees meet the goals of the company or department for reasons of compatibility with their own interests and objectives.

Motivation can also be identified by the measurement of achievement, affiliation, and power. A basic understanding of these motives is necessary in order to understand worker behavior. Productivity may vary depending upon the presence of a high or low sense of any one of these motives combined with the nature of a particular job or task. McClelland describes the higher achiever as a person who likes situations in which he or she takes personal responsibility for finding solutions to problems; wants concrete feedback on how well he or she is doing; and tends to set moderate achievement goals and to take calculated risks.

Persons with an affiliation motive have a tendency to focus upon the quality of personal relationships; persons with a power motive tend to maneuver for a position of authority. According to Livingston, power seekers will work hard to reach a position where they can have authority over a large number of people. People with affiliation motives, on the other hand, do not place as much emphasis on actions that will allow them to climb up the managerial ladder. They tend to devote their energies to noncompany policies and activities that are more satisfying to them.

Cognitive dissonance theory provides some insight into how worker attitudes are developed. This theory, which was developed by Festinger, has been interpreted by Maier as the perception that when our experiences do not agree with the expectations we have accumulated throughout a lifetime, we try to reduce the inconsistency; we may change our attitudes or opinions. In fact, we may even go as far as to change our recollection of the experience or distort the information that we received regarding the experience. This theory is important because, since it motivates behavior, it provides another look at how people function in an organization. Dissonance can be used to create controls and rewards, and that can have either a positive or negative effect on the success of an organization.

Individual Behavior Individual behavior relating to attitude has been identified and categorized by Kazanas as "affective work competencies." These competencies can be identified as five factors: self control, organization, conscientiousness, initiative, and ambition.

- ☐ Self control is the ability to stay calm and not lose his or her "cool."
- ☐ Organization is the ability to finish work correctly, accurately, and on time; to carry out instructions; and to make corrections when and where necessary.
- ☐ Conscientiousness is the ability to do what is assigned with pride and without avoidance.
- ☐ Initiative is the ability to make decisions and complete work without help or supervision.
- ☐ Ambition is a person's ability to set his or her own goals and work hard to achieve those goals; to develop new skills for improvement; and to accept training and be receptive to more difficult assignments.

SUMMARY

1. Any social system is made up of a nomothetic, or organizational, and an idiographic, or personal, dimension.
2. A leader is someone who can effect change and initiate and implement the goals and objectives of the organization.
3. Leadership can be either trait or situational, and can be categorized into the types of autocratic, democratic, or laissez-faire.
4. The direct functions of supervision are staffing, directing, coordinating, and reporting. Other functions are planning, organizing, and budgeting.
5. Human factors that a leader should have include communication and interpersonal relationship skills, the ability to motivate, challenge, listen, maintain high morale, credit others for accomplishments, promote the profession, and be fair.
6. An understanding of worker attitudes and individual behavior is essential to employee motivation.
7. Maslow's Hierarchy of Needs and Herzberg's Motivation/Maintenance theory are significant motivation and needs theory models.

8. Individual behavior relating to attitude can be classified in terms of self-control, organization, conscientiousness, initiative, and ambition.

STUDENT ACTIVITIES

Active Orientation

1. Develop a survey that identifies the human factors and functions of supervisors. Ask an individual whom you perceive as being in a leadership role to identify the amount of time spent on various supervision functions, and rank the human factors of supervision from most important to least important. From that information and any other information that you want to include in your survey, attempt to identify the person's leadership behavior and motivation/maintenance level. Be sure to justify your choices!

Independent Problems

1. Cognitive dissonance theory provides some insight into how the attitudes of workers are developed. Write a scenario using this theory as a background.

2. Where do you fit on Maslow's hierarchy? Why? Identify and justify three realistic goals that you could set for yourself that could help you to get to the next level.

3. In your two previous office management jobs, you worked for a boss who believed in good interactive communication. Your new boss, however, is very autocratic. How might this affect you, your work, your interaction with him or her, and your corporate effectiveness? Hint: Use cognitive dissonance theory and leadership behavior theory as a starting point.

REFERENCES

Festinger, L. *A Theory of Cognitive Dissonance.* Evanston, IL: Row Peterson, 1957.

Getzels, J. W. and Guba, E. G. "Social Behavior and the Administrative Process." *School Review* LXV, Winter, 1957.

Hersey, P. and Blanchard, K. H. *Management of Organizational Behavior: Utilizing Human Resources.* 3rd ed. Englewood Cliffs, NJ: Prentice-Hall, Inc., 1977.

Herzberg, F., Mausner, B., and Snyderman, B. *The Motivation to Work.* John Wiley and Sons, Inc., 1959.

Kazanas, H. C.; Beach, D. P.; Frazier, E. L.; Sapko, J. Jr.; Lucas, J. J.; and Petty, G. C. *Affective Work Competencies for Vocational Education.* Columbus, OH: ERIC Clearinghouse on Vocational and Technical Education, 1978.

Livingston, J. S. "Myth of the Well-Educated Manager." *Harvard Business Review* 49 (1971): pp. 78–89.

McClelland, D. C. "The Two Faces of Power." *Journal of International Affairs* 24 (1970): pp. 29–47.

McGregor, Douglas, *The Human Side of Enterprise.* New York: McGraw-Hill, 1960.

Maier, N. R. F. *Psychology in Industrial Organizations.* Boston, MA: Houghton Mifflin Company, 1973.

Maslow, A. H. *Motivation and Personality.* NY: Harper and Brothers, 1954.

Ouchi, William G., and Price, Raymond L. "Hierarchies, Clans, and Theory Z: A New Perspective on Organization Development." *Organization Dynamics* VII, Autumn, 1978, pp. 24–44.

Tannenbaum, R. and Schmidt, W. H. "How to Choose a Leadership Pattern." *Harvard Business Review,* March–April, 1957, pp. 95–101.

Wenig, R. E. and Matthews, J. I. "Ideals of Leadership and the Individual's Function." In *The Dynamics of Creative Leadership for Industrial Arts Education,* edited by R. E. Wenig and J. I. Matthews. Bloomington, IL: McKnight Publishing Company, 1983.

17 Administrative Job Analysis

OBJECTIVES At the conclusion of this chapter, you should be able to:

1. List the reasons for conducting an office job analysis.
2. Identify the elements of job descriptions and specifications.
3. Discuss the procedures for establishing an effective job evaluation method.
4. Discuss the importance of establishing work standards in today's modern business offices.

INTRODUCTION

Job analysis is the procedure used to determine specific information about a given job. This data can be gathered by using questionnaires, interviews, or direct observation techniques. This information identifies the principal characteristics of each job, such as the job title, a description of duties, the education of the individual performing the job, the experience level necessary to perform the job, the training required to perform the job, and the physical demands of the job. A job analysis usually results in the establishment of four documents which are used by management to address the concept of productivity in a given area such as the business office. These documents are job descriptions, job specifications, job evaluation forms, and work standards manuals.

JOB DESCRIPTIONS

A job description identifies the tasks performed by the worker holding a position, the level of skill required of the worker, and the relationships of authority and responsibility between the worker and the organization. This information is usually presented as an official document of the organization. Figure 17.1 shows a sample job description form.

FIGURE 17.1
Typical job description

Job Title: ____________________ Job Code: ____________

Department: ____________________

Supervisor: ____________________

Grade Level: ____________________ Point Range: ____________

Pay Range: ____________________

Job Tasks:

1. ________________________________
2. ________________________________
3. ________________________________
4. ________________________________

Required Skills:

1. ________________________________
2. ________________________________
3. ________________________________

Writing the Job Description

Although there is no absolute amount of job data that must be included in each job description, enough information should be included to accurately describe the job. It is important to remember that when a job description is written, the job itself is being described and not the person currently holding the job.

The U.S. Department of Labor offers two documents which will help individuals prepare job descriptions. These documents are the *Dictionary of Occupational Titles* (*DOT*) and the *Occupational Outlook Handbook*. The *DOT* contains nearly 20,000 standardized job descriptions, and the *Occupational Outlook Handbook* provides information for those individuals seeking recent employment trends.

JOB SPECIFICATIONS

The job specification is an instrument that identifies the minimum requirements of the job, including characteristics such as the educational level, experience, and personal qualities of the job holder. The job specification is often used to rate jobs during evaluation, identify training and promotional activities, and match prospective employees with available jobs. Figure 17.2 illustrates a sample job specification form.

FIGURE 17.2
Typical job specification

Job Title: ______________________ Job Code: ______________

Department: ______________________

Supervisor: ______________________

Grade Level: ______________________ Point Range: ______________

Pay Range: ______________________

Qualifications:

Knowledge: ____

Experience: ____

Effort: ____

Job Tasks:

1. ____
2. ____
3. ____

JOB EVALUATIONS

Once job descriptions and job specifications have been developed, job evaluation can take place and attempts can be made to provide an effective salary administration policy for the organization. It is important that employees who perform similar work under similar working conditions be paid approximately the same salary, because it is required by law (Equal Pay Act) and it helps to maintain a high level of morale and reduce employee turnover. The job descriptions and specifications provide the documentation necessary to aid the salary administrator in this endeavor.

Other factors, however, make salary administration more difficult than just reviewing job descriptions and specifications for salary determination. Factors such as government regulations, collective bargaining agreements, and supply and demand of workers with special skills require that employers develop additional structures to evaluate jobs within their organizations.

Administrators have agreed that there is no one best method of job evaluation. However, the alternative to job evaluation is no job evaluation. This strategy leaves the organization without a rational basis for determining what tasks their workers are performing, what employee skills exist within their own organization, and the organization's ability to keep dedicated, productive employees. The result of no job evaluation procedure could be disastrous to a business organization. Leon Megginson prescribes a behavioral approach to administration, listed below.

Advantages of Job Evaluations

1. Job evaluations help develop a fair and equitable scale of wages.
2. Job evaluations develop limits for the relative value of the job to the organization.
3. Job evaluations provide information to determine the qualifications necessary for promotions, demotions, and job transfers.

Disadvantages of Job Evaluations

1. Job evaluations cannot measure worth precisely.
2. Job evaluations sometimes do not address higher level employees.
3. Job evaluations sometimes do not separate the person from the job.

JOB EVALUATION METHODS

There are numerous types of job evaluation methods in operation today in business organizations across the United States. The following three examples are presented to illustrate the diversity of job evaluation methods.

FIGURE 17.3
Rank order method—office positions

Rank	Job Title	Median Salary —Monthly
1	Office Manager	$2,500
2	Administrative Assistant	1,900
3	Executive Secretary	1,650
4	Word Processing Supervisor	1,575
5	Accounting Supervisor	1,550
6	Records Supervisor	1,500
7	Micrographic Supervisor	1,490
8	Word Processing Specialist	1,100
9	Accounting Clerk	1,000
10	Records Clerk	950
11	File Clerk	700

The Rank Order Method

The rank order method is the simplest form of job evaluation. Using this method, jobs are listed in order from the most demanding to the least demanding or important. This method makes some assumptions that are not always true. For example, it is assumed that there is an increase in the salary paid to a worker as his or her job becomes more difficult. Figure 17.3 shows sample office positions listed in the rank order method.

The Guideline Method

The guideline method all but ignores the internal nature of jobs. It merely addresses the "going rate" for a position in the local or national job market. Obviously, this method could not be used without current job market data. The key feature of the guideline method is its minimum–midpoint–maximum range of dollar values for each set of similar jobs, or job grades. The establishment of a midpoint dollar amount allows for the overlapping of certain job classifications within the organization. This overlapping makes it possible for administrators to adjust for internal differences in job duties and conditions without distorting the entire wage scale. The guideline method is illustrated in Figure 17.4.

FIGURE 17.4
The guideline method

Job Grade	Minimum	Midpoint	Maximum
1	$ 8,500	$ 9,800	$ 11,100
2	$ 8,900	$ 10,100	$ 11,300
3	$ 9,300	$ 10,700	$ 12,100
4	$ 10,100	$ 11,200	$ 12,300
5	$ 10,990	$ 12,990	$ 13,490
37	$118,500	$125,000	$131,500

The Point Method

The point method of job evaluation identifies the factors associated with each job and then assigns points to the factors. Because certain factors may take on different meanings or emphases in different situations, the factors are therefore usually subdivided for easier interpretation. Most point method systems use the following factors and subfactors for analysis.

Knowledge includes:

- education and job knowledge;
- experience; and
- training.

Responsibility and accountability include:

- budget responsibility;
- span of control;
- safety; and
- planning and forecasting.

Effort includes:

- working conditions;
- physical/mental stress;
- initiative; and
- creativity.

Each of the subfactors can also be assigned degrees, which are assigned points to further quantify the effort among the various levels of jobs within the organization. Figure 17.5 shows a sample knowledge section in the point method.

FIGURE 17.5
Typical point method

The Point Method: Knowledge Section

Degree	Knowledge	Points
1	College Degree	
	BA General Business	15
2	Experience	
	5 yrs. Admin. Asst.	
	2 yrs. Office Manager	45
3	Training	
	Product Center (6 wks.)	
	Mgt. Seminars I, II, III	
	Sensitivity Training I	53
Total points for knowledge section		113

MAKING JOB EVALUATION WORK FOR YOU

It would probably be a mistake for a company to adopt a job evaluation plan from another organization or source such as a professional journal simply because of those activities within the company which are different or unusual. However, using another organization's job evaluation method as a guideline for establishing your own system is highly advisable. Regardless of the method selected, each organization should do its homework. The organization must identify the types of jobs being performed, the demands of the jobs, and the skills of the employees now performing these jobs. In other words, the organization must perform an effective job analysis.

WORK STANDARDS AND TODAY'S BUSINESS OFFICE

Recent studies have shown that the much maligned factory productivity has increased approximately 86 percent in the past decade. During the same period, office productivity has increased by only 4 percent. The U.S. Bureau of Labor Statistics indicates that more than one-half of all available jobs are in the information field. These jobs are primarily office or administrative positions. More important, however, is the prediction that by 1990 three-fourths of all available jobs will be in the information field. It appears that this nation is in the middle of a sweeping transition away from assembly or industry jobs and toward administrative office jobs. At this time, however, little data is being gathered concerning improving productivity in the business office.

In order for any business office to address the concept of productivity, it must first perform an effective job analysis and then use the data to establish work standards. Work standards are figures that indicate how much work is being completed and at what cost to the organization. These data will not be available to the office administrator unless a job analysis of the office is conducted.

CONDUCTING A WORK MEASUREMENT PROGRAM

In order for an effective work measurement program to take place, a commitment from management is necessary. This commitment can manifest itself in a letter of authority which authorizes the work measurement program. This letter helps the people conducting the work measurement study gain the support and cooperation of the many people throughout the organization who must take part in the effort.

Setting the Stage

Each worker, from the top executive to the file clerk, should be made aware of the nature and purpose of the work measurement study. They should all understand that this is not a spy mission that is aimed at eliminating jobs. Communicating the genuine intention of the work measurement activities creates an atmosphere of trust and cooperation instead of fear and mistrust. Small group meetings between employees and the work measurement team can effectively disseminate information about the study and answer any questions or concerns that the employees may have.

The Scope of the Study

Work measurement studies can vary in scope. A full-fledged study would encompass time studies, motion studies, and methods time measurement. However, most office work measurement studies do not have to include these scientific applications. In fact, it is a rare occurrence to find an administrative office that is willing to commit to the time and expense necessary to conduct such a study. A more common type of work measurement study uses the following format.

Gathering the data. The first step in an effective work measurement program is to perform the office job analysis. This data is gathered by observing office personnel at work, interviewing them concerning specific job performance, and, if necessary, surveying the office staff with a questionnaire. Once each job has been defined and documented, data can be gathered concerning the volume of work performed for each job description and the cost of performing each office task. This very basic information provides the framework for the work measurement analyst. The analyst can then make comparisons, on a job-by-job basis, with data from other firms or published reports to determine any significant differences in the types of work performed and the costs of these activities.

Analyzing the data. Unfortunately, this very basic information is not readily available. Most business offices do not keep track of this type of data in their organizations. It has not been a United States business practice to address the concept of productivity in an administrative environment. Furthermore, many office administrators are unfamiliar with the practice of determining efficiency through a logical systems analysis of the administrative office. This is one of the major reasons why office computer systems have moved into the administrative office so slowly.

Once the specific job data are available, the work measurement analyst can work side-by-side with office personnel to determine problem areas, bottlenecks, and duplications of efforts in an attempt to design alternatives to the present method of operation. Often new technology is the logical answer to some of the problem areas encountered. However, on many occasions, new strategies can be discovered merely by observing the whole picture for the first time. Groups of workers observing a flowchart of the office paperflow, for example, in the presence of the analyst, can provide some effective insights into new strategies for solving problems in the business office. This approach provides an outlet for creative, innovative office employees.

Putting work measurement to work. The whole purpose of gathering data through job analysis and work measurement is to determine specific information about the types of jobs being performed, how jobs are being performed, and the cost of performing the jobs. This appears to be very basic information, but this information must be collected before any new strategies can be considered. This is especially true of the business office with its wide variety of functions. The data gathered through job analysis and work measurement should be used as the foundation for conducting a systems analysis of the entire business office to address the following questions.

1. Are the business office activities consistent with the stated goals and objectives of the organization?
2. Are the present business office activities being conducted in the most efficient manner possible?
3. Are the methods used to conduct the activities of the business office adequate or is computerization necessary?
4. Are the employees properly trained for their positions?
5. Are the business office operations manuals up-to-date?
6. Is there a plan in place to monitor business office productivity?

Procedures for conducting office systems analysis and design is addressed, in detail, in Chapter 8.

Implementing the results. Once the data have been reviewed and new strategies have been developed by the employees and the work measurement analyst, the new strategies can be implemented. This implementation is subject to approval by management, of course. Successful implementation of any new system requires support from both the people who are performing tasks under the new system and from management.

It is critical that the new system be monitored closely, including prompt feedback from the office employees concerning the positive and negative aspects of the new office system. Figure 17.6 shows a flowchart of the job analysis–work measurement system study.

Although many offices do not have the ability to conduct full-scale job analyses, the structure illustrated in the classic job analysis proce-

FIGURE 17.6
Flowchart of office job analysis

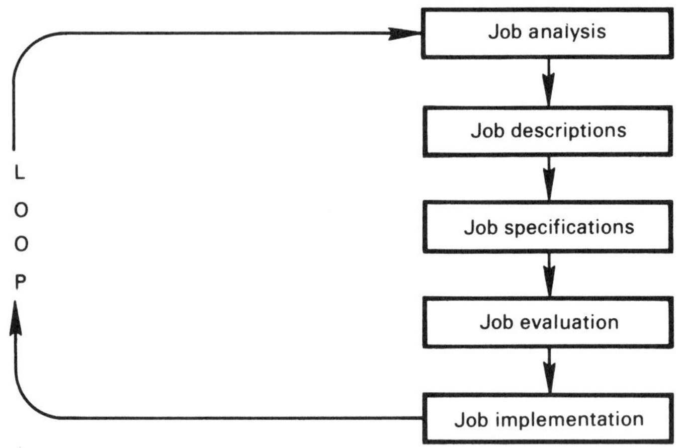

dures provided in this chapter can benefit office administrators in identifying the essential items necessary for the proper design of office work patterns. The information gathered from a comprehensive job analysis will be valuable to the office administrator as he or she begins a search for new office employees.

SUMMARY

1. Job analysis is the procedure used to determine specific information about a specific job.
2. Job analysis usually results in the establishment of four job-related documents: the job description, the job specification, the job evaluation form, and the work standards manual.
3. The *Dictionary of Occupational Titles* and the *Occupational Outlook Handbook* are two government publications which aid office managers with employment data.
4. Three common types of job evaluation methods are the rank order method, the guideline method, and the point method.
5. Establishing work standards provides the office manager with the essential data to conduct a systems study of the office.
6. Conducting an effective work standards study requires an understanding of the human factors involved in office work.
7. Implementing the results of work measurement studies in an office environment includes providing feedback to workers.

STUDENT ACTIVITIES

Active Orientation

1. Using the *Dictionary of Occupational Titles* and the *Occupational Outlook Handbook,* prepare a job description and a job specification for the position of office manager. Include considerations for office automation applications. Discuss the documents in class.

2. Visit a local company and determine its method of job evaluation for office employees. Discuss your findings with your class.

Independent Problems

1. Visit a local company and identify the procedures used to establish work standards for the office personnel. Compare these procedures with information found in this text and in professional journals.

2. Research the job evaluation efforts of Edward Hay in your local library (check the *Personnel Journal*). Compare your research findings with other point methods discussed in current human resources literature. Discuss your findings in class.

REFERENCES

Megginson, Leon. *Personnel: A Behavioral Approach to Administration.* Homewood, IL: Richard D. Irwin, Inc., 1972.

18 Administrative Productivity

OBJECTIVES At the conclusion of this chapter, you should be able to:

1. Describe the need for establishing productivity standards for administrative positions.
2. Identify the administrative tasks that are difficult to measure.
3. Describe the procedures for establishing a productivity measurement program for administrative positions.
4. List the anticipated benefits of establishing project teams.
5. Describe the implications of a productivity measurement program for the administrative office manager.

INTRODUCTION

The importance of analyzing the various administrative tasks was stressed in Chapter 17. These analyses provide the foundation for determining work standards and productivity measurement for administrative office positions. Productivity can be defined as the relationship between the output produced by a given organizational system and the quantities of inputs or resources utilized to produce that output. This chapter identifies specific procedures which utilize the work measurement concepts from Chapter 17 to construct an administrative productivity program. The productivity program compares the administrative output produced with the level of input expended by the organization to produce that output.

CAN ADMINISTRATIVE PRODUCTIVITY BE MEASURED?

When senior management personnel investigate administrative costs, they are likely to find few real productivity measurement programs in place, largely because executives, managers, supervisors, and secretaries are not accustomed to analyzing their work activities. The most common excuses given for not establishing work measurement and productivity standards for administrative positions are that administrative personnel have too many different tasks to perform or that they don't perform the same tasks every day. The fact of the matter is that administrative tasks *can* be quantified and productivity statistics can be developed for administrative positions.

Chapter 17 provides us with procedures for identifying the tasks that are being performed and determining how long it takes personnel to perform each task. Although this information is important, it is not the first step in developing a sound productivity management program. Productivity measurement is not merely an administrative task; it is an organizational objective, or company goal or plan. Therefore, it must be developed according to company policies for establishing a program. This usually means that a management team will be developed to make sure that the goals and objectives of the productivity program mesh with the goals and objectives of the organization.

Shafique Jamali from the Public Service Company of New Mexico has developed a six-step procedure for putting a productivity program into action. This six-step procedure addresses not only measurement strategies, but also techniques for implementing the strategies.

Step 1: Create Awareness

To ensure that an organization's productivity program gets off to a good start, the program must be communicated to the individuals within the organization. Management should articulate the benefits of the productivity program for both the company *and* the employees.

Benefits to the company. A well-developed productivity program benefits the organization because it:

1. provides better organization and control of each department;
2. allows more effective planning and allocation of resources;
3. creates a basis for effective supervision;
4. helps eliminate backlog and overtime;
5. creates a consistency of workflow; and
6. improves methods of work scheduling.

Benefits to the employees. It is extremely important for the employees of an organization to know how they can participate and share in the benefits of a productivity program. A well-developed productivity program benefits employees because it:

1. provides opportunities for participation in the decision-making process;
2. gives recognition for achievements;
3. provides opportunities for job enlargement, enrichment, and satisfaction; and
4. improves working conditions.

It is important to remember that the term *productivity* means different things to different people throughout the organization. Unless employees feel that they will share in the rewards of a more productive company, they may be less motivated to participate in the program.

Step 2: Measure Productivity

As stated earlier, productivity is the relationship between the outputs produced and the inputs generated. The job analysis strategies described in Chapter 17 identified who was performing the task, how the task was being performed (input), the level of work performed (output), and the cost of performing each task. The statistics generated from such an analysis provide the organization with a good foundation for establishing productivity ratings for the various tasks performed within an organization. Figure 18.1 illustrates the equation for determining a company productivity ratio. An overall productivity ratio provides only limited information about the productivity of the organization. The same relationship between inputs and outputs described in Figure 18.1 can be applied both at the departmental level and for almost every task performed within departments. Figure 18.2 illustrates a productivity ratio established for word processing applications. Establishing productivity statistics for different tasks provides

FIGURE 18.1
Company productivity ratio

$$\frac{\text{Total Output}}{\text{Labor + Materials + Energy + Capital + Miscellaneous Input}}$$

management with data that represent the relationship of inputs to outputs. However, these statistics do not provide management with an indication of the desired levels of productivity for each task. This factor requires additional evaluation.

Step 3: Evaluate Productivity

Step 2 told us how much it costs to perform each task and the level of output generated from each task. Step 3 evaluates the relationship of inputs to outputs by comparing the statistics with established norms for the industry base data from prior studies within the company. These ratios are illustrated in Figures 18.3 and 18.4. Productivity statistics that are developed for an organization and compared with industry or company standards provide only a comparison or trend in the productivity effort for the organization. Management is responsible for conducting the additional analyses necessary to determine

1. what factors are contributing to the increase/decrease in the productivity statistics;
2. what unexpected circumstances contributed to the increase/decrease in productivity; and
3. what management strategies can be developed to modify existing problem areas.

Many organizations fail to appreciate the importance of the evaluation phase of a productivity program. Once productivity statistics are generated which determine an increase or decrease in productivity, many managers tend to react to the results before a complete analysis can be conducted to ascertain why productivity increased or decreased. The result of this premature action can result in inadequate or misdirected management decisions which may turn out to be counterproductive.

Once productivity increases or decreases are determined, managers should utilize a systems approach to ascertain the true nature of the productivity effort. The systems approach to productivity measurement implies a substantial planning effort on the part of the manage-

FIGURE 18.2
Word processing productivity ratio

$$\frac{\text{Word Processing Assignments Completed and Approved}}{\text{Labor + Materials + Capital (Prorated)}}$$

FIGURE 18.3
Productivity ratio, company versus industry

$$\frac{\text{Company Productivity Ratio First Quarter, 1987}}{\text{Industry Productivity Ratio First Quarter, 1987}}$$

ment team. This approach is described in detail in Chapter 8. The communications program that is necessary to facilitate the productivity program throughout the organization is described in Chapter 10.

Step 4: Plan Productivity

The productivity planning effort is used in conjunction with the results of the systems analysis data gathered by management. The planning effort should outline the actions to be taken, the individuals responsible for each activity, the items to be delivered by the individuals responsible for the activities, and the anticipated completion dates of each activity. Figure 18.5 illustrates an action plan.

Effective planning practices. A study by Robert M. Ranftl for the Hughes Aircraft Company identified twenty effective planning practices for enhancing organizational productivity. Managers in the organization should:

1. involve all organizations and individuals in planning;
2. quantify plans whenever possible;
3. examine all pertinent trade-offs;
4. eliminate all unnecessary items and avoid excessive detail;
5. ensure realistic cost and schedule parameters;
6. optimally time-phase all important elements of a plan;
7. examine plans critically before implementing them;
8. develop contingency plans in advance of potential events;
9. recognize that plans can succeed only if they are communicated effectively, understood, and properly carried out;
10. orient budgets toward future needs, and not past expenditures;
11. make sure that planned budgets adequately represent the realities of effective operation;
12. assign specific responsibilities for adherence to budgets and stress accountability;
13. make potential return on investment a major consideration in selecting and planning projects;

FIGURE 18.4
Productivity ratio, current period versus base year

Period 1	Period 2
$\frac{2.17}{2.63 \text{ (Base Year)}} = .825$	$\frac{2.50}{2.63 \text{ (Base Year)}} = .951$

FIGURE 18.5
Planning phase: action plan

Action Plan for Developing and Implementing a Work Management Program by December, 1983

Action steps/tasks	Responsibility	Deliverables	Comp. date
Select from existing staff personnel to be trained as analysts	Plant manager	Names of employees	Jan. 1983
Train analysts	Internal consultants	Analysts trained in the use of industrial engineering tools/techniques, such as work simplification, work standard development, and process charting	March 1983
Supervisor/managerial seminar	Internal consultants	Manager/supervisor gets overview of the work management program	Feb. 1983
Work force orientation	Plant manager, internal consultants	Written goals and objectives of the program circulated to the employees involved	Feb. 1983
Analysts start documenting present plant's work activities	Analysts	Documentation of: a. What is done? b. What processes exist? c. How is workload distributed?	May 1983
Analysis of current work	Analysts	Identification of: a. How is the work done? b. Causes of work backlog and frequent work force delays Work improvement methods	July 1983
Development of work standards (use of selected and acceptable measurement techniques such as MTM, predetermined time standard, etc.)	Analysts	Work standards for identified work activities/tasks	Aug. 1983
Analysis of present work planning and scheduling procedures	Analysts	Recommended improved planning and scheduling procedures	Aug. 1983
Work management program implementation and performance control reporting	Analysts	A reporting system capable of: a. Collecting actual work data b. Comparing actual with standards c. Disseminating the performance results among concerned personnel d. Identifying activities/tasks for improving unfavorable performance and recommending positive correction actions	Sept. 1983

Courtesy of the Salt River Project

14. optimize cash flow in financial planning;
15. plan major capital investments well in advance of actual needs;
16. have managers annually prepare plans for the overall improvement of their organizations in the upcoming year and review progress against their plans at the end of the year;
17. maintain an ongoing program/plan for the replacement or updating of obsolescent plants and facilities;
18. plan for proper maintenance of the plant and facilities;
19. make optimum use of computers as an aid to planning; and
20. avoid overplanning.

The entire planning effort must address areas which need improvement. These areas include improving work methods by providing the necessary tools, materials, and technology; improving efficiency; and improving the quality of work life.

Step 5: Improve Productivity

All levels of employees must accept responsibility for improving productivity within an organization. This step identifies specific objectives for improving productivity for managers, supervisors, and employees. The following objectives are the more salient points made by Ranftl in his study of the Hughes Aircraft Company described earlier.

Improving managerial productivity. The following objectives are recommended for improving managerial productivity:

1. establish high performance standards, and promote personnel and product excellence;
2. determine what objectives to pursue, based on a thorough knowledge of the technology, market, competition, and available resources;
3. optimize the use of all available resources, and be alert for unused and underutilized resources, particularly with regard to involvement of the entire workforce.
4. delegate authority, responsibility, decision making, control, and accountability as far down the organizational ladder as is practical;
5. manage time effectively by setting priorities and deadlines and stopping nonproductive efforts as soon as possible;
6. invest in future technology through sound basic and applied research and development programs;
7. keep the organization tuned up by always searching for more productive ways of doing things;
8. be alert for, and correct, counterproductive factors within the organization;
9. apply work elimination, simplification, and standardization techniques wherever appropriate;

10. make sure that no individual or facet of the organization gets short-changed or overemphasized;
11. maintain effective, equitable compensation and promotion policies;
12. review regularly the need and justification for overhead and capital expenditures, and keep both in line with efficient operating practices; and
13. critique past performance, and learn from both the successes and mistakes of earlier efforts.

Improving supervisory productivity. Supervisory personnel must serve as key liaisons between the managerial effort and the employees of the organization. In order to improve productivity, supervisors should:

1. make a genuine effort to understand subordinates, know their strengths and weaknesses, their primary sources of motivation, and their career goals;
2. effectively integrate the abilities of all individuals within the organization;
3. involve subordinates in planning, goal-setting, and decisions that affect them;
4. let employees demonstrate their capabilities and grow professionally, and help subordinates prepare themselves for the jobs to which they aspire;
5. keep subordinates fully, but not excessively, loaded with work;
6. avoid treating all tasks as maximum efforts or special cases, rushes and overtime followed by delays, and surprises and unexplained changes;
7. be available to subordinates through an open-door policy;
8. provide subordinates with feedback on their performance, recognize and reward achievement, and cite mistakes fairly and tactfully;
9. represent equitably all subordinates and their work to higher management;
10. be sensitive to factors that cause employee dissatisfaction and frustration, and get to the root of such factors and resolve them in a timely manner;
11. maintain an effective flow of two-way communication;
12. serve as a catalyst to ensure effective technology exchange within the organization;
13. keep employees informed of the broader aspects of company operations; and
14. encourage team-building while being careful not to create provincialism.

Obviously, any effort to increase productivity within an organization will be affected by the attitudes and motivations of the employees. In order for managers and supervisors to design an effective productivity program, they will have to understand employee motivations and thus, structure work assignments and incentives to match these motivations.

The following list of job assignment practices is designed to meet productivity objectives by addressing employee motivations. Managers and supervisors should:

1. provide assignments that lead, through successful completion, to a feeling of accomplishment and a sense of contributing or belonging;
2. make sure that assignments are pertinent to the organization's overall objectives and have management's active interest and support;
3. assign work in keeping with individual capabilities and interests, thus avoiding misemployment;
4. make sure that assignments make effective use of employees' existing skills and talents while, at the same time, affording them an opportunity to develop new skills and grow;
5. make sure that assignments are clearly defined and involve specific responsibilities, thus avoiding open-ended assignments whenever possible;
6. focus on end results such as technical performance, costs, and schedules, thus giving the employee as much freedom and opportunity for work planning and decision making as possible;
7. make schedules tight but realistic, allowing adequate time to do the job effectively;
8. provide employees with the necessary resources to do the job;
9. use the most capable people for the most critical jobs;
10. strive for equity of workload among employees, avoiding overloading good people just because they "always come through";
11. change or expand employee assignments periodically;
12. establish work teams of people who are particularly productive when working together; and
13. provide job security consistent with the employee's job performance.

An often overlooked aspect of productivity programs is the follow-up aspect. Productivity programs must be looked upon as continuing projects which require constant monitoring and evaluation. The efforts described in steps 1 through 5 will be of little long-term value to the organization unless procedures are established for controlling program performance.

Step 6: Establish Control Reporting

An effective control reporting procedure gives managers the opportunity to monitor the productivity improvement measures which were established in step 5. In order to establish a control reporting program, managers should:

1. report regularly on the progress of the productivity program in their areas;
2. prepare productivity charts which address their area's progress as compared to the goals of the overall productivity effort for the organization; and
3. prepare a report that lists problem areas and strategies for addressing these problem areas.

Management will have the greatest impact on the success or failure of any productivity program, because management may be a major contributor to the problem of low productivity. Managers are ultimately responsible for the overall productivity of any organization. Therefore, the success or failure of a productivity program relies on the ability of managers to communicate the needs and benefits of organizational productivity, as well as establish an effective, ongoing program of work analysis, work measurement, and work incentives. If a manager fails in any one of these tasks, he or she will become a contributor to the problem of low productivity.

SUMMARY

1. Productivity can be defined as the relationship between the output produced by a given organizational system and the quantities of inputs or resources utilized to produce that output.
2. A management team should be organized to make sure that the goals and objectives of the productivity program coincide with the goals and objectives of the organization.
3. The six steps for developing an effective productivity program are: create awareness, measure productivity, evaluate productivity, plan productivity, improve productivity, and establish control reporting.
4. An effective productivity program benefits the company by providing better control, allowing for better planning, creating a basis for better supervision, eliminating overtime and job backlogs, and improving work scheduling.
5. An effective productivity program benefits employees by providing opportunities to participate in decision making, giving recognition

for achievement, providing opportunities for job enlargement, enrichment, and satisfaction, and improving working conditions.

6. Productivity measurement can be made against either industry data or base data gathered from within the company.
7. Once productivity statistics are determined, management should use a systems approach to ascertain the true nature of the productivity effort.
8. The productivity planning effort is used in conjunction with the results of the systems analysis data to plan strategies for improving productivity in those areas of deficiency.
9. All levels of employees must accept responsibility for improving productivity within the organization.
10. Any effort to increase productivity within an organization will be affected by the attitudes and motivations of the employees of the organization.
11. An often overlooked aspect of productivity programs is the control reporting or follow-up aspect.
12. An effective control reporting procedure gives managers the opportunity to monitor the productivity improvement measures which were established.
13. Of all the employee groups, managers will have the greatest impact on the success or failure of a productivity program.

STUDENT ACTIVITIES

Active Orientation

1. Invite an office manager from a local company to speak to your class concerning administrative productivity problems. Discuss the strategies used by the manager in terms of their measurement features and their costs to the organization.

2. Divide the class into research teams of four people and conduct primary and/or secondary research into the area of problems of executive productivity. Each research group should report its findings to the class.

Independent Problems

1. Why is it important to communicate the needs and benefits of organizational productivity programs? Answer this question from the point of view of both management and employees.

2. Should employees be asked for their input on productivity matters? Why?

REFERENCES

Jamali, Shafique. "Putting a Productivity Improvement Program into Action: A Six-Step Plan." *IE,* February, 1983, pp. 67–77.

Ranftl, Robert M. *R&D Productivity: An Investigation of Ways to Improve Productivity in Technology Based Organizations,* 2nd edition. Hughes Aircraft Company, 1978.

19 Compensation Administration

OBJECTIVES At the conclusion of this chapter, you should be able to:

1. Identify the components of an effective compensation program.
2. List the objectives of an effective compensation program.
3. Cite some sources of compensation data.
4. Describe the "cafeteria" benefit program.
5. Identify methods used in pricing office jobs.

INTRODUCTION

Effective compensation programs have always been elusive. The ability to fairly compensate employees within an organization not only aids the organization in recruiting capable workers, but also motivates current employees to be productive and reduces employee turnover. Given the projected job market for office workers, it appears that an organization's compensation program will play a key role in the successful operation of the administrative office.

OBJECTIVES OF A COMPENSATION PROGRAM

Compensation programs must strike a delicate balance between meeting the needs of employees and making payments within the company's means. Thus, organizations should develop compensation programs with the following objectives in mind:

1. to provide competitive compensation packages for all employees regardless of job title;
2. to meet all legal requirements of compensation programs;
3. to make payments within the company's means;
4. to motivate and compensate employees for exemplary work performance;
5. to promote employer–employee relations;
6. to aid the organization in planning and controlling the cost of the company's compensation program; and
7. to communicate the compensation program to *all* employees.

COMPONENTS OF A COMPENSATION PROGRAM

An effective compensation program encompasses more that just a competitive salary schedule. Compensation programs include salary schedules, health and medical benefits, retirement programs, career planning modules, vacation packages, and incentive programs. Although salaries play a very important role in the compensation program, the other employee benefits can be packaged for office workers to provide an attractive compensation portfolio for each employee. Figure 19.1 provides an example of an employee compensation portfolio.

ADMINISTERING COMPENSATION PROGRAMS

The administration of an organization's compensation program is a full-time job which requires dedicated professional personnel. Many

FIGURE 19.1
Employee compensation portfolio

Compensation portfolio Mr. John Smith Employee Number 34412	
Salary	$23,450
Medical Coverage	Major Medical Plan
Dental Coverage	No Election
College Reimbursement	Plan A Election
Stock Program	Plan B Election
Vacation	2 weeks paid
Sick Pay	Plan A Election

times, organizations fail to provide adequate budget dollars to staff and operate their compensation programs. The result is usually a hit-or-miss compensation program which manifests itself in inequitable salary schedules, outdated benefits packages, and high employee turnover.

In order to effectively operate a compensation program, the organization must hire a full-time Director of Compensation. In addition, an appropriate number of personnel department staff must be hired to conduct job analyses, develop job descriptions and specifications, conduct job market research, structure salaries and benefits packages, and communicate the program throughout the organization.

Gathering Job Data

Chapter 18 discussed the importance of determining what work is being conducted, how it is being conducted, how much it costs to perform each task, and how to evaluate work performance. This information is extremely valuable to the individuals who are charged with the responsibility of compensation because it provides them with the titles of the jobs performed, descriptions of the tasks performed, and the salaries of the individuals performing the jobs. This information can then be compared with data gathered from other sources outside the organization.

Internal data gathered through job analysis tells you where you are. Outside sources, such as government reports, professional association surveys, and local salary surveys, provide compensation personnel with information from the community and the nation. This information is then used by compensation personnel to update the salary and benefits packages so that they can stay competitive. Figure 19.2 gives a list of outside sources of information about office salaries. In addition to these published sources, compensation personnel may decide to contract with a private consulting firm to conduct compensation surveys either in their local area or within their specific type of industry on a national level. If the organization has enough money and personnel, they may choose to conduct their own research.

FIGURE 19.2
Outside sources of office salary data

- ☐ U.S. Bureau of Labor Statistics
- ☐ Administrative Management Society
- ☐ Association of Information Systems Professionals

The reality of all compensation programs is that only limited funds are available for use. Therefore, compensation personnel must work closely with the organization's budget personnel to determine the firm's ability to pay employees. In recent years, generally poor economic conditions have forced many organizations to substantially reduce the salary offerings to valuable employees. In an effort to make up for the lack of salary dollars, some companies have turned to the benefits package as a means of keeping valued employees from leaving the firm. Increased life insurance benefits, company car allowances, more vacation time, and more flexibility in the work schedule are examples of how compensation personnel have attempted to keep the hard-working employee with the firm during periods of economic crisis.

Structuring Salaries

The key feature in any compensation program is its ability to adjust to current conditions. Compensation systems cannot be adjusted unless compensation personnel know how each employee is being compensated in relation both to others in the organization and his or her peers in the open labor market. Thus, it is important that compensation personnel develop job evaluation points and associated pay scales to monitor the compensation process, as was described in the previous chapter. Figure 19.3 illustrates the use of a job evaluation instrument to identify the positions which need adjustment.

Automatic adjustments. Some organizations have chosen to adjust salaries automatically. These programs are usually tied to a type of predetermined calculation such as length of service. Other automatic adjustments, such as the cost-of-living adjustment, adjust the pay of the employee based on the consumer price index (CPI). These adjustments are reviewed quarterly or semi-annually, and salaries are adjusted according to the performance of the CPI during the previous period.

Incentive programs. Incentive programs have been utilized in factory or assembly line positions for many years. These programs are also useful in the administrative office. For example, many high production offices could utilize incentive programs such as the piece-rate

FIGURE 19.3 *Salary/evaluation scatter chart*

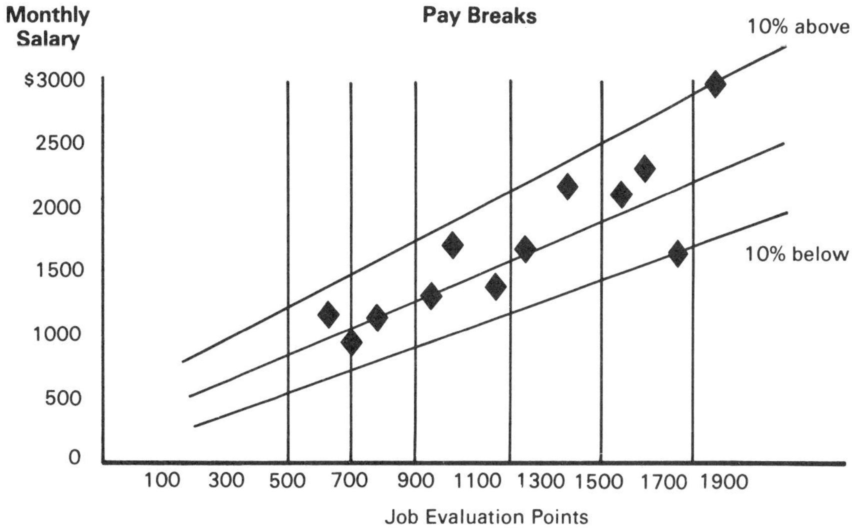

system, which pays bonus money for correspondence production over a certain number of documents per day or per week. Incentive programs can be very useful, but they require careful maintenance to ensure equitable pay for the work performed.

Another aspect of incentive programs which is applicable to the administrative office is the group incentive approach. Bonus money or benefits are made available to groups of individuals who may be working on special projects or tasks that require a large number of people. Many times this type of incentive program includes profit sharing or stock option payments.

Structuring Benefits

As was stated at the beginning of this chapter, salaries are only one part of the compensation package. The complete spectrum of available benefits is a creative and often desirable method of compensating employees. Figure 19.4 is a list of some of the benefit items that are part of today's compensation programs.

In the past, benefits packages were, for the most part, items negotiated with union representatives. Today, however, benefits packages are being used as substitutes or supplements to salary packages. A popular benefits strategy is to offer the employee a "cafeteria" benefits arrangement like the one in Figure 19.5. The cafeteria approach allows the employee to choose his or her own set of benefits. For example, one employee may value educational assistance, while another will opt for child care or additional vacation days. The saying goes ". . . there's no such thing as free lunch." The benefits package costs money, and compensation personnel must structure the benefits package within the company's ability to pay, just as it does with the salary packages.

FIGURE 19.4
Benefits packages

- ☐ Additional holidays or vacation days
- ☐ Profit sharing
- ☐ Educational assistance or grants
- ☐ Child care
- ☐ Legal aid
- ☐ Discounts on company products
- ☐ Life, health, and accident insurance
- ☐ Parking and transportation allowances

COMMUNICATING THE COMPENSATION PROGRAM

Compensation programs, especially those used as alternatives to larger salary increases, are usually not effective if they are not communicated to all the employees. Generally speaking, every employee can tell you how much he or she is earning, but few employees can tell you anything about their benefits package. Thus, a major function of every compensation program should be the communication of the entire compensation package. This can be achieved in a number of ways. The following list provides a sample of some compensation communication strategies.

- ☐ supply information in paycheck envelopes
- ☐ conduct meetings at various locations throughout the company
- ☐ prepare audio-visual materials for showing by department heads
- ☐ use company newspapers to announce benefits options
- ☐ prepare a compensation listing for each employee

Compensation personnel must constantly review the wide spectrum of opportunities available in order to provide a competitive compensation package for today's office employees. This requires a dedicated staff person with strong research skills.

FIGURE 19.5
Cafeteria benefits package

- ☐ Major Medical
- ☐ Dental
- ☐ Eye Care
- ☐ Educational Benefits
- ☐ Child Care

SUMMARY

1. Effective employee compensation programs enhance recruiting, motivate employees, and reduce employee turnover.
2. Compensation programs must strike a balance between meeting the needs of employees and making payments within the company's means.
3. Comprehensive compensation programs include competitive salary schedules, retirement programs, profit sharing, career planning and educational allowances, vacation options, and incentive programs.
4. Compensation programs require full-time staffs.
5. Compensation data can be gathered from the U.S. Bureau of Labor Statistics, the Administrative Management Society, and the Association of Information Systems Professionals, as well as through private research firms.
6. Salary and benefit structures are developed from job analysis data, labor market statistics, and the company's ability to pay.
7. The "cafeteria" approach to benefits packages allows employees to create the package that best suits them.
8. A major task of compensation personnel is to communicate the compensation program to all employees.

STUDENT ACTIVITIES

Active Orientation

1. Interview a personnel director at a company near you to determine:

- ☐ how office compensation packages are prepared;
- ☐ how office salaries are determined; and
- ☐ the educational background of the compensation personnel.

2. Contact five office employees from companies in your city to determine:

- ☐ the types of benefits available to them;
- ☐ how the employees are informed of the benefits available to them; and
- ☐ which benefit is the most important to them.

Independent Problems

1. Why are benefits important to young employees?

2. List three sources for gathering labor market data for office positions in your city.

20 Administrative Labor Relations

OBJECTIVES At the conclusion of this chapter, you should be able to:

1. Discuss the forces and movements that have aided in the development of labor legislation in this country.
2. Identify the current trends in white-collar unionization.
3. Define the term *management prerogative.*
4. List the steps involved in addressing employee grievances.
5. Define the role of an arbitrator.

INTRODUCTION

The blue-collar workforce, including factory, warehouse, and industrial workers, have traditionally made up the largest portion of union membership in the United States. As this portion of the workforce continues to shrink, labor unions are seeking new groups of workers to organize. One such pool of workers is the office worker, or white-collar worker. Richard Perry of United Food and Commercial Workers was quoted by *Forbes* magazine in 1982 as saying, "Last year we organized 6,000 private-sector white-collar workers. In the first quarter of this year we organized 7,000."

As shown in Figure 20.1, the U.S. Bureau of Labor Statistics indicates that union growth in white-collar jobs is on the increase and blue-collar union membership is declining. Although white-collar union membership is growing, the National Labor Relations Board statistics indicate that unions generally win less than fifty percent of white-collar campaigns. It remains to be seen whether white-collar personnel will become unionized on a large scale; however, America's unions have clearly targeted white-collar positions, especially office workers, for organization.

MAJOR LABOR LEGISLATION

Workers and employers have struggled to gain control of the workplace since the early days of the United States. From the craft and trade unions of the early 1800s to today's international unions, a seemingly endless battle rages. This section of the chapter highlights some

FIGURE 20.1
Blue-collar/white-collar union membership

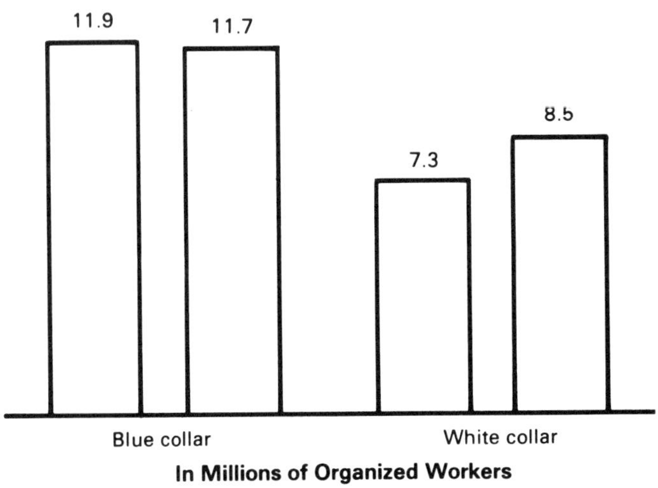

of the major labor legislation that has developed in the United States during the past fifty years.

Norris–LaGuardia Act of 1932

Prior to the Norris–LaGuardia Act, a common practice on the part of companies that were trying to discourage union organization was to seek court injunctions prohibiting union activities. The Norris–LaGuardia legislation placed severe limitations on the conditions under which injunctions could be issued. The major limitation required that hearings be held prior to the granting of an injunction. Furthermore, the Norris–LaGuardia Act forbade the use of "yellow dog contracts." *Yellow dog contract* was the name given to pre-employment agreements between employers and potential employees which required that the job applicant sign a statement indicating that he or she would not join a union. This condition of employment was ruled illegal under the Norris–LaGuardia Act.

Wagner Act of 1935

The Wagner Act (National Labor Relations Act) was the major labor legislation which supported employees' rights to unionize. Specifically, the Wagner Act established the employees' rights to:

1. self-organization;
2. form, join, and assist labor organizations in developing collective bargaining representation; and
3. engage in concerted activities for mutual aid and protection.

In addition to establishing employees' rights to organization and collective bargaining, the Wagner Act established the following as being unfair labor practices.

1. Employers cannot interfere with the rights of employees to organize for union purposes.
2. Employers cannot fail to hire or promote an individual based on any condition of employment.
3. Employers cannot penalize (discharge or demote) an individual for filing charges or testifying against an employer.
4. Employers cannot refuse to bargain collectively with union representatives.

The Wagner Act established the legal right for unions to exist in this country. Although significant pro-labor legislation has been passed since 1932, the Wagner Act was the first legislation which clearly legitimized union activities.

Social Security Act of 1935

The Social Security Act and its subsequent amendments have provided workers with unemployment insurance, retirement benefits, disability benefits, and health insurance such as Medicare and Medicaid.

Fair Labor Standards Act of 1938

The Fair Labor Standards Act established the forty-hour work week for workers. This legislation became known as the "wage and hour law" because it made provisions for minimum wage payments to workers, overtime pay at one-and-one-half times the pay rate, and child protection in hazardous work areas.

Taft–Hartley Act of 1947

The Taft–Hartley Act (Labor-Management Relations Act) was passed into law to address some of the limitations of the Wagner Act. Specifically, the Wagner Act outlined unfair labor practices on the part of employers but did not address potential labor violations on the part of labor organizations. The Taft–Hartley legislation firmly established employees' rights to refrain from union activity.

The Taft–Hartley Act uses the National Labor Relations Board (NLRB), which was established by the Wagner Act to consider violations by either the employer or the union organization. Following is a listing of some of the provisions of the Taft–Hartley Act.

1. Both employers and labor organizations can be sued by the NLRB for violations of the labor agreement.
2. Wages cannot be paid for services not performed.
3. Union organizations cannot charge excessive fees.
4. The following items must be included in the collective bargaining effort: wages, hours, working conditions, discipline, demotion, promotion, suspension, discharge, transfers, layoffs, recalls, safety and health, and grievance procedures.
5. The union cannot refuse to bargain collectively with the employer.
6. Payroll deductions for union dues can be established with the written consent of the employee.
7. The President of the United States can envoke an eighty-day emergency injunction against any strike which threatens the safety and security of citizens.

Landrum–Griffin Act of 1959

Just as the Taft–Hartley Act amended the Wagner Act, the Landrum–Griffin Act (Labor–Management Reporting and Disclosure Act) was established to amend the Taft–Hartley Act. The Landrum–Griffin Act was initiated as the result of a federal investigation into corrupt labor practices in the United States. The major provisions of the Landrum–Griffin Act are:

1. Each union member has the right to attend union meetings.
2. Each union member has the right to nominate candidates for union offices.
3. Each union member has the right to one vote in union elections.

4. Union members may use the federal court system to settle differences with the company or the union.
5. Annual union financial reports must be filed with the Secretary of Labor.

Equal Pay Act of 1963

The Equal Pay Act effectively amends the Fair Labor Standards Act. The Equal Pay Act was designed to provide equal pay policies between the sexes within an organization. The provisions of the Equal Pay Act make it illegal to

1. have unequal pay policies (wages and benefits) for men and women who, under similar working conditions, perform jobs which require equal skill and responsibility; and
2. reduce the wages and/or benefits of one group as a means of reducing pay discrimination.

The Equal Pay Act, however, allows employers to pay different salaries for work shift differentials, seniority factors, and merit pay programs.

Civil Rights Act of 1964

The Civil Rights Act addressed many forms of discrimination. However, Title VII of this act specifically addressed employment considerations. The major employment provisions of the Civil Rights Act of 1964 are:

1. It is illegal to discriminate against a job applicant or employee on the basis of race, color, religion, sex, or national origin.
2. It is illegal to advertise for employment indicating a preference for race, color, religion, sex, or national origin.
3. It is illegal to discriminate against an individual who has spoken out against an employer who has discriminated against someone.

Age Discrimination in Employment Act of 1967

The Age Discrimination in Employment Act addresses an obvious omission of the Civil Rights Act. Individuals between the ages of forty and sixty-five cannot be discriminated against in hiring, wages, benefits, or other conditions of employment as a result of this legislation.

Equal Employment Act of 1972

It became apparent that, with all the employment legislation that had been enacted, there was a demonstrated need for the establishment of an agency to investigate potential violations and to enforce the law. The Equal Employment Act created the Equal Employment Opportunity Commission (EEOC) to enforce all legislation against employment discrimination. The EEOC has the power to bring civil suits against violators of employment laws.

RECOGNIZING UNIONS

Before a union organization can legally operate, a union election must be held to determine if the majority of workers desire union representation. Usually a group of workers initiates union activity by discussing plans for unionization with fellow employees and union organization representatives. Occasionally, union representatives, called *organizers,* contact workers in nonunion companies for the purpose of union organization.

If it appears that a majority of workers want to unionize, company officials may establish contact with the union to form a collective bargaining arrangement without a formal election. However, if the workers are divided as to unionization, an election is called. Secret ballots are marked, indicating the workers' desire for or against union organization. A simple majority vote determines the existence or absence of a union.

Occasionally, more than one union will wish to represent the employees. Under these circumstances, only the union winning a majority of the votes is chosen to represent the employees of the company. If no majority is achieved, a run-off election is held between the two organizations that receive the most votes in the original election. Figure 20.2 illustrates the election process.

UNION HIERARCHY

National unions establish charters which clearly outline their purpose and operating procedures. Typical provisions of national union charters are:

1. procedures for establishing local chapters of the union;
2. procedures for the nomination and election of union officers;
3. procedures for establishing and collecting union dues; and
4. procedures for reporting financial data.

Local unions normally have elected officers such as president, vice president, secretary, and treasurer. A business agent is usually appointed to negotiate the labor contract. This person may be one of the

FIGURE 20.2
Union election voting procedure

- ☐ Call for vote by secret ballot
- ☐ Majority vote is required, or else a run-off election between the two unions with the most votes
- ☐ Winner is declared collective bargaining unit

local officers. These individuals usually represent the only full-time members of the local union. Union stewards are employees working throughout the company who represent the needs and concerns of their fellow workers to the local union officials. The union stewards are normally elected by their fellow workers.

THE LABOR CONTRACT

The labor contract is the document that lists the agreements reached during negotiations between the company and the union. It is important that each party clearly understands the clauses of the contract so that there will be few problems interpreting the agreement during the life of the contract. Labor contracts, therefore, are frequently lengthy and redundant because both parties insist on re-emphasizing their items of concern.

As stated earlier, labor contracts must contain certain provisions required by the Taft–Hartley Act. These provisions require that labor contracts contain clauses addressing wages, hours, working conditions, discipline procedures, promotion, demotion, suspension, discharge, transfers, layoffs, recalls, safety and health, and grievance procedures.

Obviously, all possible situations cannot be anticipated, not to mention negotiated. Any situation that is not covered in the contract and is not addressed in the Taft–Hartley Act becomes an item called a *management prerogative*. This means that the item in question can be controlled by management; management does not have to negotiate the item with union representatives during the life of the existing labor contract. Many times management prerogatives become items for negotiation in the next labor contract.

The labor contract is the legally binding agreement between the employees and the company for a specified period of time. This specified period of time is known as the "life of the contract." The life of a labor contract varies; however, most common labor contracts are for two or three year periods.

GRIEVANCE PROCEDURES

One of the most structured provisions of labor contracts is the procedure for processing grievances between the employees and the company. A *grievance* can be defined as any complaint against the company filed by an employee. Grievance procedures provide both the company and the union with a structured format for resolving conflicts in the workplace without the union having to resort to boycotts, work slowdowns, or strikes. Many grievances are filed because one or both of the parties involved does not clearly understand the provisions of the labor contract.

Resolving the Grievance

If the labor contract has been properly drafted, it will contain specific provisions that outline the procedures both parties are to take when a grievance is filed. Although these procedures, often called *steps,* vary from organization to organization and contract to contract, the following procedures, which are also illustrated in Figure 20.3, represent common provisions for resolving grievances.

Step 1. The first step in most grievance procedures is for the employee to file a grievance with his or her superior. This filing should be in writing and prepared in cooperation with the employee's union steward. Many organizations do not require that first step grievances be in writing. However, because written grievances reduce the potential for errors in interpretation, memory, and intent, it is recommended that even the first step of the grievance process be in writing.

Step 2. If the grievance is not resolved between the employee, the union steward, and the employee's immediate superior, the next step of the grievance procedure is utilized. The employee is represented by the business agent or a local union officer in the second step of the grievance process. Normally, the employee and his or her representative meet with the personnel manager or the employee relations person from the company to address the written grievance. If the grievance is not resolved at this point, it is carried to the third step.

Step 3. The employee and local union officers meet with the general manager, plant manager, or president of the company during the third step of most grievance procedures. This step is usually the last step in the process before outside intervention is required.

Step 4. If both parties are unable to resolve the pending grievance during the third step, an arbitrator may be called in to resolve the

FIGURE 20.3
Four-step grievance process

- ☐ Step 1: File grievance with supervisor
- ☐ Step 2: Business manager meets with personnel manager
- ☐ Step 3: Local union officials meet with general manager
- ☐ Step 4: Arbitration

issue. Arbitrators are third party representatives who offer solutions to the grievance, given the available information. Organizations can hire an arbitrator or an arbitration board consisting of representatives from management and the union.

IMPLICATIONS FOR THE ADMINISTRATIVE MANAGER

It would appear that many office positions are prime targets for union organization efforts. Whether or not an administrative office becomes unionized is really not the issue. Certainly an office union will force office managers to address specific employer-employee issues. However, many of these important issues will surface with or without an office union.

The projected job market for office personnel indicates the potential for tremendous job mobility throughout this century. This will allow office workers to lobby for higher salaries, more management responsibility, and fringe benefits such as medical coverage and child care. These items will either be negotiated through union representation or individual contract, and, if they are not available, the employee will merely seek employment elsewhere. It is imperative, therefore, that the office manager adopt a management style which addresses the complete spectrum of needs of office workers if he or she is going to be successful in hiring and keeping productive office workers in the future.

SUMMARY

1. Union growth in white-collar occupations is increasing while union membership in blue-collar jobs is decreasing.
2. The Norris–LaGuardia Act of 1932 required that hearings be held before injunctions prohibiting strikes were issued. This legislation also prohibited "yellow dog contracts."
3. The Wagner Act of 1935 established employees' rights to organize themselves and to organize unions for collective bargaining.
4. The Social Security Act of 1935 and its amendments provided American workers with unemployment insurance, retirement benefits, disability benefits, and health insurance.
5. The Fair Labor Standards Act of 1938 made provisions for minimum wage payments, overtime pay, and child protection in the workplace.

6. The Taft–Hartley Act of 1947 provided the guidelines for the National Labor Relations Board (NLRB), which was created under the Wagner Act to investigate and prosecute violators of labor law.
7. The Landrum–Griffin Act of 1959 amended the Taft–Hartley Act to protect workers from illegal union practices.
8. The Equal Pay Act of 1963 makes it illegal to pay individuals different amounts for work performed under similar working conditions which require similar skills and responsibilities.
9. Title VII of the Civil Rights Act of 1964 makes it illegal to discriminate in the workplace because of an employee's race, color, religion, sex, or national origin.
10. The Age Discrimination in Employment Act of 1967 makes it illegal to discriminate in hiring, wages, benefits, and other conditions of employment of people between the ages of forty and sixty-five.
11. The Equal Employment Act of 1972 created the Equal Employment Opportunity Commission (EEOC) to enforce all types of employment legislation.
12. Unions are recognized as bargaining agents for workers through an election process. The union must receive a majority of votes from the workers in order to be established.
13. The labor contract contains agreements between the company and the union as well as provisions outlined by the Taft–Hartley Act.
14. Grievance procedures should be clearly established in the labor contract.
15. The administrative office manager should prepare for the unionization of the office.

STUDENT ACTIVITIES

Active Orientation

1. Visit a local union office to determine the following information:

- ☐ the number and type(s) of workers represented;
- ☐ which national union the local union is affiliated with; and
- ☐ the role of each of the local union officers.

2. Interview a local office manager to determine his or her opinions concerning:

- ☐ office unions;
- ☐ preventing office unions; and
- ☐ working with office unions.

Independent Problems

1. Role play a union organization effort in the classroom. Have different students take the roles of management personnel, office workers, and union organizers. Have each group meet individually to determine strategies for dealing with a possible union representation vote.

2. Develop a list of issues which you feel would be the critical issues faced by office managers during a union organization effort.

REFERENCES

Brophy, Beth. "Rank and Filers," *Forbes,* May 10, 1982, p. 172.

Nussbaum, Karen. "Coalition Gears Up to Organize Women," *Industry Week,* March 23, 1981, pp. 136–37.

21 Training and Development of Administrative Personnel

OBJECTIVES At the conclusion of this chapter, you should be able to:

1. Define *training* and its effects on both employee and employer.
2. List and describe the areas of office training.
3. Identify and describe the six steps of the training process.
4. Describe the functions of the various types of trainers.
5. Distinguish between the five training methods.
6. Identify and describe the various training techniques.
7. Have an awareness of the need for equity in business and office organizations.

INTRODUCTION

From the moment that a mutual employment decision has been made, through the retirement of the employee, training should be an essential part of the employer-employee relationship. As the automated office becomes a reality due to the ever decreasing costs of automated office equipment, managers are recognizing the value of this type of equipment in the race for efficiency and productivity. In order for a company to keep the competitive edge, automated equipment and skilled employees are a must. Training must become equally sophisticated and productive so that companies can handle, for example, a sevenfold increase (from 2.5 million to 17.5 million) in on-line word processing equipment in the next decade. Training may become a major chapter in a corporation's success story before the end of this century.

Training is an organized process which should provide experiences that result in productive growth for both the employee and the organization. The employee should benefit through increased knowledge and improved skills and attitude. The organization should benefit from greater effectiveness, efficiency, and a more goal-oriented informal organization, resulting in greater productivity.

TYPES OF OFFICE TRAINING

When people in business and office occupations hear the words "office training," they usually envision the teaching of office systems and procedures. In fact, training encompasses much more than these skills and technical training areas; other areas include entry training, management and subject matter training, and motivational training.

Entry Training

Entry training may be thought of as an employee's baptism into the organization. This process may last up to six months and it is most intensive during the first week of employment, when the employee is exposed to corporate policy, procedures, and benefits. During the first few months of employment, the employee should also begin to feel a sense of responsibility and loyalty to the company. It is expected that, by the end of the first six months of employment or sooner, the employee will be productive.

Management and Subject Matter Training

Management training prepares qualified employees to enter supervisory and middle management positions within the organization. It is also used to update and refresh current supervisors and middle managers. Subject matter at these levels of training includes communication, problem solving, decision making and employee appraisal methods. All of this subject matter is geared toward making the shift from being a worker to being a leader as fulfilling and rewarding as possible for employees who are being considered for promotion into the ranks of supervision or middle management.

Motivational Training

Motivational training generally encompasses an employee's work values, habits, and attitudes as described in Chapter 16. In recent years, motivational training has also become the prime business and industry delivery system for Human Resource Development; this program operates under the premise that the total person is a resource to the organization, and if that person is experiencing difficulties at work or in other settings, his or her effectiveness is lessened. Human Resource Development covers a wide range of areas, from alcohol and drug-related problems to programs on death and dying, as well as personal growth assistance.

Skills and Technical Training

The case for skills and technical training is generally a strong one; most people assume that it is needed because they realize that increased productivity requires either improved equipment and processes or gains in worker knowledge and skills. Skills and technical training is provided to business and office organization members who must possess specific knowledge and skills to meet business objectives. The organization invests in its human resources for the purpose of producing financial gains for itself.

In the business and office world of work, the skills and technical training area is essential because of rapidly changing office technology. Efficiency and productivity will be very closely tied to the understanding and use of electronic systems by every level of employee within the business and office hierarchy. Examples of business and office skills and technical training that fit into this category would be telecommunications services, reprographic procedures, word processing procedures, and data processing procedures.

THE TRAINING PROCESS

Although the training process that will be described in this chapter relates to all of the areas of training, it will seem more relevant if it is discussed with respect to a specific area. Therefore, the training area of skills and technical training will be used as an example where necessary.

The training process envelops the whole concept of training; why it's done, how it's done, was it done properly and effectively, and so on.

It usually involves the six steps of: identifying the need; determining objectives; developing activities; determining resources and materials; evaluation; and feedback. Each step will be discussed in the following paragraphs.

Identifying the Need What is going to be taught to whom and why is it going to be taught? These simple questions become very complex when a manager attempts to justify spending thousands of dollars for office employee skills and technical training. In most companies, top management officials have the responsibility for determining the needs of the company. These needs are usually based upon profit and relate to a lack of productivity or efficiency in one or more departments within the company. For example, a reduction in overall sales may be traced to an ineffective change in a marketing strategy. The need would be to reverse this trend by changing the strategy. Needs are sometimes based on growth projections of a company; if a company knows that expansion will occur in the budgetable future, a need may be felt for the training of additional personnel. In any event, the needs that can be satisfied by training will eventually be filtered down to the training executives for consideration.

Cost-effectiveness must also be considered as a need in determining who will train whom. It may be appropriate for a medium to large company to develop an in-house training system that will result in the transformation of an office with traditional equipment to an office capable of using the latest word processing equipment or accounting system. However, it may not be cost-effective for the same company to develop its own program for mail processing because of the limited number of personnel who are directly involved in such activity in the company.

Determining the Objectives Once needs are identified, they must be clarified into objectives which answer the questions Where are we going? How are we going to get there? and How will we know that we've arrived? An objective for a word processing example under skills and technical training might be: "At the conclusion of the word processing training program, the word processing secretary will be able to efficiently and effectively use dictation/transcription equipment and text/editing equipment to produce a textual product suitable for distribution." At this stage of the training game, objectives shouldn't be too specific, but should give the trainer the guidance needed to proceed to the next step.

Developing Activities Activities relate specifically to the objectives; they answer the how we are going to get there question. At this stage, the trainer should identify the techniques that will be employed, describe the trainees who will participate and benefit from the training, and identify and qualify the training instructors. An activity that is related to the word processing objective would be to have each word processing secretary make a transcription from a recording device using an automatic typewriter with a memory device.

Determining Materials and Resources

In office skills and technical training, more than in any other training area, you can't just talk about it; you must do it! It is essential that, during this phase of the training process, there are enough materials for use by everyone. This doesn't mean that there must be twenty of everything if there are twenty trainees; the training program must be coordinated so that each trainee is rotated through each piece of equipment. This can be done without the trainees waiting for equipment by having different groups of trainees do different training activities in the same time frame.

As you might imagine, determining materials and other resources for a training program can become a major challenge for the trainer. The trainer must:

1. determine the number of trainees per training session;
2. efficiently group and schedule the trainees so that meaningful activities will occur simultaneously in a number of training areas;
3. determine the quantity of equipment with appropriate materials and supplies; and
4. have back-up equipment available on short notice if needed.

When determining materials and resources, the cost of the training program must be considered. Some cost related items are:

1. time—for both trainees and instructors (is training taking place during working hours or, if not, is the company paying for the trainee's time off of the job?);
2. instruction (use and development of materials and equipment); and
3. the use of facilities for training as well as trainee per diem.

It is essential that the trainer realize that the types of materials and resources to be used should be based upon the types of activities that are needed to meet the objectives of the training program. There is no room in training programs for "It would be nice for everyone to know this" material. If it is not in an objective, it shouldn't be taught!

Evaluation

How do we know that we have arrived? Evaluation of the office training program must be geared to the objectives of the program. In order to find out if the training program has made any difference, it is necessary to evaluate the trainees before and after the program with respect to the objectives of the program. If more than one major skill or technical concept has been taught, such as transcribing and editing, periodic evaluation called "unit evaluation" should take place. Trainers should remember that they are dealing with individuals, and should obtain information from each trainee regarding not only his or her progress through the program but also his or her feelings concerning the methods, techniques, equipment, and instructors used in the program.

Feedback So we've done all of this evaluating. So what! This statement is a valid one if evaluation is not followed up with feedback. It doesn't do the trainer any good to evaluate unless the information is used to improve the business training program or justify the existence of the training department. Feedback is essential as soon as instruction begins. If trainees are not getting the basic information that they need to build upon, feedback from evaluations will allow the trainer to correct the problem. If trainees are turned off by a particular instructor, a situation that can affect learning, feedback can be given to the instructor so that either behavior modification can occur or a new instructor can be hired. Feedback, therefore, is the process of operationalizing evaluation for the purpose of improving or justifying the training experience.

The training process must begin before any training takes place. Once the needs are determined and objectives are established, several inputs must be considered either before or when resources and materials are determined. The next three sections of this chapter will describe these inputs.

SOURCES OF TRAINING

It should be obvious by this time that in all but the largest organizations, some training functions must be contracted out. This occurs because they either are not cost-effective to the company or the company does not possess the necessary resources and/or personnel to adequately perform the training function. Most organizations use one or more of the following types of trainers.

- ☐ **Job Trainer.** This person from within the organization is considered to be an expert at a certain skill or technology. He or she will perform on-the-job training (OJT), usually on a one-on-one basis.
- ☐ **Corporate Trainer.** This is a generic trainer who may provide entry training for a specific program that is needed by a large organization.
- ☐ **Training Provider.** This person is usually a vendor who provides training packages for direct consumption to departments. The "package" may include an instructor or out-of-house training and is

often the result of a major purchase of new or innovative equipment, such as word processing equipment.

- □ **Training Broker.** This is a person or organization whose function is to link up people with specific expertise to organizations that have specific needs.

TRAINING METHODS

Everyone learns different things at different rates through the use of a variety of means. Different subject areas, by their very nature, also lend themselves to a variety of training methods. In the business and office world of work, training methods that are most often used are on-the-job training (OJT), department or corporate training, corporate-wide training programs, vestibule training, and programmed instruction.

On-the-Job Training (OJT)

This is the most common method of training found in the business and office world. The advantage of this method is that the trainee receives knowledge and skills training in using the actual equipment and materials required for the job while he or she is working "on the job." The trainee can also be exposed to both the problems and benefits of the job. The one-on-one relationship with the trainer can provide a communication link that extends beyond the OJT time; the trainee usually feels free to ask questions or voice concerns to his or her OJT trainer for many years.

The only major disadvantage to this type of training can be found in the qualifications of the trainer. Content knowledge, personality, and a willingness to teach and allow others to experience are characteristics that an OJT trainer should possess. A poor trainer can make OJT a meaningless and frustrating experience.

OJT is a good training system to use when a job is specific to a department or organization, such as billing, mail sorting, and switchboard, and the number of persons who perform the job is limited.

Department or Corporate Presentations

This type of training is usually considered as a lesser evil than the corporate-wide memo. It is used when information such as new insurance forms must be presented to a great many people in a short period of time. This one-way communication process usually gives people enough awareness about the new procedure to consult a handbook or human source for further clarification regarding the procedure.

Corporate-Wide Training Programs

Very large companies often have their own training department which is usually a subset of Human Resources. This type of organizational structure ensures a supply of properly trained individuals in different departments. Large companies, for example, employ hundreds of clerical workers, all of whom have different ideas and perceptions regarding their role within the organization. The subject areas of line of authority, proper attire, and telephone etiquette can be presented, discussed, and clarified in training programs.

Many companies form links with schools and universities to obtain a pool of skilled workers. The advantage of this type of relationship for the schools is reflected in the placement opportunities for students. The company receives an additional advantage of being able to look over the field of candidates without expending a great deal of financial energy.

Companies also use schools and universities for personnel training. For example, Temporaries Inc. offers word processing training opportunities to any temporary employee meeting their selection criteria. After completion of the course and 300 hours of satisfactory employment, the employee is reimbursed for one-third of the tuition fee. Western Temporary Services Inc., which is based in California, will also train a promising temporary employee in a traditional business school when the need for specific skills is required.

Vestibule Training

Vestibule training involves trainee activities that occur in an environment that typifies the real job, and may even be an exact copy of the real job. This expensive training technique is used when trainees know very little about the job. The jobs are either very complex or they require a high level of expertise or accuracy; in these cases, practice on the real job would jeopardize or interfere with the orderly flow of work. Electronic mail sorting training by the U.S. Postal Service is an example of this type of training.

Programmed Instruction

In recent years, programmed instruction, computer-assisted instruction, and teaching machines have become very popular and effective in business and office training programs. This type of training has various levels of sophistication, from a linear program which is not much more than a recyclable flow chart to a branching program which has an instructional path for the trainee to follow that depends upon how each question is answered. Add to this the use of computers and a variety of media, such as television, films, and video tape recorders, and you'll find that almost any type of training can be performed in a self-paced manner using programmed instruction. The limitations relate to high production costs, and generic use and usefulness for specific occupations. According to Robert Norton, there are many advantages to using programmed materials in training.

- ☐ Programmed materials are self-paced, permitting each trainee to move independently through each sequence.

- ☐ The trainer is freed from routine instructional tasks, which leaves more time for interaction with trainees.
- ☐ Materials are efficient and objective-oriented.
- ☐ The information presented is organized and sequenced for individual readiness and is based on sound psychological theories.
- ☐ Learning can be independent and informal.
- ☐ A single trainer can monitor and help individuals who are working on different programs.

The main disadvantage to the use of programmed materials can be directly linked to the cost of this type of instruction; software is expensive and the initial capital outlay for the teaching machines, which are usually microprocessors, is high. Another disadvantage relates to the difficulty that some employees have in taking directions or instructions from a machine; they feel a lack of personal interaction and, as a result, have a difficult time with the self-paced materials.

TRAINING TECHNIQUES

The most common training techniques fall under the heading of simulation and include in-basket, equipment, case studies, gaming, and role playing. Other types of training techniques are group and panel discussions and symposiums. At times more than one training technique may be considered appropriate for the type of training objective that is to be accomplished. This is always a good situation for the trainer because using more than one technique increases the chances of a successful training experience.

Simulation

Simulation involves the creation of a realistic business and office setting using appropriate problem-solving activities which are related to real occupational experiences. According to the Center for Vocational Education (CVE) at Ohio State University, some of the advantages of simulation are that it:

- ☐ provides a degree of realism and immediacy which is often lacking in the presentation or discussion of ideas;
- ☐ allows trainees to experiment in a safe, simplified, and realistic environment with minimal fear of failure;
- ☐ permits trainees to get feedback on their performance in a non-threatening manner;
- ☐ affords a realistic experience at a cost which is generally less expensive than that involved in an actual experience;
- ☐ offers short-term experiences and feedback in what are often long-term processes in the real world;

- ☐ presents a conflict situation which can involve the trainee more actively in the learning process than other instructional techniques;
- ☐ allows the trainee some control over the events in the situation;
- ☐ allows the trainee to assume and experience other roles;
- ☐ controls the situation and structures it so that it may be handled by the trainee;
- ☐ emphasizes team learning and trainee interaction; and
- ☐ provides immediate feedback to the trainee.

The major disadvantage of simulation can be found in the cost of developing a realistic environment through the use of a simulator. In addition, employees may not take the simulation activity seriously because they feel that the setting is not real.

In-basket simulation. In-basket simulation is a decision-making experience that is particularly appropriate for business and office training. In this type of training, participants assume the role of decision makers and react to materials provided to them such as letters and memos that can typically be found in a person's in-basket. The trainee, based on the type of materials or instructions placed in the in-basket, must make decisions, set priorities, and accomplish tasks. In-basket simulation can be used as part of the personnel promotion selection process or for supervisory and managerial training.

Equipment simulation. The best example of an equipment simulator is the Driver Training Simulator used in schools throughout the country. At times it is impossible to have an actual piece of equipment in a training session because of size, cost, or danger. In these situations, a simulator may be designed that allows the operations that must be learned to be performed in the same way that they would be performed in real life; however, the extra features that don't relate to the task at hand are eliminated. Companies like IBM or NCR who have large repair and maintenance staffs use this type of simulation in their training of personnel in these areas.

Case study. In a case study, trainees are given an account of a realistic situation and are asked to solve the problem, either independently or as a group. Case studies are appropriate to business and office training if the case is relevant to the trainee and is possible to solve. The best case studies play upon a trainee's experience base, allowing that person to put a number of concepts together in order to arrive at a correct solution. Care must be taken by the trainer not to frustrate the trainee by posing too great a problem or accepting too narrow a response.

Gaming. Almost everyone of every age loves some type of game. The simulation known as *gaming* attempts to profit from this observation. Board games, card games, and the good old spelling bee type of games seem to be the most popular at getting trainees involved in teamwork and making decisions toward a training objective. The problem with this type of simulation relates to the difficulty in finding or developing an appropriate type of game for the trainees' level. An appropriate game for business and office training may be entitled "The Office"; here, trainees would be exposed to all of the various job responsibilities and duties throughout the office hierarchy.

Role playing. Role playing is a common and effective type of business and office simulation. It involves the acting out of a particular situation that reflects a training objective. Role playing is performed unrehearsed, allowing the trainee and trainer to get a clear picture of the realities of the situation. According to the Center for Vocational Education, when used properly, role playing can:

- stimulate interest and participation;
- provide a kind of laboratory in which roles can be examined and experimented within situations where a semblance of reality exists;
- give insight into the roles a person plays in real life and how effectively one plays those roles;
- teach trainees to perform new roles and thus be able to adjust more adequately to the groups of which they are a part;
- provide examples of behavior, which can be more effective than merely talking about a situation;
- help develop clearer communication, because it is sometimes easier to act out a situation than to put it into words;
- help trainees to have a more sympathetic attitude toward others and to understand other points of view;
- help students learn to express themselves;
- acquaint students with problems and possible solutions;
- provide a means of extending emotional insights among group members and between groups; and
- demonstrate in advance how students will probably react under real conditions.

Disadvantages of role playing relate to:

- the difficulty in staying on task or focusing directly on the training objective;
- the possibility of a person using a role in a nonsympathetic manner toward others, a situation which gives valuable information to the trainer, but may cause a morale problem among the trainees; and

- ☐ the possibility of the participants not "getting into" the role because it is perceived as being "just a game."

All of these disadvantages can be eliminated through careful preparation and monitoring on the part of the trainer.

Group and Panel Discussions This type of training technique is found in almost every type of training. Group discussions involve the entire training class and are concerned with the sharing of information on a specific topic or the evaluation and analysis of information. Panel discussions are merely small group discussions that are used for the purpose of getting across differing points of view to a larger audience. In either type of discussion, it is important to make sure that all trainees are given the opportunity to participate.

Symposiums A symposium is a more formal type of panel discussion in which several speakers present different aspects of an issue or problem. These speakers are usually considered to be experts in their area, and they usually respond to questions from each other and the audience. An example might be a manager, supervisor, union representative, and office worker speaking on the topic of improving morale.

EQUITY

The training and development of office personnel must address sex and minority equity in all of its training programs. Guidelines from the Equal Employment Opportunity Commission (EEOC) on these issues should be addressed during both employee orientation and general training programs. Trainers should pay special attention in all of their programs to statements and terminology that have potentially biased overtones. They should also make a concerted effort to discourage sexual harassment and any type of bigoted behavior among trainees by stating the internal and external regulations against such behavior as a part of the introduction to every program.

SUMMARY

1. Training is an organized process which should provide experiences that result in productive growth for both the employee and the organization.
2. The types of office training are entry training, skills and technical training, management and subject matter training, and motivational training.

3. The training process involves the six steps of identifying the need, determining objectives, developing activities, determining resources and materials, evaluation, and feedback.
4. The sources of training are the job trainer, corporate trainer, training provider, and training broker.
5. In the business and office world of work, training methods that are used most often are on-the-job training (OJT), department or corporate training, corporate-wide training programs, vestibule training, and programmed instruction.
6. Simulation is a training technique that includes in-basket, equipment simulations, case studies, gaming, and role playing. Other training techniques are group and panel discussions and symposiums.
7. Training should increase all employees' awareness regarding the dignity of all work and workers.

STUDENT ACTIVITIES

Active Orientation

1. As a class or in small groups, work on the following case study.

The Arthur Bigg company wishes to begin a training program for their office personnel that will allow each individual to have at least a working knowledge of the following technological office innovations and their present use in their organization: word processing, data processing, and electronic mail. The company has already decided that it is willing to allow groups of up to ten employees to be away from their desks for one day; therefore, the training must not take longer than eight hours per person.

A team of five members of the training department (your class) has been assigned to get the job done and you must be ready for presentation in two weeks. Using the information from this chapter, develop a training strategy for Mr. Bigg. Hint: Start with the training process; you've already got the need and a few other bits of information.

2. As a class or in small groups, work on the following panel discussion.

As a "training provider," your company has invited its potential clients to a luncheon panel discussion where five experts will speak on the topic of either "Improving worker productivity through training" or "Improving worker morale through training." You are responsible for the following:

- ☐ Selection of the topic.
- ☐ Selection of five subtopics that relate to the topic and have an information base in this chapter.

- ☐ Selection of five panel members who must each prepare five-minute presentations on the subtopics.
- ☐ Each member of the remainder of the class must prepare three questions on at least two of the subtopics that will be presented.

3. Review, and be prepared to interpret in a group discussion in class, the guidelines of the Equal Employment Opportunity Commission (EEOC) on the subject of sexual harassment. Develop, as a group, a class policy statement prohibiting sexual harassment.

Independent Problems

1. Write an essay that addresses this question: Why is training important to management, workers, and people seeking promotions?

2. Visit a training department or section in a company. By using observations and interviews, determine at least five of the following:

- ☐ the topics for training;
- ☐ the extent of training in-house and out-of-house;
- ☐ the types of training conducted;
- ☐ the training process that is followed;
- ☐ the sources of training; and
- ☐ the methods and techniques used in training.

REFERENCES

The Center for Vocational Education. *Employment Simulation Techniques.* Athens, Georgia: 1977, p. 6.

Norton, Robert E. *Using Programmed Instruction in Occupational Education.* Albany, NY: Bureau of Occupational Education Research, The State Education Department, The University of the State of New York, 1977, pp. 12–13.

Epilogue

The world is witness to an unusual phenomenon which has been observed by only a few generations in human history. It is a "changing of the guard," a "shifting of gears," or a significant alteration of world order. This phenomenon has been given many names: "the Third Wave," "the Information Age," and "the Computer Revolution," just to name a few. Regardless of the label, one clear fact remains: the worlds' people are experiencing a dramatic change in the way they do their work.

Alvin Toffler quite accurately documents these shifts in the human work effort from the Agriculture Age through the Industrial Age to the present Information Age in his book entitled *The Third Wave*. These shifts represent significant and irreversible technological advances resulting in substantial increases in human productivity.

We Americans have been the greatest beneficiaries of technological change largely because we have been the innovators, creators, and users of the tools of modern science. We have been free to create and enjoy the fruits of our technology without serious foreign competition. In recent years, however, the ability of foreign countries to compete technologically with the United States in the free enterprise market has created a significant realignment of economic power among the nations of the world. No longer does the United States control the automobile and steel manufacturing markets of the world. No longer does the label "Made in Japan" indicate an inferior product.

As Americans we find ourselves in a precarious position. Behind us we see our outmoded automobile and steel factories lying idle or operating at a fraction of capacity. Ahead of us we see not only fierce foreign competition, but also as many as ten million American workers who are virtually unprepared for the jobs that are available in information-related technologies.

Information-related technologies now account for more than *fifty percent* of all United States workers. This percentage is expected to increase to seventy percent by the year 1990. Industrial workers represent only seventeen percent of today's United States labor force. These startling figures clearly indicate the scope of the employment shift from the Industrial Age to the Information Age. Many of the traditional job markets associated with the United States, such as automobiles, steel manufacturing, and copper mining, will never again employ human workers in the numbers that were common in the 1960s.

The rapid technological innovations of recent years have caught United States workers and industry napping. Our inability to provide long-term training and development for our workforce has severely handicapped our efforts to compete in the world economy. The troubling paradox of high unemployment and high underemployment in specific job areas is further evidence of a world in flux. We can expect sustained high unemployment throughout this decade, not because the jobs aren't there, but because we must retrain our industrial age workers for information age jobs. It will take a substantial amount of time and money to retrain this estimated ten to fifteen million workers. It will be worth the effort, however, since most of these workers have more than twenty-five years of work life remaining.

One of the fastest growing areas of employment opportunity in the United States, according to the U.S. Department of Labor, is the office occupations. Government figures indicate that office occupation opportunities will grow from 18.9 million to 23.9 million during the 1980s. The office will be the cornerstone of the Information Age for the United States. However, recent data indicate that managerial productivity lags far behind the much maligned factory productivity rates established in this country in the last decade; we have been doing an even poorer job of managing our workers than we have of managing our products.

It is imperative, therefore, that the United States establish effective administrative system structures to increase the productivity rates of our business and government leaders. It is hoped that this text will play a valuable role in aiding business persons, government workers, educators, and others in the creation of more productive administrative systems. The key to a bright and prosperous future for any nation in the Information Age will be the ability of its people to harness technology. It is our hope that this generation and future generations never again lose sight of the American work ethic.

Keller and Savage
Phoenix, Arizona
June 1986

Glossary

ACTIVE FILES. Those files used in the day-to-day operation of an organization.

ADMINISTRATIVE ASSISTANT. An employee responsible for giving administrative support to a manager.

ADMINISTRATIVE INFORMATION SYSTEMS. The term used to describe the automated word processing, records management, budget analysis, and communication systems of the administrative office.

ADMINISTRATIVE OFFICE. That part of the organization which provides clerical, records management, and information systems skills.

ADMINISTRATIVE OFFICE MANAGER. The person who has direct responsibility for the entire administrative office.

AMBITION. A person's ability to set his or her own goals; to work hard to achieve those goals; to develop new skills for improvement; and to accept training and be receptive to more difficult assignments.

ARBITRATOR. A third party representative who, given the available information, offers solutions to a grievance.

ARITHMETIC LOGIC UNIT (ALU). A unit that controls all arithmetic functions needed to process data.

AUDIO TELECONFERENCING. The least expensive teleconferencing method, it requires only telephones and/or speakerphones.

BEHAVIORAL SCIENCE ERA. A period in the 1960s and 1970s which reflected strategies addressing worker needs as well as organizational concerns.

BIDDERS' CONFERENCE. A meeting, held after bids have been received and before they are due, to clarify the true needs of the buyer.

BID SPECIFICATIONS. The official set of requirements for each item requested by the buyer.

BLOCK MOVE. This occurs when a word processing operator designates a block of text within a document and moves that block to a new location within the document.

Blue-collar worker. A classification for a worker traditionally employed as a non-professional, such as a factory or warehouse worker.

Budget. A financial plan for conducting the affairs of an organization.

Budget analysis. This provides useful information which can be used to predict future revenue and expense levels in an organization.

Capital budget. A budget that outlines and allocates those anticipated funds for the projected budgeting period.

Centralization. A method of functional control in which a person or department performs its function throughout the organization.

Centralized approach. When word processing workstations are established in one location (such as a typing pool).

Central processing unit (CPU). A computer's processor unit.

Chief information officer (CIO). The title given to the person in charge of the information processing activities of an organization.

Cognitive dissonance theory. A theory that provides insight into how worker attitudes are developed.

Collective bargaining. The term used to describe representative bargaining of wages, hours, working conditions, etc., on behalf of the employer and the employees. Representatives negotiate collectively for their respective sides.

Communication. The transfer of information, thoughts, and emotions among people.

Compensation. Payment programs for employees which include salaries, health and medical benefits, retirement programs, career planning modules, vacation programs, and incentive programs.

Computer assisted retrieval (CAR). A micrographic process utilizing the speed of the computer to reduce microrecord retrieval time and cost.

Computer fraud. The misuse of a system by criminals outside or within a company.

Computerized records system. A records system developed specifically to process the majority of business records via computer equipment.

Computer networks. They allow computers to communicate with each other through cabling, usually consisting of coaxial cables or twisted-pair wiring.

Computer output microfilm (COM). A fast and accurate micrographic process for building a microrecord.

Conscientiousness. A person's ability to do what is assigned with pride and without avoidance.

CONTROLLING FUNCTION. This monitors and makes adjustments to the actual operation of various functional units of a business enterprise.

CONTROL UNIT (CU). This supervises or monitors all the functions of the computer system, including peripheral devices.

DATABASE. A "pool" of computerized data designed to be shared by the various administrative support systems in an organization.

DATABASE MANAGEMENT. A form of computer processing that allows for the "pooling" of files for use by numerous individuals throughout an organization.

DATA COMMUNICATION. The ability to link computer systems together through telephone systems for the purposes of entering, processing, retrieving, storing, and transmitting information.

DECENTRALIZATION. A method of control in which several individuals or departments have responsibility over specific functions.

DECENTRALIZED APPROACH. Occurs when provisions are made for word processing equipment and support where needed within the organization.

DEPARTMENTALIZATION. When the activities of organizations are grouped to facilitate the various tasks.

DIRECTING FUNCTION. The supervision of employees through formal and informal lines of authority.

DISK/DISKETTE. A recording medium for use with most microcomputers, often used as auxiliary storage.

DISTRIBUTION PHASE. Occurs when an edited and approved document is distributed.

ELECTRONIC MAIL. A software application for transferring mail-related documents such as letters, memos, etc., via computer technology.

ELECTRONIC TYPEWRITER. A device which utilizes microprocessors to perform limited text editing of typed documents.

ERGONOMICS. The study of people's relationships to their working environments.

EVALUATION PHASE. Occurs when the originator of a document receives the edited document for review and evaluation.

FEEDBACK. The response from the receiver of a message.

FILES. The official documents of an organization.

FILES ANALYSIS. The first step in developing a workable record maintenance system.

FILES DISPOSITION. This procedure controls the proliferation of files and eliminates unneeded files.

FILES INVENTORY. A physical inventory of existing files done to produce a master list of all files by title.

FILES MAINTENANCE. A series of activities performed to maintain the existing files of an organization.

FILES RETENTION. A predetermined date placed on each file indicates how long the file should be maintained in the file area.

FINANCIAL BUDGET. This charts the anticipated flow in revenue and expenses throughout the budgeting period.

FLOWCHART. A process used to describe the flow of an operation or a procedure, which utilizes symbols for the various activities of the operation.

FLUID DUPLICATOR. An inexpensive means, usually of marginal quality, of reproducing multiple copies of documents.

FORMAL ORGANIZATIONAL STRUCTURE. A structure represented by an organizational chart and by written operations manuals.

GANTT CHART. A chart which represents the activities performed and the time frame for performing them. Developed by Henry L. Gantt.

GLOBAL SEARCH AND REPLACE. The word processing option used when editing to search a document for specific items.

GRIEVANCE. Any complaint filed by an employee against the company.

HARDWARE. The component machine parts which make up the computer system, i.e., disk drives, monitors, printers, keyboards, etc.

HUMAN RELATIONS ERA. An era that spanned the 1940s and 1950s and emphasized the needs of the individual within an organization.

HUMAN RESOURCES. A reference to a person as a resource in the business environment.

IDIOGRAPHIC (PERSONAL) DIMENSION. This represents the personality and need/disposition of the individual within an organization.

INACTIVE FILES. Those files no longer used for the day-to-day operation of the organization, but not marked for destruction.

INFORMAL ORGANIZATIONAL STRUCTURE. The actual method of operation as perceived by the employees of an organization.

INFORMATION CENTER. The area within an organization which coordinates the computing resources of the company. These activities include computer acquisitions, and training and development of employees.

INFORMATION-RELATED JOB. A position associated with the administrative office, such as accounting, budgeting, records management, etc.

INITIATIVE. A person's ability to make decisions and complete work without help or supervision.

INPUT PHASE. Occurs when information is supplied to word processing specialists in rough draft form.

JOB ANALYSIS. The procedure used for determining specific information about a given job.

LABOR CONTRACT. The legally binding agreement reached between the company and the union for a specified period of time.

LEADER. Someone who can effect change, and initiate and implement the goals of the organization.

LINE-AND-STAFF ORGANIZATION. The most popular form of organizational design, in which top-down authority indicates essential support staff positions.

LINE ORGANIZATION. The basic form of organizational structure in which direct authority flows vertically from top to bottom.

MACHINE KEYS. The counting and security devices for xerographic copy control.

MAGNETIC CARD. A storage device used primarily with magnetic card typewriters during the 1960s and 1970s.

MAGNETIC DISK. A storage device used with micro, mini, and mainframe computers which allows for sequential and random access of data.

MAGNETIC TAPE. A storage device used with micro, mini, and mainframe computers which allows only sequential access of data.

MAINFRAME COMPUTER. The largest type of computer system compared to micro and minicomputer systems.

MAIN MEMORY. The memory cells that are available for storage until a secondary storage device is available for data or text.

MANAGEMENT. The process of organizing people's activities to achieve goals.

MANAGEMENT INFORMATION SYSTEM. A structure which organizes the functions of the organization through computer technology to process and disseminate information for decision making.

MANAGEMENT PREROGATIVE. Any situation not negotiated by the company and the union which is not addressed in the Taft-Hartley Act; item in question can be controlled by management.

MANAGER. An individual who plans, organizes, and staffs a department, and directs and controls others in the department.

MASTER BUDGET. This charts the financial operation of every department for every anticipated expense within an organization.

MEDIA. The means by which a message is delivered.

MESSAGE. The thoughts, ideas, and emotions of the sender in written or oral form.

MICROCOMPUTER. A computer system, usually costing less than \$10,000, designed primarily for the small business user.

MICROFICHE. A type of microform used in micrographics.

MICROFILMING. A popular type of microform used in micrographics.

MICROGRAPHICS. The process of copying selected business documents in miniaturized form.

MICROIMAGING. The process of reducing an image to miniature size.

MICRO-JACKET. A type of microform used in micrographics.

MICROPROCESSORS. Extremely small integrated circuits on silicon chips.

MIDDLE MANAGEMENT. Those persons with direct responsibility for the supervisory staff.

MINICOMPUTER. A computer produced, at a lower cost, with a smaller memory capacity and reduced processing speed.

MODEM. An electronic device which allows the digital-based computer to be linked with the wave-based telephone system.

NOMOTHETIC (ORGANIZATIONAL) DIMENSION. This illustrates the role expectations of the individual within the organization.

OFFICE COMPUTER SYSTEM. The technical capability to gather, process, file, and retrieve information in an efficient manner.

OFFICE LAYOUT CHARTS. Pictorial descriptions of the positions of offices, furniture, and equipment, used for design purposes.

OPERATING BUDGET. This funds the expenses anticipated within each department necessary for day-to-day operation.

ORGANIZATION. A person's ability to finish work correctly, accurately, and on time; also refers to a business endeavor.

ORGANIZATIONAL STRUCTURE. This depicts the relationship among people, their duties, and their responsibilities.

ORGANIZING FUNCTION. This coordinates the people, equipment, and procedures of an organization.

OUTPUT PHASE. Occurs when the edited document is sent to originator for review (hard-copy form or computer terminal hook-up).

PERT CHART. Stands for Program Evaluation and Review Technique; a useful tool for managing the scheduling of projects along a time line.

PLANNING FUNCTION. This allows to effectively plan for the future.

PRIVATE EMPLOYMENT AGENCIES. Agencies that charge a fee for providing business organizations with potential employees.

PROCESSING PHASE. Occurs when a word processing specialist edits an input document and prepares an edited document.

PRODUCTIVITY. The relationship of the output generated to input expended by an organization.

PUBLIC EMPLOYMENT SERVICES. Local or regional employment offices which provide employee information at no charge to the employer or the prospective employee.

RECEIVER. The person(s) to whom a written or verbal message is sent.

RECORDS MAINTENANCE. The proper maintenance of files to provide essential information for decision making within an organization.

RECORDS MANAGEMENT. Those functions which create, maintain, store, retrieve, and dispose an organization's documents in order to furnish accurate and complete information.

RECORDS MANAGEMENT CENTER. Consists of the employees who are responsible for the creation, maintenance, storage, and disposition of business records.

REPROGRAPHICS. The process of duplicating or copying documents.

REQUESTS FOR PROPOSAL. The official solicitation of bids from prospective suppliers of a given commodity by a prospective buyer.

SCIENTIFIC MANAGEMENT ERA. A task-oriented period which extended into the 1930s and saw the development of mechanical methods of producing goods.

SELF-CONTROL. A person's ability to stay calm and not lose his or her temper.

SENDER. The person responsible for starting the communication process.

SHARED-LOGIC WORD PROCESSOR. A system designed to allow many people to use one word processing software package stored in a central computer memory.

SIMULATION. A training technique that approximates the actual job tasks.

SOFTWARE. Sets of instructions, written in various computer languages, that direct the hardware to perform certain tasks. The three basic types are operating system software, applications software, and communications software.

SPAN OF CONTROL. This refers to the number of subordinates that an individual can effectively manage.

STAFFING FUNCTION. The ability to determine job requirements, tasks, and responsibilities along with employee selection, orientation, and training and development.

STAND-ALONE WORD PROCESSOR. A system designed to operate independent of other machines.

STENCIL. An inexpensive document reproduction process, usually of marginal quality.

SUPERVISION. The act of supervising (controlling, directing, guiding) the activities of employees.

SYMPOSIUMS. A formal panel discussion in which several expert speakers present different aspects of an issue or problem.

SYSTEM. A set of related procedures designed to meet specific objectives.

SYSTEMS ANALYSIS. A strategy devised to coordinate the various activities of all of the administrative support systems.

SYSTEMS CHART. A common monitoring tool, usually developed in graphic form, that is used by systems analysts.

SYSTEMS ERA. The present management era that incorporates the electronic computer into management strategies.

SYSTEMS EVALUATION. The final phase of a systems project that evaluates the new system design.

SYSTEMS IMPLEMENTATION. The phase of the systems project in which the new design is placed into operation.

SYSTEMS INVESTIGATION. The phase of a systems project where data is gathered about the existing system in order to determine problem areas.

SYSTEMS THEORY. An understanding of information flow and available technology, used in order to process and disseminate that information.

TASK-AMBIENT LIGHTING. A combination of the best characteristics of direct and indirect lighting; provides a flexible, inexpensive, easily installed option to overhead lighting.

TASK CHART. A chart designed to diagram specific tasks; it provides detailed information about specific jobs.

TASK FORCE. A structured involvement technique that can be used to create worker involvement.

TASK LIGHTING. Built-in lighting to accommodate a specific area.

TELECOMMUNICATIONS. Thc transmission of all sounds, pictures, and data by wire or satellite.

TELECONFERENCING. A technique that utilizes the telephone to transfer voice or voice and pictures to individuals located at different sites.

TELEPHONE AUTOMATED SWITCHING SYSTEM. A telephone system utilizing computer technology to receive, hold, override, and queue multiple incoming calls.

TEMPORARY HELP AGENCIES. Agencies that provide the office manager with temporary or short-term office employees.

TOP-DOWN DESIGN. A term synonymous with line organization.

TRADITIONAL BUDGETING APPROACH. This provides for a percentage increase or decrease to the prior budget based on present market anticipation.

TRAINING. An organized process which should provide experiences that result in productive growth for the employee and the organization.

UNIONS. Bargaining agents for workers through an election process.

VIDEO DISPLAY TERMINAL (VDT). A computer screen.

VIDEO TELECONFERENCING. A technique which utilizes various forms of video (picture) and sound communication between two distant points.

WATS LINES. WATS stands for Wide Area Telecommunication Service.

WEEKLY COPYING LOG. A counting device for xerographic copy control.

WHITE-COLLAR WORKER. A classification of worker usually describing professional workers, such as doctors, lawyers, businesspeople, office workers, etc.

WORD PROCESSING. The clerical activities in today's office; the utilization of people, procedures, and equipment to produce written business documents while containing their costs.

WORD PROCESSOR. A stand-alone or shared-logic system which possesses large memory capacity, removable memory media, large visual displays of text, and multiple print styles; also refers to a worker who inputs data onto a word processor.

XEROGRAPHIC. One of the most common document reproduction processes.

ZERO-BASED BUDGETING. This requires that each budgeted item be justified every budget period.

Index